ANIMAL
SPIRIT GUIDES

Hay House Titles by Steven D. Farmer, Ph.D.

Power Animals:
How to Connect with Your Animal Spirit Guide

Power Animals Oracle Cards (a 44-card deck)

Sacred Ceremony:
*How to Create Ceremonies for Healing,
Transitions, and Celebrations*

Hay House Titles of Related Interest

Animals and the Afterlife, by Kim Sheridan

Contacting Your Spirit Guide, by Sylvia Browne

The Journey to the Sacred Garden (book-with-CD),
by Hank Wesselman, Ph.D.

Magical Mermaids and Dolphins Oracle Cards,
by Doreen Virtue, Ph.D.

Spirit Messenger, by Gordon Smith

All of the above are available at your local bookstore,
or may be ordered by visiting:

Hay House USA: **www.hayhouse.com**®
Hay House Australia: **www.hayhouse.com.au**
Hay House UK: **www.hayhouse.co.uk**
Hay House South Africa: **www.hayhouse.co.za**
Hay House India: **www.hayhouse.co.in**

ANIMAL
SPIRIT GUIDES

AN EASY-TO-USE HANDBOOK FOR IDENTIFYING
AND UNDERSTANDING YOUR POWER ANIMALS
AND ANIMAL SPIRIT HELPERS

STEVEN D. FARMER, Ph.D.

HAY HOUSE, INC.
Carlsbad, California • New York City
London • Sydney • Johannesburg
Vancouver • Hong Kong • New Delhi

Published and distributed in the United States by: Hay House, Inc.: www.hayhouse. com • *Published and distributed in Australia by:* Hay House Australia Pty. Ltd.: www.hayhouse.com.au • *Published and distributed in the United Kingdom by:* Hay House UK, Ltd.: www.hayhouse.co.uk • *Published and distributed in the Republic of South Africa by:* Hay House SA (Pty), Ltd.: www.hayhouse.co.za • *Distributed in Canada by:* Raincoast: www.raincoast.com • *Published in India by:* Hay House Publishers India: www.hayhouse.co.in

Editorial supervision: Jill Kramer • *Design:* Amy Rose Grigoriou
Photos: www.shutterstock.com, www.corbis.com, www.jiunlimited.com, www.photos.com, www.jupiterimages.com, www.gettyimages.com, www.seapics.com, www.nigeldennis.com

Library of Congress Cataloging-in-Publication Data

Farmer, Steven.
  Animal spirit guides : an easy-to-use handbook for identifying and understanding your power animals and animal spirit helpers / Steven D. Farmer.
      p. cm.
  Includes bibliographical references.
  ISBN-13: 978-1-4019-0733-4 (hardcover)
  ISBN-10: 1-4019-0733-4 (hardcover)
  1. Guides (Spiritualism) 2. Animals--Miscellanea. I. Title.
  BF1275.G85F365 2006
  133'.259--dc22   2006009441

ISBN 10: 1-4019-0733-4
ISBN 13: 978-1-4019-0733-4

11 10 09 08   10 9 8 7
1st printing, September 2006
7th printing, August 2008

Printed in the United States of America

For Jaden and Gena:

May you and the generations
to come live in peace and
harmony with all life

*"All things share the same breath—the beast, the tree,
the man . . . the air shares its spirit with all the life it supports."*

— Chief Seattle

*"If you talk with the animals they will talk with you,
and you will know each other. If you do not talk to them,
you will not know them, and what you do not know,
you will fear. What one fears one destroys."*

— Chief Dan George

Editor's Note:

10% of the the author's profits from this book
will be donated to Defenders of Wildlife,
People for the Ethical Treatment of Animals,
and The Humane Society.

Contents

PART I: The Animal Spirit Guides
(in alphabetical order)

PART II:
Whom to Call On for Specific Needs
Calling on Animal
    Spirit Guides.................. 411

APPENDIX

Introduction
Animal Spirit Guides as Teachers, Guides, and Healers

FOLLOWING THE PUBLICATION OF MY BOOK *Power Animals,*
many people asked me the meaning of spirit animals that weren't
contained in that book, and in my workshops whenever I did power
animal readings, various animal spirits would come through that I
wasn't as acquainted with as I wanted to be. Although there were a
lot of excellent books, DVDs, and Websites in which to get information about the animal kingdom and the meaning of animal spirit
guides (whether they're called totem animals, power animals, spirit
animals, or familiars), none were as simple and straightforward as
I would have preferred.

I found that when someone had an unusual experience with an
animal or had repeated sightings—whether the animal appeared in
physical or symbolic form—their first priority would be to understand what that visitation meant and what possible messages the
spirit world was trying to convey to them through the essence of
that particular animal. Another question that most people had was
to understand why a particular totem or power animal was with
them and what that said about their personality and character. A
third area of interest was to know which animal spirit helpers to
call on for a particular purpose, such as whom to call on to increase
self-confidence or to interpret dreams.

It became evident that to have such a book, I'd have to create it, along with the help and contributions of the animal spirit
guides themselves. My intention, as the subtitle suggests, was to
write a practical, accessible, and easy-to-use handbook or guide that
would cut to the chase and respond to these concerns in a simple,
straightforward format. You won't find any detailed descriptions
or information on the 200-plus animal spirit guides represented
in this book; rather there is simply a photo of each animal. Most
of us know what the more common animals look like, but what if
one that isn't so common appears to you as a spirit guide? Written
descriptions are sometimes a little harder to visualize, but as has
been said, a picture is worth a thousand words. And if you desire
more details about the actual animal, you can easily find more
information through books, Websites, and DVDs, many of which
I've listed in the Resources section in the Appendix.

I trust that you'll find this book—and the animal spirit guides
represented here—helpful on your spiritual path. I know that these
incredible beings have guided, taught, and helped heal me in ways

far too numerous to count. In fact, I've had a lot of help from them in putting this book together, one of the most prominent being Hawk spirit.

Hawk Brings Focus

It was the morning of Christmas eve, and my wife, Doreen, and I were saying our morning prayers, a sacred ritual we do every morning before we get going into the day, when out of the corner of my eye I caught a flurry of wings as all the birds that had been feeding outside our bedroom window quickly scattered. Since we leave birdseed there, it's not unusual to see doves and a smattering of other birds on our deck and in the tree just outside. Obviously something had alarmed them, so I was naturally curious to see what had caused all this ruckus. As I looked outside, there perched on one of the branches a few feet away was a magnificent red-tailed hawk, solemnly gazing about, surveying his kingdom, supremely confident and poised, awaiting some instinctual signal for his next move.

It had been several months since I'd last seen this hawk, and since Hawk for a number of years has been a consistently profound and accurate messenger and spirit guide, I asked Hawk spirit the meaning of this visitation. What I heard in my head was, "Stay focused and don't get distracted. Keep things in perspective."

Straightforward and simple. Not cryptic or abstract at all. That's the way I like my messages from Spirit—whoever is the messenger—and Hawk has always proven to be a trustworthy teacher and guide.

Given that I was working on the book you're holding in your hands and the manuscript was due in just five short weeks, I very much appreciated this counsel from Hawk. It takes discipline to write, and I confess that sometimes it's easy to get distracted with any number of other seemingly important things, such as reorganizing my office, checking e-mail, or playing computer games (any of which I'd highly recommend if you ever want a pointless diversion from accomplishing your mission).

So that morning I sat down at my computer and enthusiastically and diligently began writing, appreciative of my friend's visit. My attention span lasted about 30 minutes, at which point I decided to check my e-mail. When I clicked the button to access my account, however, nothing happened. The Internet wasn't working! Suddenly I panicked, feeling as if this were a crisis of immense proportions. I called our Webmaster, but he wasn't available for the next few hours, so I proceeded to spend the next three hours on the phone with the Internet company and Apple Computer, trying this and that with no success, growing increasingly frustrated and doing a lot of muttering and clenching of my fists and my gut. That morning following Hawk's gentle reminder, I'd set an intention to get ten pages done, and now this incredibly urgent matter had come up to delay my progress!

Just when I felt like throwing things, our Webmaster appeared, and after a few minutes of performing his computer wizardry, the Internet was up and running again. Of course, I immediately went online to check my e-mail. Since it was the day before Christmas, there was barely any at all, except a letter from a guy in Nigeria who wanted me to help him out by transferring several million dollars into my account, for which I'd get a percentage.

I tried to remember why it had been such a critical matter to check my e-mail in the first place, but I couldn't. Whatever my reason had been at the time, it was lost to what had seemed to be a matter of grave importance—getting the Internet working again. Then I heard Hawk's message again: "Stay focused and don't get distracted. Keep things in perspective."

It was like one of those old commercials where a guy slaps himself in the head and says, "I could've had a V8!" I laughed out loud at my follies. I had completely forgotten about Hawk's beautiful and purposeful message and had created an entire drama around a very minor dilemma! The Internet could have easily waited, but instead became a convenient diversion from my writing. Oh, well—joke's on me. Maybe Coyote was around, working his medicine.

So I dumped my computer games, put e-mail at the bottom of the list, and industriously and productively wrote for the rest of that day and every day for the next week. On the morning of January 1, guess who appeared once again in the tree outside our window? You got it—that same hawk. A gentle reminder from Hawk spirit—stay focused, don't get distracted, and keep writing!

As if that weren't enough, about two weeks later on a warm Southern California day, I was at my desk plunking away on the computer, when out of the blue I heard a loud commotion between the front of my desk and the sliding-glass door that leads to the backyard. Startled, I looked up and saw what appeared to be wings furiously flapping away. I got up, walked around my desk, and sure enough, there was that same hawk I'd seen before, flailing away at the glass with his wings and talons, trying to make a quick exit. I spoke calmly to him, as he was obviously quite terrified. Doreen came in about then, both of us awestruck by this highly unusual event. I said, tongue in cheek, "Do you think this means something?" and we both laughed. After a couple of minutes, I opened the sliding-glass door and the hawk immediately flew away.

Then we spotted a dove tucked away between the desk and the printer, who exited very quickly as soon as there was an opportunity. We realized that the hawk had been after the dove, and both had flown in through the open sliding-glass door at the front of the house, down the hallway, and into my office, and had come to a halt due to the door being closed. So just in case I'd missed the meaning of the first two appearances, Hawk spirit in this third visit provided a dramatic exclamation point for the previous messages.

Once all this activity had settled down, I thought about what had just happened. In addition to Hawk's earlier communications, he was also saying to pursue the goal (of this book) with relentless focus and diligence, no matter what happens, just as he had done with his prey. Dove as animal spirit guide also conveyed a couple of messages through her visit: first, that there will be a happy outcome; and second, to remain peaceful and calm throughout the process, in spite of any disruptions or disturbances.

Our Natural Connection to Animals and Spirit Guides

It's amazing how animals permeate our consciousness and are with us all the time, either in their physical form—like the hawk and the dove in the story, the hummingbird that flits about and blesses the flowers blooming in the backyard, or the dolphins that frolic in the ocean just outside the surf—or in symbolic form, like the tiny raccoon, tortoise, owl, and hawk totems that are sitting on my computer observing me right now; the painting of the Rainbow Serpent on my office wall; or the bronze rendition of a raven with his wings spread that looks at me from the corner of the room.

This intimate connection we have with the animal kingdom shows itself in a variety of ways. Even in congested urban settings, the birds in the trees sing away, the pigeons gather around the man on the park bench feeding them, and the squirrels scamper about doing squirrel business. Taking a walk in the forest, we might see rabbits darting through the bush, a quick glimpse of a deer before it charges away, or wild turkeys scratching for grubs. Dogs, cats, goldfish, and hamsters are some of the more common domesticated animals that compel us to remember this relationship. Then there are zoos and wild-animal parks that give us a safe and contained glimpse of the wildness that abounds in Nature.

Go into any number of stores and you'll see animal icons depicted in pictures, jewelry, and fabric. Many sports teams are named after animals, such as the Philadelphia Eagles or Sydney Roosters, as well as various organizations such as the Lions club or the Loyal Order of Moose. Fairy tales are rampant with animals, ones that communicate readily with each other and with the humans in the stories. In our everyday language, animal metaphors abound. The stock market is either a bull or bear market; someone is busy as a beaver, or a person is trying to weasel his or her way out of things. You may be trying to outfox someone, but because your idea sounds fishy, others probably think you're just horsing around and trying to get their goat, so once they find you out, you'll have to eat crow.

Okay, enough examples. You get the picture. We're so intertwined with our animal brothers and sisters that most of the time we remain unaware of their presence in our lives, and the bountiful gifts they give us.

Not only are animals around us in all these ways and more, but also *we* are animals ourselves—the human kind. We only need to pause for a few moments and feel our heart beating; notice our breathing and our movements; and consider that we eat, sleep, eliminate, and procreate in the same basic manner as nearly all other animal beings. We breathe the same air and live together on the same planet, whether on land, in the air, or in the water. Like every other being, we eventually die, the substance of our bodies returning to the earth as our spirit goes to the spirit world.

The Spirit World and Spirit Guides

The spirit world is another dimension that exists alongside our material reality and is populated with nonphysical beings, or spirits. It's not some place up in the sky or removed from us, but is present and accessible at all times, requiring only the willingness, intention, and openness to make contact with those beings that reside there. Our awareness and consciousness are the vehicles that allow us to accomplish this.

In this alternate nonphysical reality called the spirit world, you'll find ancestors, archangels, ascended spiritual masters, religious figures, deceased loved ones, fairies, and for our purpose, spirit animals. These beings are extensions of God, Great Spirit, Source, or whatever name you give to All-That-Is, just as those of us and everything else in the material world are. What we call matter is denser and more tangible to our usual senses, whereas accessing this other dimension requires greater receptivity, heightened awareness, and a consciousness that allows for the existence of this aspect of being.

The term *spirit guide,* also known as a *helping spirit* or *guardian spirit*, is a term for any of these spiritual beings that help us in a life-positive way. We can call on them for guidance, protection, healing, encouragement, and inspiration. Some have been with us since childhood, while others have appeared at various periods in our life, perhaps to help us through a difficult transition. We may see them, hear them, feel them, or just know they're with us, and we can have any number of spirit guides throughout our life whether we're aware of them or not. They want to help us have a more peaceful, harmonious, and happier life, yet will not interfere with our free will. They are happy to serve and willingly do so whenever called.

Animals as Spirit Guides

Those spirits that are in animal form that teach us, guide us, empower us, and help us heal are called *animal spirit guides* or *spirit animals*. In shamanic and indigenous cultures, they may be called *totem animals* or *power animals*. Often these terms are used interchangeably, although there are subtle differences in meaning.

The term *totem animal* has two meanings. First, a totem animal is typically one that is shared by a family, clan, or group. In many indigenous cultures, often the family you were born into will have a totem animal in common. In modern societies, various groups also have communal totems, such as sports teams or clubs that identify with a totem animal. A second meaning of *totem animal* is a representational object of a particular animal, such as the small tortoise, owl, raccoon, and hawk glass figures I mentioned earlier that are sitting on my computer. We often give our children totem animals, such as teddy bears or bunny rabbits to give them comfort.

The term *power animal* has its origins in shamanism. This is a specialized animal spirit guide that shamans or shamanic practitioners acquire early in their initiation into their practice. Their power animal travels with them whenever they go on a shamanic journey, which is an altered state of awareness in which the practitioner sends their soul or consciousness into *non-ordinary reality*—a shamanic term for the spirit world—to receive teachings, guidance, and healings. You can, however, have a relationship with a power animal even if you're not a shaman or shamanic practitioner. They may come to you in meditations, visions, dreams, or shamanic journeys. It's a highly personal and specialized relationship with an animal spirit guide, one in which the personality and characteristics of the particular power animal that you've attracted to you is typically reflective of your own personality and characteristics.

Although every creature on the planet can be an animal spirit guide, in some traditions domesticated animals can't be power animals because they've lost much of their wildness and are removed from the natural world. Likewise, some traditions believe that insects are to be excluded from being power animals because of their size and nature. I have, however, included both domesticated animals and some insects such as Butterfly and Dragonfly in this book, and even two mythological animals, Dragon and Unicorn, to account for those who work with them as animal spirit guides.

To experience the tremendous value of working with animal spirit guides, you don't need to be a shaman, have any interest in shamanism, or be associated with an indigenous culture. For most purposes, you don't even need to be concerned as to whether an animal spirit guide is a totem or power animal. Instead, consider these wonderful beings as spiritual allies that want to reach out to each and every one of us who are open to their guidance and, when called with sincere intent, will respond.

One of the great advantages of working with animal spirit guides is that the actual animal is physically and symbolically present in so many ways throughout every society and culture on Earth. Because of their abundant representations in third-dimensional reality, they're continually in our consciousness. Depending on how and in what way they show up in the material world, either in the flesh or symbolically, their appearance may be as a representative of the spirit of that animal.

When an animal shows up in an uncommon way or repetitively, that animal isn't just the single animal, but is representing the spirit of the entire species. For example, the hummingbird that flits about and then hovers for several seconds directly in front of you isn't just a hummingbird, but is carrying with her the essence of *all* hummingbirds, and is therefore Hummingbird with a capital "H." That's also why when we speak of an animal spirit guide, we leave out the "a" or "an" as a way of recognizing and honoring that spirit animal. The hawk that visited me wasn't only a hawk, but in those instances was representing the essence of all hawks, and is, therefore, called Hawk.

Not only do these spirit animals help us in many ways, but another positive effect is that you'll deepen your appreciation for the magic and mystery of all animals, whether they're of the air, water, or land. Every being on this beautiful and majestic planet has its place in the web of life, and as you develop your consciousness and awareness of the unique quality of animal spirit guides, you'll enhance your relationships with all of our animal brothers and sisters.

Messages from Animal Spirit Guides

When an animal or a symbol of that animal shows up to you in an unusual way or repeatedly (at least three times in a short period of time), it's most definitely trying to convey a message from the spirit world to you. The hawk that visited me around the holidays did both. He showed up three times in a short period, and in one of those visits performed the very unusual act of flying into my office. In spite of my facetious comment to Doreen, it was evident that this was a strong message meant for me, particularly since Hawk has been a consistent and recurring animal spirit guide.

In another instance, my friend Melody described how, after her father's death, she went to a spot on the beach located in front of her dad's favorite restaurant, and a single dolphin was frolicking in the water unusually close to shore. As she walked on the beach, the dolphin followed her for several meters, then swam farther out to sea and joined his pod. This was a very reassuring message from Dolphin to Melody that her father was just fine in the spirit world.

My friend Tim and his wife, Beth, provide another illustration. Less than a year ago they were preparing a major move to a new city, and Tim was feeling extremely anxious about it, to the point of losing sleep and dropping weight. One night a raccoon showed up in their backyard. He looked up the message from Raccoon in my book *Power Animals,* and discovered that it was about resourcefulness. At that point, Tim realized that he did in fact have all the necessary resources, both internal and external, for this move. It relaxed him a great deal, and he and his wife are now living very successfully in their new home in a new city.

I've had the good fortune to have a number of personal experiences like these and have also heard a number of stories from others with respect to these miraculous interventions on the part of an animal spirit guide, either represented and embodied by the physical animal or a symbol of that animal. An example of a repetitive symbolic representation would be when you have a vivid and colorful dream about a bear, go to the market the next day and overhear hear two strangers in a conversation talking about bears, and that evening turn on the television and there just happens to be a program about grizzly bears. An experience like this counts just as much as three literal sightings, and since most of us who live in urban areas will never actually encounter live bears or come close to a number of wild animals, the spirit of that animal has to reach us in some other way to get a message across.

How You Get Messages from Spirit Guides

There are four major ways in which you can get messages from the spirit world: visual, auditory, kinesthetic, and cognitive. As your receptivity to the spiritual dimension opens and develops, you'll discover that one of these pathways is the strongest and feels the most natural, with a secondary one that works fairly well. The more you practice and the more you attune to the spiritual dimension, you'll find that you can receive input through the other channels as well. What's required is that you hold a clear intention to receive these messages and simply remain receptive, and they will come to you, often in unexpected and surprising ways.

Here is a detailed description of the four ways:

1. Visual: When you see that dolphin a few yards from shore or the crow that lands a couple of feet away from you and you know these are unusual visitations and meant for you, this is the animal spirit coming through a visual channel. *Clairvoyance* is another way, where you see spirit animals that are in the nonphysical realm in your mind's eye or as an apparition, such as having a vision of a bear or a mythological animal like a dragon, or having a vivid dream where a wolf makes an appearance.

2. Auditory: You hear the voice of an animal spirit guide in your mind giving you some advice, or a sound in the environment triggers a thought about an animal spirit guide. Another means is for you to overhear a conversation or listen to someone talking and intuitively know that what is being said is a message from a spirit animal. Hearing spirit's communication is called *clairaudience*. Messages coming in this way are typically short and to the point, without excess verbiage.

3. Kinesthetic: This is when you feel or sense something, sometimes called a gut feeling and often termed *intuition*. You feel or sense the presence of the ethereal form of one of your more common animal spirit guides or your power animal, and get a sense of what they're trying to communicate to you. This is also called *clairsentience*.

4. Cognitive: This is a "knowing" through our thought processes, also called inspiration or insight. If your primary mode of input is through this pathway, your animal spirit guide is communicating with you by generating a thought or thought pattern, also called *claircognizance*. Often someone doesn't exactly know how they know, and if asked, will tell you that they just somehow know.

So unless you're already aware of which of these channels is your primary avenue for spiritual input, for the next several days simply observe how you make the simplest of choices. What are the most important considerations about where you live? How do you shop for things? How do you decide what to wear? As you observe yourself, you'll gradually notice the primary way(s) in which you connect with the spirit world. Do you *look* for and *see* the communications from your animal spirit guide or other spirit helpers? Do you *hear* their voice? Or *feel* them? Or for you is it more of a contemplative or insightful *thought* process? Keep in mind which channels are your primary spiritual conduits, and with practice, you'll develop greater trust in how you get messages from spirit animals.

Interpreting and Understanding the Messages from Animal Spirit Guides

As I've noted, when an animal shows up in ordinary reality in an uncommon way or at unusual times, such as a dove landing on the balcony two feet away, a raccoon that's walked into your back door, or a fox that darts across your path as you're walking in the woods, it's definitely a sign from that animal spirit guide. The dove may be reminding you to stay calm, the raccoon may be letting you know that you've got what it takes, while the fox may be suggesting that you be discerning about whom to trust. Or if you spot a crow in the tree outside your window three mornings in a row when there's usually none, it could mean that you're going to be seeing more magic occur. Seeing a hummingbird repeatedly could mean that you need more joy and sweetness in your life.

Animal spirit guides will teach you in both cryptic and dreamlike ways and also offer their counsel by hitting you right between the eyes with a message that's obvious. However, when it isn't clear what the message is or you want to understand more about it, there are several options. One is to look for the animal in this book or in *Power Animals* and see what the possible meanings are with respect to the visitation. I've also listed other books and Websites in the Appendix that offer interpretations, as well as other resources that have excellent information on the animals themselves that can give you clues about what the message is.

One of the most useful and direct ways is to communicate with the spirit of that animal that you've sighted and ask them. When you know that you're getting a communication from an animal spirit guide, the first thing to do (unless you're driving) is to close your eyes, imagine that animal's spirit is in front of you, and in your mind ask the question, "What do you want me to know?" Take a deep breath, relax your body, and see what sort of impressions and information you get—whether visual, auditory, kinesthetic, or cognitive. By doing so, you'll often get a "hit" on what the meaning of the visitation is. Also, by contemplating the sighting over the next few hours, you'll discover further insights about the experience. If you know how to do a shamanic journey, that's another means of understanding what the message was. The more you practice deciphering the messages, the easier it becomes.

In the Appendix, there's a guided-meditation journey called "Messages from Your Animal Spirit Guide" (a version of which is on my CD of the same name) that you can use to visit an animal spirit guide, whether it's the one that came to you in your dreams or your waking state, or one that wants to contact you when you do the meditation. This is another way in which you can go directly to an animal spirit guide or power animal and find out what they want to communicate to you. You can also use this meditation if you have any kind of question that you want to ask and receive advice from any animal spirit guide.

I encourage you to practice any of these methods in addition to looking to this book or other resources for the meaning of the spirit animal's communication with you. These remarkable beings want to help us and teach us and will do so in myriad ways.

The Layout of This Book

This book is divided into two main sections plus an Appendix. Part I is a listing of more than 200 animals from around the world, all of which have pictures accompanying them. There's no identifying information about, or descriptions of, every animal, as this is beyond the scope of this book. There are hundreds of other easily accessible resources where you can get detailed information about the animals themselves, and I urge you to do so if you're interested.

For each of the animals represented, there are three sections:

1. If [ANIMAL SPIRIT GUIDE] shows up, it means: This is where you first look when you've had a sighting or visitation. It lists several possible messages, synthesized from communications I've received from that particular animal spirit guide and other sources. When you're looking in this section, one or more of the messages will be the most relevant for you. You'll intuitively discern which of these messages is most significant as you read through them.

2. Call on [ANIMAL SPIRIT GUIDE] when: This will give you some conditions or issues with which this particular animal spirit guide can help when you call on it through prayer, meditation, contemplation, or journeying.

3. If [ANIMAL SPIRIT GUIDE] is your POWER ANIMAL: If you've identified this spirit animal as your power animal, this section will tell you about yourself and how your power animal is reflective of your personality and characteristics. If you call your primary animal spirit guide your totem animal, these descriptions will also fit.

In some cases, there are two or more names for each animal. Whenever this occurs, you'll be referred to the primary name of the animal by "*see* ___," following the alternate name, such as "Mountain Lion (*see* **Cougar**)." There are also separate entries for different types of the same animal (such as Barn Owl or Great Horned Owl), which not only have their individual readouts, but also refer you to the generic animal, as in "Barn Owl" (*also see* **Owl**). Similarly, for a generic animal (such as **Owl**), in some instances you'll be referred to the more specific types of animal.

In Part II, you'll find a list of which animal spirit guides to call on for help with conditions you may have to deal with, such as discerning whom to trust or dealing with criticism, or qualities that you want support and reinforcement for, such as clear communication or manifesting your dreams. This list is alphabetized to make it easy to search for what you're looking for, and most of the listings give several animal spirit guides to choose from so you can find one that feels most compatible and appropriate for your particular needs.

The Appendix contains a guided meditation journey that will help you get a message from your spirit animal and a list of resources, including books, Websites, and DVDs to help you develop a better understanding of various animals and the meanings of animal spirit guides.

How to Use This Book

There are a few different ways to use this book. The first way is when you've had a sighting of an animal and you suspect that it's trying to give you a message. When this happens, find the animal in Part I and review the possible meanings. As you read these, pay attention to which ones jump out at you as the most pertinent. Once you've identified the most helpful message, you can read the other sections for that animal, which are some conditions you might call on that spirit animal to help you with and the information about the animal as a power animal. You may glean further information from these other sections that's helpful in discerning the message that the particular animal spirit guide is trying to convey to you.

Another way to use the book is as a divination tool. Close your eyes, take a deep breath, relax your body, and think of a question. Once the question is clear in your mind, flip through the pages of Part I until you get a sense of when to stop. Whatever page you've landed on, read the messages from the animal spirit guide that's on that page and see how they're applicable to your question. You can use this method in conjunction with other oracle tools, such as the *Power Animal Oracle Cards.*

If you know who your power animal is or you think you know, look for it in Part I and review each of the three sections, particularly the one that suggests what this says about you if this is your power animal. At the same time, you may discern some additional information or messages from reading each of the segments under that animal.

In Part II, you can look up any condition that's listed there to see which animal spirit guides might best be called upon to help with that condition, or find qualities and characteristics that you want to reinforce in yourself or bring out, and which spirit animals to call on in order to do so. Most of these listings have more than one entry, so when you look at the list of animal spirit guides to call upon, you're welcome to call on any and all of them, or intuitively discern which one would be the most significant in helping you with your condition or embellishing a characteristic that you want. Once you've identified the spirit animal or animals that you want to call on, you can then cross-reference them in Part I to get additional information or inspiration.

Calling on an animal spirit guide requires only a sincere intention and openness to receiving their help and guidance. It's very simple to do so, whether through prayer, meditation, contemplation, or through doing a shamanic journey. You may not get instant results (although this does sometimes happen), but observe what happens for some time after you've made your appeal. When you invoke an animal spirit guide for help or guidance, the assistance often comes in unexpected ways from surprising sources.

When you want to get more information and get further acquainted with your animal spirit guide or your power animal, use the listings in the Resources as a guide. There's a wealth of information about the animal kingdom, and the more you work with spirit animals, the more useful it is to research and get additional information about your favorite animal spirit guides. As you become more acquainted with the traits and characteristics of your favorites, you become that much more intimately involved with them both in third-dimensional reality and as spirit helpers.

Honoring Your Animal Spirit Guides and Your Power Animals

Anything you do on behalf of our animal brothers and sisters will be looked on very kindly by the spirit world and especially by the spirit animals. Thanking them at each and every opportunity through prayer is a subtle but very powerful way of honoring them. Donating your time, energy, and/or money to any reputable animal-rights or environmental organization whose mission is in alignment with your ethics and philosophy is an active way to give something back to the animals. Intervening in any way when you know of an animal brother or sister that's being mistreated scores high as well.

If you're guided to forego using animal products in order to become a vegetarian or a vegan, this is another way to say thank you. However, if you continue to use animal products, be sure to say a prayer of gratitude for that animal's contribution to your life and pray that their soul is readily transported to the spirit world. If you do eat animal flesh, it's particularly important to offer prayers of gratitude before ingesting their bodies and do what you can to assure that these animals were treated kindly and fairly before they gave their lives so that we can sustain ours.

To honor the animals is very simple. All it takes is a consciousness and awareness of the tremendous contributions that they make to our lives each and every day. It's a simple gesture to thank them and honor them in these ways and more.

PART I
The Animal Spirit Guides

AARDVARK

© Nigel Dennis

If AARDVARK shows up, it means:

Trust your instinctual senses to "sniff out" what's right for you and what's not.

It's best to be slow and cautious when starting a new project or relationship until you feel that it's safe to move ahead.

This isn't a time to be particularly social, but rather one to spend in quiet and solitude.

Look below the surface of appearances and find out what's underneath.

Evenings will be the most productive time for whatever project or creative effort you're working on.

Call on AARDVARK when:

You're having difficulty discerning the truth from the falsehoods of a situation or of what someone is communicating to you.

You're attempting to unearth some important information that will help you resolve some questions you've had.

You've been assigned to investigate a particular subject related to your work or role and have to get the most relevant information quickly.

You have to get to the bottom of a recent incident or a problem very quickly.

If AARDVARK is your POWER ANIMAL:

You're a night person, which is when your energy is at its peak.

You're a solitary individual, only seeking the company of others on occasion.

You enjoy delving into any subject that attracts your interest and will explore it in depth.

When you meet people for the first time, you're very cautious and timid, yet once you feel comfortable, you open up to them.

You don't settle for long in any one place, instead preferring to move about regularly.

ALBATROSS

If ALBATROSS shows up, it means:

Whatever issues have been in the way of your spiritual or emotional growth are now cleared.

You're going through a chaotic period in your life, but you'll be able to sail through it and come out the other side stronger and even more adaptable.

This is a cycle in your life when you're wandering about without clear goals or direction, yet one that is necessary for your personal development and spiritual growth.

Be patient with yourself as you meander on your quest, trusting that you'll find what you're looking for just over the next horizon.

Call on ALBATROSS when:

You're facing a burdensome task or a period in your life where there are some unpleasant things to deal with.

You're getting itchy feet and want to do something adventurous without necessarily having a specific destination in mind.

Others are pressuring you to find stability and purpose, but in your heart of hearts you know that you're just not ready to do so.

You feel weighted down and trapped by all your responsibilities and obligations, and want to break out of the rut you're in.

If ALBATROSS is your POWER ANIMAL:

You're capable of going the distance when involved with any long-term project.

You have a great deal of resilience, and are able to bounce back from any hardship very quickly.

You seem to be perpetually on a search, even though you're not always sure what you're seeking.

As you mature, you attain greater and greater clarity about your life purpose, goals, and direction, even if these change from time to time.

For you to thrive, you must always be involved in some type of artistic and creative pursuit.

ALLIGATOR
(Crocodile)

If ALLIGATOR shows up, it means:

Take your time to digest what you're now learning rather than rushing ahead to pursue further education or gather more information.

You need to be very protective of your personal territory and assertive about setting boundaries.

This is a time for renewal and new beginnings as you emerge from a dark period of your life.

Be sure to gather all the facts and look at the situation from all sides before passing judgment, making any decisions, or taking action.

It's an important time to honor your ancestors in any way you choose.

Call on ALLIGATOR when:

Someone has confided something very personal to you, and you need to keep it hidden and secret.

You're clearly at the end of one cycle or phase of your life and moving into a new era.

You've transgressed your own ethical guidelines, and in doing so have hurt someone else and sincerely want to make amends.

You're feeling drawn to a study of ancient wisdom and knowledge but are not sure where to begin.

If ALLIGATOR is your POWER ANIMAL:

You may seem a bit cold to others upon a first meeting, yet given enough time, you can warm up to them.

You keep to yourself most of the time, but when you do reveal yourself, others feel your strong presence.

You move rather slowly and deliberately until someone invades your personal space.

You're quite shy and a bit of a loner, and when you're in social situations you tend to go unnoticed.

You take your time assessing any troubling situation, taking action only once you're satisfied that you have all the necessary information, but when you do act, you do so swiftly and without hesitation or equivocation.

ANT

If ANT shows up, it means:

It's time to get to work on that project that you've been thinking about and see it through to completion.

Seek support from your closest friends and family rather than isolating yourself.

Trust that you'll succeed in accomplishing your dreams.

Be patient with yourself, those around you, and with any work projects in which you're involved.

Call on ANT when:

You're involved with a project that seems daunting and you need motivation to get the job done.

You're responsible for coordinating efforts between several people.

You've been highly adaptive, always trying to please others, and know that it's now time for you to become the architect of your own life.

You're feeling frustrated that things aren't moving along much faster, and want to be more patient.

If ANT is your POWER ANIMAL:

You're very meticulous and tend to scrutinize everything very carefully.

You do your best work when you participate in a group effort.

You tend to make decisions based on your assessment of what's the greatest good for everyone, rather than solely on what's in it for yourself.

You trust the universe to provide, having faith that whatever you need will come to you when you need it.

ANTEATER

If ANTEATER shows up, it means:

Modify your eating habits so that you have smaller and lighter snacks or meals throughout the day rather than the standard three squares.

Beware of anything that "smells" funny or is out of place, and use extra caution if this is so.

In order to complete the project you're working on, dig in and charge ahead until it's done.

Be conservative in your use of any supplies and goods, not using more than you need.

If you feel afraid, stand erect with eyes straight ahead and take several slow, deep breaths.

Call on ANTEATER when:

You want to dig in and get under the surface of what's obvious and apparent.

You need to take a stand with someone who's pushing your buttons and irritating or threatening you in some way.

You have any problems with ants or termites, even if you use other methods as well.

You want to take your time and enjoy walking along the road, enjoying the scenery.

If ANTEATER is your POWER ANIMAL:

Although you don't like to stay in one place for too long and prefer to wander about, when you do settle down for a stretch you're very guarded about your personal territory.

You're careful about your food intake, never eating more than makes you feel comfortably full.

You're a solitary individual, preferring to go it alone most of the time.

When you find yourself feeling claustrophobic during the day, you adapt by operating more at night, when there are fewer people around.

You lumber along at a leisurely pace most of the time, but when you need to you can move a lot faster.

ANTELOPE
(Pronghorn)
(*Also see* Gazelle; Gnu; Impala)

If ANTELOPE shows up, it means:

Be cautious around anyone with harsh or aggressive energy, and if you find yourself in such a situation, surround yourself with golden light to psychically insulate yourself.

Pay attention to new opportunities that show up and take advantage of them.

Whatever your heart's desire, make a clear and firm decision to begin it, and then go for it with gusto.

Whatever you've begun, follow through and finish it as quickly as you can.

You've been spending too much time in solitude and need to seek out the company of friends.

Call on ANTELOPE when:

You feel sluggish and lethargic and want an extra charge of energy.

Something doesn't "smell" right and you want to find out what it is.

You feel blocked or stymied in your efforts and need to take action in order to get things moving.

You're starting a new project or job, or else you're approaching a new phase of your life.

You're confused about something that's happening in your immediate surroundings, and you need to be attentive and watchful in order to sort it all out and make sense of it.

If ANTELOPE is your POWER ANIMAL:

You're quick-witted and can think on your feet, enabling you to deal effectively with any situation you find yourself in.

You're innately psychic and highly intuitive, having been born with the gift of clairvoyance and clairsentience.

You're highly adaptable, at ease, and able to survive in any environment you're in.

Although you're shy, you don't like to be alone for too long a time, and will seek out the company of those you feel safe and comfortable with.

Your judgment is quite sound, and you have confidence that actions you take will be successful.

ARMADILLO

If ARMADILLO shows up, it means:

You need to set clear boundaries with those whom you feel are intrusive or invasive.

It's a time to retreat rather than trying to make headway or directly influence the circumstances at hand.

There's a situation that requires you to dig deeper to discover any underlying deceit or evasiveness.

It's important to be discerning right now about whom you can trust, especially with particularly sensitive or highly personal issues.

Define to others not only what you *don't* want, but more important, what you *do* want.

Call on ARMADILLO when:

You need extra emotional or psychic protection from unwarranted and unwanted harassment or criticism.

The best choice is to take flight in order to feel safe.

You need to discriminate between what is safe and what's not.

You feel that you're being overly sensitive and reactive to the energies and feelings of others, picking up on them in such a way that it's difficult to tell what's yours and what's theirs.

If ARMADILLO is your POWER ANIMAL:

Although you present a rather tough exterior, you're actually quite sensitive and a soft touch.

You're easygoing and move about life more slowly than others, unless threatened, in which case you either withdraw or beat a hasty retreat.

You prefer to stay in the background and will do anything to avoid the spotlight.

You have the unique ability to dig in and unearth secrets and hidden motives in others.

You're very wary of exposing your vulnerabilities, keeping those parts of you protected and hidden.

BABOON

If BABOON shows up, it means:

You've been involved in an intense mental process and need to get grounded and back into your body.

Your family needs your attention and your presence now.

At this time, significant teachings will come about as a result of what you initially thought were foolish mistakes.

You need to protect your recent creations by keeping them to yourself, sharing them only with those you completely trust.

It's a good idea to create a sacred space in your home, if only a small area that's out of the way of normal traffic, and build a sacred altar in that space.

Call on BABOON when:

You're feeling spacey and fragmented and need to pull yourself together.

You've done something that you regret, and you want to figure out why you did it and what there is to learn from the experience.

You're in charge of taking care of a child or children, whether yours or someone else's.

You want to create a haven or refuge for yourself in or near your home.

Your family is embroiled in dissension or conflict, and you want to encourage peace and harmonious interaction.

If BABOON is your POWER ANIMAL:

You're very family oriented, with a deep commitment to, and strong protectiveness toward, your kin.

You're very effective at working out any problems or conflicts that surface in your family or close group of friends.

You're very affectionate and enjoy hugging and caressing others you're close to as a way to show your love and care.

Although you don't always seem that way to others, you're very wise and have a deep connection with, and understanding of, ancient mysteries.

BADGER

If BADGER shows up, it means:

You must be persistent and stick with your project to its completion no matter what.

Be willing to ferociously defend your beliefs and principles and meet any challenges or criticism head-on.

It's time to stop your delay and avoidance tactics and get on with what you know you need to do.

Stop always depending on others then resenting them when they don't come through, and trust that you have the capability to be self-reliant.

Turn your anger and aggression into constructive action without cutting others to shreds.

Call on BADGER when:

You have a long-term goal but feel like giving up on it.

You're feeling harassed and abused and want to stand up for yourself.

You're feeling uncertain about moving ahead with any projects.

You're put into a position of increased responsibility and need support for this new assignment.

You need a physical healing and are unwilling to try conventional methods.

If BADGER is your POWER ANIMAL:

You're very persistent and willing to stick with it for a long time in order to accomplish what you want.

You don't like confrontation, but if you're cornered, you're very willing to fight if necessary.

You're a powerful and effective healer, often using alternative and unconventional means for healing others.

You sometimes display a rather gruff exterior that masks feelings of self-doubt and timidity.

You're a very engaging storyteller, with a number of tales that make for inspired teachings.

BARN OWL

(Also see Owl)

If BARN OWL shows up, it means:

Since life is so short, treat every day as precious and live it to the fullest.

Let your heart be open, and don't let fear get in the way of expressing your love.

Do a house clearing and a blessing, one that will incorporate a way to free up any lost spirits that need to move on.

Take a silent retreat somewhere away from the usual noise, whether for a few hours or a couple of days.

You're entering into a period of considerable abundance, easily fulfilling your needs with minimal effort.

This is a time requiring considerable adaptability and ingenuity in all your dealings.

Whenever you need help, call on the spirits of your ancestors, and as long as your plea is sincere, they will help you.

Call on BARN OWL when:

You're inundated with lots of noise and need a break from it.

You feel that your emotions and intellect are out of balance.

You believe that your resources are in short supply.

You suspect that there may be unwanted spirits in your home or place of business.

If BARN OWL is your POWER ANIMAL:

You're clever and skillful about getting whatever you set your mind on.

You have the gift of clairaudience, the ability to hear messages from the spirit world.

Your hearing ability is very keen, such that you can hear sounds in the environment that others miss.

You're able to easily tune in to ancestral spirits, especially through your hearing.

You're excellent at finding resources to sustain you, even in situations where scarcity seems to prevail.

BARRED OWL

(Also see <u>Owl</u>)

If BARRED OWL shows up, it means:

Express yourself through your voice, whether singing, humming, or chanting.

Weather any storms you're now encountering with as much gentleness and grace as you can muster.

Take a walk in the forest or bush, and while doing so, notice the sounds you hear.

Make your intention cooperation, rather than competition or rivalry, in your relationships with everyone.

Call on BARRED OWL when:

You're having any difficulties or challenges with your throat or voice.

You have an interest in acting or any kind of work where you use your voice.

You're with someone who seems overly competitive.

You want to build your self-confidence without getting too brash or overbearing.

If BARRED OWL is your POWER ANIMAL:

You're very generous, willing to share just about anything you have.

You're charming, vivacious, easy to get along with, and almost everyone you meet takes a liking to you.

You're very good at acting, changing in and out of character, and mimicking vocal expressions and sounds with your voice.

You're amicable and cooperative, even with those you don't particularly care for.

BAT

If BAT shows up, it means:

Let go of those habits and attachments that no longer serve you, and welcome the changes that are long overdue.

The ordeal that you're facing is a necessary part of your transformation and an initiation into a much more spiritually directed life.

It's time to confront and conquer your fears, trusting that doing so will bring about dramatic and beneficial changes.

Mingle and socialize more with others, perhaps by joining ongoing classes or group activities that you think you'd enjoy.

Call on BAT when:

You're in a transition, where a life that you once lived is dying, and a new cycle is emerging.

You've been isolating yourself far too long and need to make contact with others.

You're feeling anxious and fearful without knowing why or what you're afraid of.

You find yourself having powerful dreams and visions but don't understand their meaning.

You're being drawn to explore shamanic practices.

If BAT is your POWER ANIMAL:

You thrive on being in the company of others and prefer groups of people to being alone.

You're able to see in others what they keep hidden, and hear what they don't say.

You've earned your gifts as a visionary and shaman through a series of difficult initiations that have been a significant part of your soul's path.

You're able to look beyond immediate circumstances and perceived limitations to see the bigger picture, as well as possibilities that others overlook.

BEAR
(Also see <u>Polar Bear</u>)

If BEAR shows up, it means:

Set clear boundaries and don't compromise, even if pressured.

Ask for what you want whether or not you feel you'll get it.

Get going on that creative project you have in mind.

Take some time out from your usual routines and spend some time in solitude.

You may be in need of physical or emotional healing.

Be gentle, and show your love to those you're close to.

To find answers to your questions, go inside rather than reading or consulting others.

— If BLACK BEAR:

- It's an important time for meditation and introspection.
- Balance your activities with periods of rest.
- Don't forget to play.

— If BROWN (GRIZZLY) BEAR:

- Stay grounded no matter what.
- It's time to bring your dreams and plans to fruition.
- It's important to trust your instincts.
- Enough hiding—it's time to come out and meet the world.
- Don't just wait for something to happen; take action now!

Call on BEAR when:

There's a need for physical or emotional healing.

You want to gather power and strength to deal with adversity.

You need physical, emotional, or psychic protection.

You want the courage to aggressively pursue your goals.

You're involved in a situation that requires you to be assertive in order to maintain your dignity and integrity.

If BEAR is your POWER ANIMAL:

You're assertive and confident, with a strong presence.

You're a powerful healer, whether your focus is physical, emotional, or spiritual healing.

You need periods of reclusiveness for your creative spark, and typically emerge from these periods with new ideas and projects.

Winter is definitely a period to honor your need for quiet, solitude, and alone time, whereas spring is a time to act on the opportunities before you.

You're very independent, preferring to do things yourself rather than asking for help.

You're a survivor.

BEAVER

If BEAVER shows up, it means:

This is a time for purposeful and directed activity, not contemplation or procrastination.

Balance your activities by providing time for resting and socializing with family and friends.

Be especially aware of wasting time, energy, and resources on unimportant matters.

Don't be busy for busy's sake; let your actions be focused and intentional.

It's time to change your environment in a way that makes you feel more secure and comfortable.

Call on BEAVER when:

There's a job to be done, and you need to get to it and stay with it until it's done.

You want to bring your ideas and visions into third-dimensional reality.

You want to extricate yourself from situations or relationships where you feel trapped.

You want to resolve conflicts with your mate, friends, or co-workers.

You're ready to clean up the clutter in your home or work area.

You want to overcome any procrastination about a daunting project you're faced with.

If BEAVER is your POWER ANIMAL:

You're a "doer," and willing to do what it takes to get the job done.

You work much better as a team player, and prefer projects that involve others.

The work you do contributes to and benefits the greater good.

You're very resourceful, organized, and focused.

You're very loyal to your friends and tend to make lifelong friendships.

You genuinely try to get along with everyone.

You'll stick with a task until it's completed, no matter what obstacles may appear.

BEE

If BEE shows up, it means:

It's time to get organized and get to work on that idea that you want to implement and develop.

Approach your projects with commitment, diligence, and dedication, and you'll succeed beyond your wildest expectations.

Involve several others in a cooperative and life-affirming venture, one in which everyone who participates will benefit—and if possible, one that includes the entire community.

Take the time to appreciate and enjoy the sweetness of life.

This is a very fertile time for you physically and creatively, one where you can bring your ideas into fruition.

This is a very productive cycle for you, so stay with whatever you're working on, and there will be a favorable outcome.

Call on BEE when:

You're faced with a situation that requires considerable social skills, particularly tact and diplomacy.

You're engaged in a project that requires persistence and perseverance in order to see it through to completion.

There's a need to sort through much chaos and confusion in order to get things organized.

You've been placed in a position of responsibility and need help in encouraging everyone to cooperate in the shared tasks.

If BEE is your POWER ANIMAL:

You're industrious, focused, and committed to whatever task you're working on.

You're quite capable of being successful at anything you attempt.

It takes quite a bit to get you riled up, but when you do, you have to be careful not to sting others too harshly with your words.

You have a powerful effect on others, such that when you give someone your loving attention, they blossom and open up to you.

Although you're self-sufficient, you do your best when working cooperatively with others.

BELUGA
(White Whale)
(Also see <u>Whale</u>*)*

If BELUGA shows up, it means:

Your contact and perception of Spirit will increase and become clearer, chiefly through your hearing.

Let your imagination roam into uncharted territories, and you'll feel an urge to do something unusual and creative.

Even though you mainly enjoy in-depth conversations, try engaging in light, superficial banter from time to time.

This is not a time to go it alone, but instead, a time to rely on the support and encouragement of family members or a group of friends.

Call on BELUGA when:

You find that your creativity is stifled or stagnant and you want to open it up.

You've recently experienced a spiritual revelation of some kind and want to assimilate it.

You want to call in any of your spirit helpers for guidance, protection, or comfort.

You want to keep track of your dreams or learn to have lucid dreams.

If BELUGA is your POWER ANIMAL:

You have an active imagination and the capacity to turn your visions into physical expressions and manifestations.

You have the gift of being able to sing or whistle in soothing and healing ways.

You're extremely social, always enjoying the company that you're with, and even like to go on trips with groups.

You have a great deal of depth, balanced with a strong sense of playfulness and harmless mischievousness.

BLACKBIRD

If BLACKBIRD shows up, it means:

Let go of all your inhibitions and sing, without concern for how it sounds or others' disapproval.

Archangel Uriel is with you, watching out for you and helping you connect with Nature and the Nature spirits.

Sound healing is one of your best treatments for whatever physical or emotional ailments or maladies you're experiencing.

The gateway to the world of non-ordinary reality is open, beckoning you to follow your true spiritual path and enhance your awareness of the nonphysical realm.

This is a particularly auspicious time to observe and heed any signs or omens that are shown to you.

Call on BLACKBIRD when:

You feel overwhelmed by city life and want to connect with Nature.

You're a singer about to give a performance or recital and want support so you can do your best.

You're taking voice lessons in order to improve your vocal expression or your singing voice.

You've been getting nudged to expand your spiritual exploration but are not sure how to do so.

If BLACKBIRD is your POWER ANIMAL:

You have the gift of being able to use singing and chanting for healing purposes.

You have the greatest vitality and energy during the spring and summer season, gradually easing up through fall and winter, at which time you need extra rest and quiet.

Most of the time you're very cheerful, gentle, and loving to others—unless and until they violate your boundaries.

You're very territorial, aggressively defending your personal space and very selective about when and with whom you'll share it.

BLACK WIDOW SPIDER

(Also see <u>Spider</u>)

If BLACK WIDOW SPIDER shows up, it means:

It's time for a fresh perspective on what you're doing, perhaps even a perspective that's contrary to your usual way of thinking and of seeing things.

Your intuitive powers are very strong now, so pay closer attention to the subtle sensations in your body rather than relying solely on what meets the eye.

You've done the hard work; now be patient and wait expectantly for the rewards that will come.

There's soon to be a substantial shift in the direction of your life, with a beneficial and renewed sense of purpose.

This is a good time to do a dietary cleanse and detoxification to clear out any toxicity or pollutants in your body.

Be direct and straightforward in all of your dealings, rather than dancing around the issues.

What you once thought of as threatening is really quite harmless, so there's no need to fear.

There's a situation you're involved in where it will work better for you to remain in the background.

Call on BLACK WIDOW SPIDER when:

You're impatient and anxious to see the returns that should have resulted from your efforts.

You're feeling immobilized and stuck with a creative project that up until now has been moving along nicely.

What you see and what you feel are widely incongruent, and you're not sure which to trust.

You feel very much out of balance physically, emotionally, mentally, or spiritually, and want to bring everything back to equilibrium.

There's some confusion and lack of clarity in an important relationship that has you on edge.

If BLACK WIDOW SPIDER is your POWER ANIMAL:

You're very good at looking at situations from various perspectives rather than being stuck in one way of seeing things.

You're a very engaging and expressive storyteller who can spin a tale with the best of them.

You're easy to get along with until and unless someone agitates you; then you can be rather biting and harsh.

You're intrigued by, and continually seek balance between, the various polarities we commonly face in life, such as death/rebirth, past/future, and masculine/feminine.

Although you can get along with most people, you prefer solitude.

BLUEBIRD

If BLUEBIRD shows up, it means:

This is a very rare and precious moment, so open up all your senses and simply enjoy this time.

You're so involved and bogged down with everyday events that you need to relax and lighten up.

Take a risk and speak your truth to that special someone rather than holding back, whether expressing positive or negative feelings.

Take some time to spend in a large open space, such as a meadow, and do a walking meditation there.

You're coming into your own in many different ways, so welcome this milestone with a relaxed sense of confidence and happiness.

Call on BLUEBIRD when:

The circumstances of your life feel overwhelming and weighty and you need some cheering up.

You've taken on a great deal of responsibility lately and need some support for handling it.

You're involved with facilitating a rite-of-passage ceremony for girls emerging into young womanhood.

You're out of balance because of working too much, and you need to inject more play and lightheartedness into your life.

If BLUEBIRD is your POWER ANIMAL:

You're a modest and unassuming individual, liked by nearly everyone you meet.

You work hard and you play hard.

You have the knack for speaking up at the right moment and saying the right thing.

You're a sweet and gentle person, never pushing or intimidating others, yet willing to stand up for yourself if threatened.

BLUE JAY

If BLUE JAY shows up, it means:

Pay close attention to nonverbal clues that tell you when someone is trying to deceive you.

Rather than just dabbling in the spiritual/metaphysical realm, choose a path to explore and go as far as you can with it.

Whatever the situation that has triggered some fear, attack it boldly and courageously.

Assess your main gifts and talents, develop a plan as to how you can best use them, and then take clear and purposeful action.

Choose one or two of the projects you've started and finish them.

Call on BLUE JAY when:

You're feeling threatened or intimidated by someone, particularly someone you see as stronger or more capable than you are.

You have a suspicion that someone is trying to dupe you by masking their true feelings and motives.

You're faced with a choice of giving up or continuing on with a project or relationship, and in your heart of hearts you know that you need to stay committed and see it through.

You have an interest in a number of subjects and want to explore them all to a degree.

If BLUE JAY is your POWER ANIMAL:

You're fearless and will not back down from any challenge or threat.

You're a dabbler, particularly in the psychic and metaphysical fields, knowing a little bit about a lot of things.

You sometimes convey the impression that you know more than you really do.

You're an excellent mimic, able to reproduce just about any sound or impersonate other people.

BLUE WHALE

(Also see <u>Whale</u>)

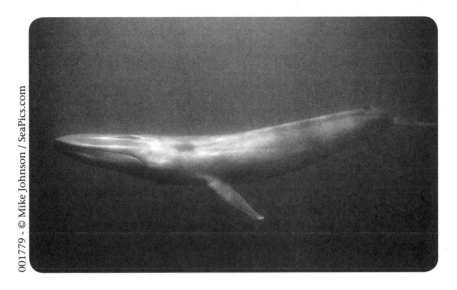

If BLUE WHALE shows up, it means:

You're going to be receiving messages from Spirit that will be so loud and clear that it will be impossible to ignore them.

Now that you've finished the plans for your creative project, take a deep breath, dive in, and watch how smoothly it grows and develops.

Be willing to help out those who ask you, whether it's giving coins to a homeless person, listening to the concerns of your friends or family members, or pitching in at a local charity drive.

Be extra careful with your communication during this time, both with listening and speaking, to make sure that you understand and that you're understood.

Take some time to investigate and understand the esoteric concept of the Akashic records and what this means for you and for our planet.

Call on BLUE WHALE when:

You want to increase the range and volume of your voice for speaking or singing.

You want to deepen your understanding of yourself by exploring and analyzing your subconscious realm through contemplation, meditation, and dreamwork.

There's been some miscommunication and misunderstanding with someone who's important to you, and you want to clear things up.

You're pursuing a course of study, formal or informal, of the ancient earth.

If BLUE WHALE is your POWER ANIMAL:

You have such a big and powerful presence that people take heed and notice you right away.

You have a lot going on under the surface that you contain very well, once in a while showing others the depth of intelligence and insightfulness that you have.

You have a big heart and are generous and compassionate, always willing to lend an ear or a helping hand to a friend.

You enjoy any type of communication and vocal expression, whether it's conversation, speaking, or singing.

You like to strike a balance between alone time, time with a mate, and socializing with a group of friends.

BOAR
(Peccary)

If BOAR shows up, it means:

Stop your procrastinating and move forward on that project that you started and have yet to finish.

It's time to meet whatever situation or person in your life is causing you distress head-on and achieve some sort of closure.

You're at the beginning of a period of wealth, prosperity, and personal growth.

Face your fears and do whatever is necessary to resolve them so that you can find peace.

Whatever controversy you're involved in will soon be settled in a fair and just manner.

Call on BOAR when:

There's someone in your life who has been mean or critical with you and you want to confront them.

You're feeling a lack of self-confidence and lowered self-esteem.

You're fearful and doubtful about being able to come up with whatever is necessary to meet your needs.

You've been personally misjudged and your efforts misperceived, and you want to straighten things out.

If BOAR is your POWER ANIMAL:

You're willing to tackle anything that makes you uncomfortable, in spite of any fear, and try to resolve it.

You have the uncanny knack for making the most of any situation, using whatever resources are available.

You're a stubbornly determined individual, persistent in pursuing your goals.

When you feel trapped or cornered, you can become quite belligerent and aggressive.

BOBCAT
(Also see <u>Lynx</u>)

If BOBCAT shows up, it means:

One of your tasks right now is to learn to live alone without feeling lonely.

This is a time to be vigilant, remaining simultaneously as alert and relaxed as you can be, with all your senses available as needed.

You'll find that you're much better at discerning what lurks behind the persona that someone presents.

If something doesn't feel right, trust your instincts rather than what others are telling or showing you.

Be careful at this time about what you share with someone else, even in confidence, as there is some risk that it will be passed on to others and either distorted or blown way out of proportion.

Call on BOBCAT when:

You want to be able to see better, particularly in darkness, both literally and metaphorically.

You're suspicious that what appears before you isn't the whole truth or else is completely deceitful.

You're studying and practicing any of the more prominent psychic or intuitive arts.

You've been around a lot of social activity and noisiness and need to withdraw into solitude and silence for a while.

You've been entrusted with confidential information from a friend and want to honor your friend's trust by keeping this information completely to yourself.

If BOBCAT is your POWER ANIMAL:

You're quiet, solitary, and a great listener, which is why friends are willing to share their secrets with you.

You're able to shift back and forth between various altered states of consciousness and everyday reality, always prepared to deal with practical matters as necessary.

You're very adept at knowing when to speak, what to share, and whom to share it with, and you use your utmost discretion in making this determination.

You have powerful psychic and intuitive gifts that you continue to develop, including clairvoyance, clairaudience, and psychometry.

You're so sensitive that you're sometimes overwhelmed with sensory input and need to retreat, yet are aware that it's not in your best interest to remain isolated and completely reclusive all the time.

BUFFALO
(Bison)

If BUFFALO shows up, it means:

Trust that you'll always have whatever you need.

Focus on being appreciative and grateful for all that you have.

Clear out any surplus goods and recycle those items.

Have faith in the natural abundance of life.

Stop feeling sorry for yourself and instead be aware of the extraordinary number of resources you have available.

Expand your interests by trying a new hobby, recreational activity, or sport.

— If it's WHITE BUFFALO:

- Expect a miracle and keep the faith.
- A period of calm and peacefulness is upon you, one that you can pass along in your contact with others.
- Your spirituality will now increase in leaps and bounds.
- You're a contributor to a new era that's being ushered in, one of peace and harmony for all people.

Call on BUFFALO when:

You're experiencing any kind of poverty or lack and need reassurance that supplies are plentiful and available.

You need extra determination when you're pursuing an important goal.

You want to restore your faith in the abundance and plenty of life.

You have an important project you're about to start.

You want help getting through a period of intense struggle and challenge.

If BUFFALO is your POWER ANIMAL:

You're confident that you'll always have whatever you need, and you don't worry about your supplies.

You're very generous and willing to share what you have.

You're very accepting and nonjudgmental with others, always trying to see the good in them.

You have a great deal of strength and endurance.

You can be unpredictable.

Once you set your mind on something, nothing will stop you from achieving it.

BULL

If BULL shows up, it means:

This is a very fertile and dynamic time, so allow yourself to indulge in any creative projects you've been considering.

Your life is headed for an upturn cycle, so welcome it and enjoy it.

This is a very prosperous time for you, and you'll soon receive an unexpected windfall.

Enjoy the material possessions you have, and release those that have served their purpose and are no longer useful.

Set your sights on your goal, get committed to it, and move toward it steadily and persistently, but don't rush ahead haphazardly.

— If OX:

- Pursue the educational course you've been considering.
- Teamwork is the best way to accomplish what you want to accomplish.
- Draw on masculine energy, whether you're male or female.

Call on BULL when:

There's a possibility of encroachment or intrusion by someone you don't want to be involved with and don't want near you.

You've been putting out a lot of energy, and you need a boost of strength and endurance.

You've been assigned to some difficult or challenging work, but you're not sure if you can do it.

You're worried about the future and whether you'll be safe and provided for.

You want to get to work on an idea you have, but you're fearful and not sure how to go about it.

If BULL is your POWER ANIMAL:

You're a very powerful individual, extremely protective toward your mate and your family.

When you want something, you're very determined and resolute, which some would even call stubbornness.

You value commitment highly, and once you commit to something, you stay with it for the long haul.

You carry yourself with an air of nobility and expect that others will respect and understand that aspect of you.

BUTTERFLY

If BUTTERFLY shows up, it means:

Lighten up and stop taking everything so seriously.

Get ready for a big change, one where an old habit, way of thinking, or lifestyle is going out, and a new way of being is emerging.

It's time to make the changes you've been considering.

In spite of the challenges, you'll get through this transition, and as always, know that "this too shall pass."

Express yourself by wearing more colorful clothing.

Call on BUTTERFLY when:

You know it's time for a change, and you need the courage to break out of your self-imposed cocoon.

You're going through a major life transition such as divorce or career change.

You want encouragement to more freely express the love you feel to those around you.

You want to put more romance into the relationship with your spouse or intimate partner.

You want help to relax more and go with the flow of the cycles in your work or your relationship.

If BUTTERFLY is your POWER ANIMAL:

You have a profound appreciation for the natural cycles of life/death/rebirth that occur within and around you.

You have a great deal of vitality, with exotic and colorful tastes in your choices of clothing, décor, art, music, and even friends.

You're very attractive to others, and people are naturally drawn to you.

You can be flighty, and generally don't form strong attachments to other people.

You don't do well in a harsh or toxic environment; as such, you have to live where the air and water are clean.

You adjust to change very readily and easily.

CAMEL

If CAMEL shows up, it means:

More than ever, it's a time to trust your own intuition for guidance, paying close attention to your senses and what they're telling you.

You have a lot more energy and durability for the task ahead than you think you do.

The road ahead may be difficult and you won't have a lot of support, yet you must take it with complete trust that you have everything you need within you and that you will succeed.

Although you'll never want for anything, it's still a good idea and a practical move to store away some supplies and money for future use.

Call on CAMEL when:

You've been on a long haul and need to replenish your energy and nourish yourself.

You're feeling lost and discouraged and need the strength to endure and the faith to know that everything will turn out all right.

You want to feel some stability and continuity in your life in spite of the shifting sands around you.

You're about to embark on a new adventure, a literal or metaphorical journey that will take you into unknown territory where you're not sure how your basic needs will be met.

If CAMEL is your POWER ANIMAL:

You're remarkably adaptable, with considerable inner strength, able to withstand and endure just about any condition life throws at you.

Although you can be unpredictable, you're generally very patient and kind.

You have the ability to succeed and even thrive in environments that others would find much too difficult to deal with at all.

You remain consistently positive amidst even the most severe or challenging times or experiences.

CANARY

If CANARY shows up, it means:

Whatever has gone before, let it all go, and greet the morning sun with a spirited welcome and a renewed sense of hope and purpose.

You're now discovering the power of your own voice and how influential and effective it is in speaking and/or singing.

You need more fresh air and sunlight for your health and vitality.

The emotional and spiritual atmosphere you surround yourself with will greatly influence your mood and your state of well-being.

Experiment with the varied uses of sound for healing, both as a receiver and as a healer.

What you say and how you say it will have considerable impact on others depending on whether you say it with love and compassion or with harshness and disparagement.

Call on CANARY when:

You have any obstructions, blockages, or discomfort in your throat chakra.

You're a professional singer or musician and want support for the clarity and power of your voice or instrument.

You feel somewhat depressed or down and want to lift your mood.

You want to improve your communication skills, particularly the sound and tone of your voice.

If CANARY is your POWER ANIMAL:

You're a powerful communicator, whether through your speaking or singing abilities.

You're very sensitive to the physical or emotional atmosphere you're in.

You're musically gifted and have to express yourself in this way to maintain balance in your life.

You have a passion for teaching and a way with words that communicates clearly what you're trying to convey.

You enjoy opportunities to have conversations with others, and they always appreciate how you bring sunshine into their lives through your presence and what you have to say.

CARDINAL

If CARDINAL shows up, it means:

Someone needs your compassionate and loving attention and has flagged you down to get it.

Stop right where you are, observe your surroundings, then notice the sensations in your body.

This is a very creative time, one where it's best to heed your intuitive guidance as to how to express this creativity.

Add color to your life in your home environment, your yard, and in your choices of clothing.

This is a good time to make a fresh exploration of the religion you grew up in, with your eyes and heart open.

Call on CARDINAL when:

Your life or the world around you looks rather dreary and you want to add some color.

You've moved around a lot and want to settle down in one place for a stretch of time.

You want to improve your diet and be more careful about eating the kinds of foods that are healthy and that your body requires.

You want to learn to listen to your intuition more closely, but you're not sure how to go about it.

If CARDINAL is your POWER ANIMAL:

One of your primary purposes for being on this planet is to bring color to this world.

You much prefer a stable living situation, so you tend to stay in the same place for long periods of time.

You have access to a powerful feminine creative energy, and are able to listen closely to your intuitive guidance.

You stand out in a crowd, and when you walk into a room, you brighten it up without even trying.

You have a past-life connection with the Catholic Church, likely in the upper echelons of the priesthood.

CARIBOU
(Also see [Deer](#))

If CARIBOU shows up, it means:

This is a time for you to act with resolve, so make a decision, stick with it, and take the appropriate action.

The long emotional and spiritual trek you've been on is about to conclude; and once it does, you'll reap the rewards, benefits, and pleasures of having done it.

There's something bugging you, and you need to address whatever it is and either try to change it, get away from it, or surrender to it.

There is solidarity and camaraderie among the people you know and trust, which is something your soul is yearning for at this time, so indulge yourself and seek out these folks.

Although your journey may seem rather lengthy, as long as you seek the support you need, you will succeed.

Call on CARIBOU when:

You're feeling an itch to wander to some place far away from home.

You're feeling pestered by something or someone that's annoying you, and you want to do whatever you can to get away from this situation or person.

You want to do something active to help yourself and your family feel more secure, but you're not sure what to do to accomplish that.

You've resolved to eliminate some self-limiting or self-defeating habits or patterns and you're ready to start the process.

If CARIBOU is your POWER ANIMAL:

You're gregarious and sociable, enjoying the company of your own kind of people.

You enjoy traveling regularly, and tend to vacation at the same places.

Once you've decided that it's time to act, you're off and running.

Autumn is your season and is the best time for you to begin any creative projects or endeavors.

You're a very determined individual, particularly when you know that you have the support of your friends and family with respect to whatever you're going after.

CASSOWARY

If CASSOWARY shows up, it means:

To refresh and restore your vitality, get away from civilization and spend some time in a forest or the bush.

It's important to give something back, such as your time, money, gifts, or recycled goods, to anyone or any organization that has provided for you in the past.

Increase the amount of fresh fruit in your diet—at least two or three portions each day—for the next two weeks.

Maintain your dignity and self-respect no matter what it takes.

The law of karma—what you put out will come back to you—is stronger than ever right now, and the return that much quicker.

Call on CASSOWARY when:

You have any doubts or concerns about the importance of your purpose and your mission.

You feel that you've been mistreated such that your dignity and self-respect have been challenged and demeaned.

Someone has intruded upon your sacred space, and you want to confront them and set your boundaries.

You've been overly aggressive with someone without due cause, and you want to make amends.

If CASSOWARY is your POWER ANIMAL:

You enjoy your solitude, whether in a relationship or not, yet you don't mind when others visit.

You carry yourself with a relaxed authority and command respect from others simply by your presence.

If you're a man, you're an active participant in your children's lives from gestation to birth and through childhood into adulthood.

You're very territorial and react strongly if someone uninvited attempts to intrude, such that you have to be careful about being too forceful and belligerent.

CAT

If CAT shows up, it means:

This is a period where self-sufficiency and trust in your own capabilities is necessary.

Honor your sensuality by dancing slowly, with graceful and easy movements, and by enjoying touch and physical intimacy.

Listen closely to your intuitive guidance, as it's most likely an ancestor who's one of your spirit guides trying to communicate with you.

This is a period of magic and mystery for you, so pay close attention to signs and omens that will guide and direct you.

Whatever you've released—relationships, material goods, self-defeating habits—will soon be replaced with something or someone entirely more suitable for who you are presently.

— If FERAL CAT:

- Do something totally wild and out of character, yet which is completely harmless.
- Break away from any unhealthy dependencies on others.

Call on CAT when:

You feel so wrapped up in someone else's life that you're not sure where you begin and the other ends.

You're feeling pressured to conform or to go along with the group, but your instincts are telling you something different.

You're in an intense period of self-reflection, exploring some new dimension of yourself.

You've been working much too hard, and it's time to play.

If CAT is your POWER ANIMAL:

You're introspective and listen to your own internal guidance more than others' advice.

You're independent, sometimes to the point of doing exactly the opposite of what others expect or want you to do.

Your most creative work is done at night.

You move very gracefully and naturally, exuding a mysterious sensuality.

At times you come across as rather self-absorbed, seeming oblivious to those around you.

CHAMELEON

(Also see <u>Lizard</u>)

If CHAMELEON shows up, it means:

This is a time to stay in the background, be patient, and not show your true colors.

You're in for a very positive change in your environment.

Trust that what you see with your eyes is the truth, rather than relying on what you hear or feel, or what others claim to be true.

Pay attention to a potential opportunity that will show up for you in the next day or two, and when it does, act on it quickly.

Be careful about getting ahead of yourself, and instead, make sure that you're solidly anchored before making any important choices.

Call on CHAMELEON when:

You need to keep track of demands and responsibilities that are coming at you from all directions.

You're in a situation where you want to blend in and not be noticed.

You want to determine an important choice based on relevant information from the past, as well as your hunch about what's to come in the future.

Your emotions are just under the surface, and you want to let yourself feel and express them.

You have a strong feeling that you're acting too hastily regarding some important choice or decision.

If CHAMELEON is your POWER ANIMAL:

You generally move more slowly and carefully than others, but when you see something you really want, you move quickly to get it.

You have this unique ability to be able to see and understand many different points of view at the same time.

You have a tendency to be moody, sometimes going through changes several times throughout your day.

You're very deliberate and purposeful in your thinking and in the way you move, willing to go as slowly as needed in order to stay grounded.

CHEETAH

If CHEETAH shows up, it means:

Things will be speeded up for a while, but be assured that you'll move gracefully through this cycle.

Increase your flexibility by daily stretching, perhaps even taking regular yoga classes for the next few months.

You must respond without hesitation to the opportunity that has recently presented itself.

Don't get caught up in the trap of rigid thinking and acting, but instead remain flexible and willing to change course quickly as the situation demands.

Call on CHEETAH when:

Getting something done quickly and efficiently is a top priority.

You've put forth an incredible amount of effort and energy and need a good rest in order to recuperate.

You're in a situation that requires you to think and respond quickly in order to adapt to the rapidly changing circumstances that are unfolding.

You need to keep your feet on the ground—literally and metaphorically—as you maneuver through a rather difficult task or challenge.

If CHEETAH is your POWER ANIMAL:

You have very quick reflexes and can move swiftly whenever you need to.

You enjoy your solitude, yet from time to time you also enjoy the company of a few people with whom you have a close bond.

You're very protective of your children and to other youngsters you're close to.

Your early years were extremely difficult, with lots of grief and tears.

You're very empathetic and compassionate with others most of the time.

CHIMPANZEE

If CHIMPANZEE shows up, it means:

Use your imagination to create fresh approaches to problem-solving the situation before you.

You have everything you need in order to tackle the responsibilities and tasks you're faced with.

Let go of any remaining anger or resentment, and forgive the person you've recently had a conflict with.

Adjust your diet to one of healthy, natural, and organic foods.

It's better to ignore some of the things that are going on around you that would otherwise cause you considerable disturbance.

This is a good time for self-assessment and self-reflection, acknowledging your strengths and limitations, and positive and negative characteristics without judgment.

Call on CHIMPANZEE when:

You've followed a particular strategy that isn't working any more in dealing with the current situation, and you need to develop a new approach.

You're involved in a creative enterprise that requires imagination, innovation, and originality.

The spiritual and mundane aspects of your life are out of balance, polarized in one direction or the other, and you want to bring them back into equilibrium.

You've had a disagreement or dispute with someone and want to make amends.

You've been feeling bored and stuck in routines and want to make some changes that will help you feel more enthusiasm and vitality.

If CHIMPANZEE is your POWER ANIMAL:

You're able to come up with innovative and practical ideas that are helpful in a number of situations.

You're very curious about a lot of things, and eagerly explore whatever holds your interest at any given time.

You're very sociable, and thrive on feeling connected to a group of like-minded people, whether family or friends.

You're a very nurturing, compassionate, and caring individual, and you show this consistently and in a variety of ways with your family and others you're close to.

CHINCHILLA

© GK & Vikki Hart / gettyimages

If CHINCHILLA shows up, it means:

Investigate and consider donating some time, energy, and/or money to animal-rights organizations.

Trust your instincts to tell you when to go forward, when to retreat, when it's the right time to act, and what the right course of action is.

It's best to stand back and carefully observe what's going on before making your next move.

Rather than relying so heavily on intellectual analysis to solve a problem or make a decision, take a deep breath, notice your gut feelings, and see how they balance and complement your analytical skills.

It's important at this time that you maintain a healthy diet and a good exercise regimen for optimal health.

There's something out of balance in your life, and it's in your best interest to do whatever it takes to bring things back in balance.

Call on CHINCHILLA when:

Timing is critical for you as far as when to make your next move.

You're due for a detoxification cleanse, particularly if it's a change of season.

You're having any kind of communication difficulties with someone and want to straighten things out.

Something is off or out of balance and you want to correct it.

Psychically, you're not feeling 100 percent and want to make some changes in your diet and in the amount and kind of exercise you're doing.

If CHINCHILLA is your POWER ANIMAL:

You're always very curious about the details of your surroundings, wherever you happen to be.

Once you feel safe and secure, you approach life with innocence and a sense of adventure.

You're very effective and accurate when it comes to discerning the meaning of signs and omens.

You're a keen observer, with a good memory of whatever it is you're seeing and hearing.

You effectively balance your remarkable analytical skills with your attention to your instinctual promptings.

CHIPMUNK
(Ground Squirrel)

If CHIPMUNK shows up, it means:

Trust that you're well protected and that there is no real danger you'll have to face.

Be curious and willing to investigate anything of interest that comes your way.

Go out for walks, and when you do, take the time to explore anything that attracts your attention, from the tiniest pebble or flower to the vista that's on the horizon.

Once you've completed a creative piece or project, keep it to yourself for a few weeks before revealing to others.

Pay more attention to the vocal characteristics of those you encounter—volume, pitch, and inflection—than the actual words as a way of discerning more about the person than speech alone reveals.

Call on CHIPMUNK when:

You're in a new situation where you feel anxious or afraid even though there's no objective threat or imminent danger.

You're doing a nature walk by yourself or with a group and want to maximize your appreciation of what you observe while on the walk.

You're not sure if what someone is saying to you is what they're actually feeling or thinking.

Someone is being bossy or pushy with you, and you need to respond clearly and appropriately.

Your fears and anxieties are keeping you from enjoying life.

If CHIPMUNK is your POWER ANIMAL:

You're inquisitive, playful, and enjoy exploring anything that comes across your path.

You do what you want when you want to do it and don't tolerate others telling you what to do or when to do it.

Noticeable and sometimes dramatic shifts and changes occur for you in either three-month or one-year cycles.

You're very chatty and love to talk with others, sometimes having to remind yourself to stop and listen to what they have to say.

You carry yourself with an aura of confidence and certainty; and your movements are quick, unpredictable, and decisive.

COBRA

(Also see <u>Snake</u>)

If COBRA shows up, it means:

You have a profound connection to goddess energy, particularly to Isis.

Expect an awakening and heightening of your intuitive abilities that will serve you well when it comes to making decisions.

You're faced with an important choice right now, so be sure to strike when the time is right, and don't hesitate when your gut tells you it's time.

Take some classes in kundalini yoga, and after a few classes, notice the difference in how this makes you feel.

Dance by turning on some slow music and allowing yourself to enjoy free-form movement.

Keep your eyes and your senses open and alert, and don't be blinded by illusions perpetrated by others.

Call on COBRA when:

You need to make a quick decision and follow it with action.

There's an unexpected opportunity that shows up and you're not sure what to do with it.

You're doubtful about what others are telling you because your instincts tell you otherwise.

You're feeling distrustful of someone and you're not sure why.

You need to detoxify your body and your emotions.

You've got an idea or a creative project in mind and you need to guard it closely and keep it contained for the time being.

If COBRA is your POWER ANIMAL:

You carry yourself with an air of nobility and dignity.

You have a gift of being able to look beyond the appearances of another person and into their soul, which can sometimes be intimidating to others.

You trust your instincts to dictate what you should do in any situation that's questionable or where there's any doubt.

You know when to withdraw and when to strike out.

COCKATOO

If COCKATOO shows up, it means:

Let go of your agenda and do something spontaneous and out of the ordinary.

Do something special to demonstrate your love and care for your mate or one of your closest friends.

You're about to embark on an important learning process, whether through formal education or self-study, which will require your dedication and perseverance and yet be very stimulating and fulfilling.

Bolster your self-esteem by refusing to demean, put down, or criticize yourself for at least one full day.

The lover you're with is a keeper, and will be a responsible and affectionate mate.

— If WHITE COCKATOO:

- You've just about completed these difficult changes and are about to launch a new beginning.

— If BLACK COCKATOO:

- This period of chaos and uncertainty that you're going through will soon be over, so be patient, as it will soon pass.

Call on COCKATOO when:

You need help in understanding and getting clarity about the signs and messages you receive.

You're having difficulty with communication in a close relationship and you want to straighten things out.

You're in a situation that requires you to exude a supreme degree of confidence.

You've found someone whom you're considering as a life partner and want to work toward that end by consciously going through a courtship with that person.

If COCKATOO is your POWER ANIMAL:

Ever since you were young, you've had a spiritual consciousness and would make an excellent minister, teacher, or spiritual leader.

You're a very caring, responsible, and nurturing intimate partner; and once you've found the right person, you stick with him or her for the rest of your life.

You're intelligent, affectionate, and enjoy socializing with others immensely.

You're unpredictable and full of hidden talents, and others never quite know what to expect from you at any given moment.

CONDOR
(Vulture)

If CONDOR shows up, it means:

In spite of the dire circumstances you find yourself in or the losses you've sustained, you'll eventually find the gifts in this experience that may not be immediately apparent.

It's time to clean up the clutter or messes that you find around you.

Develop new and creative solutions to those problems that you or others would prefer to ignore.

You'll find that your tastes, cravings, and possibly your entire diet will soon change, so pay close attention to your body's response when you eat certain foods.

You need to take all those material items that no longer serve a purpose and either recycle them or get rid of them.

— If CALIFORNIA CONDOR:

- You'll find a renewed sense of vigor, vitality, and enthusiasm about life.
- In the morning, take a few moments to greet the sun by standing with your arms out in a welcoming gesture.
- This is a good time to retreat, and enter into a period of solitude and meditation.

— If TURKEY VULTURE:

- You'll find yourself being more visually perceptive, to the point of seeing auras around others.
- It's a good opportunity to sort out and eliminate that which doesn't "smell right" in your life.

Call on CONDOR when:

You're in the midst of a crisis, one that requires you to remain calm and adjust your thinking to accept the situation as it is before moving on to a solution.

You've lost someone in your life through death and want to contact their spirit on the other side.

You see yourself as having disadvantages and want to reframe your perceptions and beliefs to see them as assets.

You feel as if you're in a mess emotionally, physically, or spiritually, and you want to clean things up.

If CONDOR is your POWER ANIMAL:

You have the unique ability to make the best of a bad situation and find the rewards that result.

You're a somber and serious individual most of the time.

You're willing to take on distasteful tasks that others are unwilling to do.

You have the gift of mediumship, whether you've developed it or not, and can communicate with deceased loved ones and ancestors.

Because of your unusual appearance and your metaphysical gifts, others don't understand you and may irrationally fear you, so they tend to keep their distance.

CORMORANT

If CORMORANT shows up, it means:

Once you have clarity about what your goal is, dive in enthusiastically and without hesitation.

When you've been immersed in the pursuit of your goals for too long, stop and take a nice stretch in the sunlight and fresh air.

You've been working very hard, so now it's time to step back and appreciate what you've accomplished so far.

There's someone who seems to be holding you back, so in order to move ahead, you first have to release any beliefs that you're somehow a victim in this situation, and if necessary, confront this person.

Own your power, because giving it away causes too much physical, mental, and emotional distress.

Don't limit yourself by thinking and believing that something isn't possible.

Call on CORMORANT when:

You have a dream or a vision that you don't yet believe is possible to achieve.

You've let some criticism get to you and you want to let it evaporate from your consciousness.

You're offered an opportunity that would require you to stretch beyond what you think you're capable of.

You're feeling tired of going it alone, and need support from friends and family.

If CORMORANT is your POWER ANIMAL:

You have a way of accomplishing things that others think are impossible.

When there's an opportunity presented to you that looks pretty tasty, you dive into it wholeheartedly.

You balance your work by making it a point to take breaks outdoors.

You're friendly and accommodating, so much so that you have to be careful of allowing others to take so much from you that you end up feeling depleted and used.

COUGAR
(Mountain Lion or Puma)

If COUGAR shows up, it means:

You're being called upon to provide leadership to your family, friends, community, or the world as a whole.

There's a need for you to be very decisive right now and not equivocate.

Stop procrastinating with respect to that important task—just get to it.

Stay strong, clear, and assertive with those who are asking or demanding that you change when you're not ready to.

Move forward with faith and courage, and keep your eyes on the goal.

Call on COUGAR when:

You need strength and assertiveness to deal with a challenging situation.

You want to have more patience and persistence when you must tackle a difficult task.

You need help in balancing your personal power with gracefulness and clear intention.

You want to gain confidence when you're called upon to give a speech or any kind of presentation.

You feel overwhelmed and need help accomplishing several demanding tasks.

If COUGAR is your POWER ANIMAL:

You're a well-balanced individual.

Once you've decided what to do about a situation, you're quick to take action.

You're often called upon to take a position of leadership in which others depend on you to provide answers and direction.

You prefer solitude to socializing.

You're a take-charge kind of person, sometimes engendering others' disapproval and criticism.

COW

If COW shows up, it means:

This is a very nourishing time for you, so be willing to partake of all that's offered to you.

You have nothing to worry about, as you're well provided for in spite of any fears or doubts.

This is a time for mending and healing the relationship with your mother, whether she's alive or has passed into the spirit world.

You may wish to work with the Hindu goddess Lakshmi, the goddess of fortune, as a means of being assured of your abundance.

Stand in your truth, and once you've made a decision, don't let others sway you.

You may be called upon to make some sort of sacrifice that will benefit the greater good.

Call on COW when:

You feel the need for nurturing and nourishment, both physical and emotional.

You're about to become a mother, already have children, or care for other people's children.

You want to have greater faith that the universe will always provide and that there will always be plenty for you and everyone else.

You're in need of healing some emotional wounds that resulted from being neglected or abandoned during your childhood.

If COW is your POWER ANIMAL:

You're very alert and aware of all that's going on around you.

You enjoy quietness and stillness, giving you a chance to simply think at your leisure.

You're very generous and giving with your heart and your time, and are known for your compassion and caring.

When there's trouble or strife, you like to seek out family and friends and stick close to them.

You're capable of sensing both danger and opportunity and are able to discern between the two.

You're very service oriented, willing to put others' needs before your own.

COYOTE

If COYOTE shows up, it means:

Lighten up—you're taking things much too seriously.

The resources you need are available.

Something quite unexpected and not necessarily welcome is about to happen.

Rather than fighting or running from this situation, it will work out better if you adjust to it.

Look for the lessons in the turmoil you're experiencing.

Forgive yourself for any mistakes or errors, and look for the gifts that have come out of the experience.

Call on COYOTE when:

You want to simplify something that appears complicated.

You're looking for the more subtle meanings behind a dream, vision, or recent experience.

You want to stay poised and remain calm in the midst of any chaotic situation.

You're feeling down, and you need to regain your sense of humor about life.

You're feeling bored because life has gotten to be too much of a routine, and you want to liven things up.

You want help in brainstorming creative solutions to a seemingly insurmountable problem.

It's unclear whether a decision you make will lead to peace or chaos.

If COYOTE is your POWER ANIMAL:

You're always looking for the hidden lessons in difficult situations.

You're a practical joker, and tend to turn just about everything into fun.

You're a survivor, capable of living through almost any experience.

You're very resourceful, able to adapt to virtually any circumstance.

You're a natural teacher, teaching mainly by example; and as you age, you gain greater and greater wisdom.

You're able to see the humor in the most challenging situations.

Your friends consider you to be a paradox, very difficult to pigeonhole or conveniently categorize.

CRAB

If CRAB shows up, it means:

You're about to experience an unexpected shift in your surroundings or in your personal life that will be beneficial for your soul's path.

You'll find yourself becoming increasingly clairvoyant, able to see things from the nonvisible realm more clearly.

You're missing a lot by staying too focused on what's directly in front of you rather than incorporating the subtleties of what you see and hear peripherally.

Pay close attention to promptings from your subconscious, which will come through dreams, visions, and flashes of insight, and bring these to the surface for guidance and to manifest them in physical reality.

Put on some of your favorite music, dress comfortably, shut the shades, and dance.

Call on CRAB when:

You've been hiding out for quite a while, and now it's time to come out of your shell.

You're going into a potentially hostile or negative emotional climate and need extra protection.

You're faced with some sudden and unexpected changes, and you need help in adapting quickly to these.

Someone is confronting you, and you want to tactfully deal with and respond to what the other person is saying without becoming defensive and verbally counterattacking.

You're cleaning out and clearing up a lot of stuff that you're not sure what to do with.

If CRAB is your POWER ANIMAL:

You have a tendency to make quick decisions and quick changes, often to the surprise of those around you.

You're incredibly durable, able to survive and thrive in just about any environment, and will adapt as necessary and very quickly to any changes.

Your hearing, vision, and physical feelings are very acute, leading you to be quite sensitive to your surroundings and other people, so you protect yourself by being reclusive or withdrawing as needed.

You're able to shift your attention very quickly and still maintain your concentration and be alert to all that's going on around you.

You're very protective of your home and personal space, guarding it carefully from any outside intrusions.

CRANE

If CRANE shows up, it means:

Do what you need to do to bring greater balance into your life.

This is a time of great abundance and plenty, one in which you won't want for anything.

A portal has opened that allows you glimpses of the future without fear or trepidation.

Maintain a relaxed vigilance at this time, paying close attention to signs and omens.

It's time to revive and restore that hobby or recreational interest you once enjoyed.

Call on CRANE when:

Everything feels off kilter and you want to restore order and balance.

You find yourself worrying to the point of feeling stressed and out of sorts.

Your attention is divided between two important aspects of your life and you want to focus on only one.

You're feeling a lack of love, money, attention, or anything else, and want to shift your attitude to one of gratitude and abundance.

You feel out of touch with your emotions or closed off to your intuitive side.

If CRANE is your POWER ANIMAL:

You're unflappable, moving through life without worrying or hurrying.

You have the uncanny gift of often knowing what will happen before it actually does.

You're very sensitive to any changes in your environment and are particularly reactive to more dramatic ones.

You can be so focused for long periods of time that you disregard what's happening around you.

You're great at successfully mediating among adversaries by appealing to their feelings and their intelligence, bringing them to a common ground of agreement and peace.

CROCODILE
(See <u>Alligator</u>)

CROW

(Also see <u>Raven</u>)

If CROW shows up, it means:

You're on the verge of manifesting something you've been working toward for a while.

Be very watchful over the next couple of days for any clear omens or signs that will guide you and teach you.

Expect a big change very soon.

You've noticed something that's out of balance or an injustice that hasn't been addressed, and it's important to speak up about it.

You're about to get a glimpse into some future event that affects you directly.

Call on CROW when:

You feel as if someone is trying to trick or con you, but you're not sure.

You're faced with some significant change in your life and need some help and guidance to get through it.

You're feeling a strong creative surge and want support in developing and manifesting this inspiration.

You know that you're receiving spiritual guidance in the form of signs and omens but aren't sure of their meaning.

You're navigating a rather treacherous path through a project or relationship and want some advance warning of any potential pitfalls.

If CROW is your POWER ANIMAL:

You're a very resourceful person, effective at using whatever is available to create what you want or need.

You're sociable, but prefer to spend time with your closest friends and family.

You view the physical and spiritual worlds as illusory and are therefore able to shift reality to suit you.

More so than by any human-made laws, you let yourself be guided by the voice of Spirit and your personal integrity.

You're very willing to speak up whenever you feel that something is out of accord with spiritual law.

CUCKOO

If CUCKOO shows up, it means:

Listen closely to what others are saying—and what they're not saying.

An unexpected turn in your life path has just opened up, or soon will, and will be even more congruent with your soul's destiny.

Be a bit more cautious about what you say and to whom, especially anything that is hearsay or gossip about others.

You don't have to suffer to grow and mature on your spiritual path.

Slow down and trust that everything takes place in divine time, no matter what your agenda is.

Call on CUCKOO when:

Something has been eating at you and you want to release it and heal it.

You've been moving so fast that your muscles are tensed, your jaw is clenched, and you know that you need to slow down.

You're at the beginning stages of a project, job, or relationship, and want to enjoy it as much as possible.

You're resurrecting a hobby, sport, or other recreational activity that you used to enjoy.

You've recently had a negative experience with someone and you need the strength and clarity to deal with it.

If CUCKOO is your POWER ANIMAL:

You're somehow able to draw people out of their shells and out from behind their personas, and in a brief time, get to know them at a fairly deep level.

You're very adept at going with the flow of life and surrendering to and moving with each new twist and turn.

You enjoy finding new projects and interests, and enthusiastically jump into them at every opportunity.

You enjoy singing, especially songs that are positive and up-lifting.

DEER

(Also see <u>Caribou</u>; <u>Elk</u>; <u>Stag</u>)

If DEER shows up, it means:

You've been involved in some aggressive, negative circumstances and need to seek out safe, nurturing situations and people.

More than ever, you need to trust your gut instinct.

You're poised for an enticing adventure, one that will take you down many different paths and lead to many important insights.

Be gentle with yourself and others.

— If WHITE-TAILED DEER:

- You're entering into a time of plenty, but the path to get there has not been without sacrifices.

— If MULE DEER:

- You're in a phase of your life where you're wandering about without a clear sense of direction, so go ahead and enjoy it.

Call on DEER when:

You need help finding inspiration and resources for any creative projects you're working on.

You need help in situations where extra vigilance and sensitivity is called for in order to avoid any harmful consequences.

You want to release any resentments, grudges, or judgments about someone.

You're charged with facilitating any women's ceremonies or rituals, such as honoring any major life passages and transitions.

You want to find strength and endurance when you're going through a difficult life passage.

If DEER is your POWER ANIMAL:

You maintain a balance of the masculine traits of mastery, authority, and protection with the feminine characteristics of love, nourishment, and surrender, yet relate most closely to those associated with your gender.

You're highly sensitive and intuitive and are often aware of the feelings of others before they are.

You can move with intention, awareness, and speed, and can change directions quickly while staying completely centered.

You're most comfortable outdoors, particularly in the woods or forest, and must frequently spend time there to recharge and regenerate.

DINGO
(Also see <u>Dog</u>)

If DINGO shows up, it means:

Lighten up, laugh at your mistakes, and don't take yourself or life so seriously.

Spend some time out in nature and make it a point to listen closely to all that you hear—and what you don't.

Stay flexible and be willing to adjust your plans as needed.

When you're pursuing a goal, be persistent and relentless in your quest until you achieve what you want.

Rather than judging yourself for your errors and mistakes, look for what you've learned from them.

Call on DINGO when:

You're involved in a project that's so demanding that at times you feel like giving up, yet you know that it's critical to stay with it.

You're finding it difficult to accept what life has brought your way, feeling victimized by these occurrences, yet wanting to regain a sense of power.

You're taking life much too seriously and want to regain your sense of humor.

You feel that you've messed things up somehow, and not only do you want to rectify the situation, but you also want to discover the lessons that have come out of this experience.

If DINGO is your POWER ANIMAL:

There are times when you know something without having a logical reason as to why it is you know.

You're very adaptive, quite able to accommodate whatever circumstances you find yourself in.

You're intelligent and persistent, willing to experiment with different ways of getting the job done.

You're a very good public speaker and do well in a job that requires you to use this talent.

You work with sound in some form, whether music, singing, or sound healing.

DOG

(There are so many different types of dogs that only
the general meanings are offered here. Meditate on and
research the characteristics of any particular dog to
discover the specific meanings and purpose.)

If DOG shows up, it means:

Keep your faith strong no matter what's going on in your life.

It's important for you to volunteer for something purely in the
spirit of service.

Remain determined and resolute even if you face some negativity or disappointment.

Show your love and appreciation in creative ways to those you're
closest to.

Give your loyalty to those you love and cherish.

Call on DOG when:

You've been working on a project and your resolve is beginning
to fade.

You're feeling lonely and in need of companionship.

You feel the need for immediate and strong protection.

You're facing some difficulty or challenge and feel like giving up.

If DOG is your POWER ANIMAL:

You're very loyal to your friends, work situation, and community.

You do your best when you do work where you can serve humanity in some way.

You thrive when you're living and working in groups of people rather than by yourself.

When someone needs something, you're often the quickest to respond.

DOLPHIN
(Porpoise)

If DOLPHIN shows up, it means:

Take a few minutes today to meditate while playing one of your favorite pieces of music.

Listen more and talk less, especially to the more subtle levels of communication from other people and from the natural world.

Think and behave more lovingly and positively toward that person you're having difficulty with.

Smile more at others, and notice how they smile back at you.

Try Dolphin breathing by taking three slow, deep breaths, each time exhaling with an audible "Puh!" sound. Then observe how you feel.

Call on DOLPHIN when:

Things have become routine and monotonous and you need to breathe some freshness into your life.

You're having a conflict with someone close to you and you want to clear things up.

You're feeling uptight and want to release all your tension.

There's been a problem with or a blockage of communication in any relationship.

You're being prompted to move into some deeper spiritual work.

If DOLPHIN is your POWER ANIMAL:

You're a master communicator, mainly because you're able to listen at several different levels simultaneously.

You're sensitive and keenly aware of people's feelings, even those that others would prefer to keep hidden.

You live very much in the present.

You're a guardian of the waters, which means that your soul's assignment is to do anything you can to protect and clean up the oceans, rivers, lakes, and streams.

Because of your compassion and empathy, people seek you out for advice and counsel.

You're highly intuitive, psychic, and even telepathic, with both people and animals.

You rarely take things too seriously, turning everything into a game, sometimes to the point of annoying others.

You're flirtatious in a playful and innocent way.

DONKEY

If DONKEY shows up, it means:

Volunteer and give your time and physical energy to a service organization that's compatible with your philosophy and beliefs.

Listen to and respect your intuition, particularly when it comes to doing something that has potential risks.

Take your time and proceed cautiously and slowly, but keep on moving ahead, pausing only to determine the best direction to go toward your destination.

The more you express and honor your inner truth, the more recognition and acknowledgment you'll receive.

Call on DONKEY when:

You've done a lot for someone and now you need to set limits by saying no.

There's a task you have to do that seems like it will be burdensome and exhausting, yet you need to get motivated to get on with it.

You're having trouble finding your way to your destination because you've been overly focused on the goal rather than the best way to *get* to that goal.

You're in a precarious and potentially dangerous situation that requires caution and steadiness to extricate yourself from it.

If DONKEY is your POWER ANIMAL:

You're a hard worker, dedicated to the tasks put before you and very willing to be of service.

You're always willing to help others when and where needed, although sometimes you take on more than you can handle.

You're a very patient and unassuming individual with a tremendous depth of character.

You will persevere and get the job done no matter how difficult, as long as it's safe to do so.

DOVE

If DOVE shows up, it means:

Express your love to as many people as possible in words and in deeds, even in small yet significant ways.

The soul of someone who's recently passed is making a smooth, peaceful, and joyous transition.

This is a powerful time of prophecy and clear vision, and now more than ever you're able to glimpse the future.

You're experiencing a spiritual renewal that's the result of a period of intense self-examination and challenges.

This is a good time to stay at home and enjoy your domestic side.

It's important to nurture yourself with loving care.

Call on DOVE when:

You feel troubled, worried, distraught, anxious, or upset, and need to have some peace and calmness in your life.

You feel anxious about your partner's love for you, and want to instill a greater feeling of security into the relationship.

You're experiencing doubt and uncertainty about your spiritual life and want to deepen your faith.

Someone close to you has recently died, and you want to find some comfort and somehow connect with this person's spirit on the other side.

If DOVE is your POWER ANIMAL:

You're usually very serene, imparting this calmness to others by your mere presence.

You're a paradox in that you're quite evolved spiritually yet also very grounded and down-to-earth.

You love staying at home and involving yourself in various domestic pursuits.

Your maternal instincts are very strong, whether you're male or female.

You're both gentle and very passionate, expressing these qualities in quiet yet powerful ways, not the least of which is as a lover.

DRAGON

© Sue Dawe

If DRAGON shows up, it means:

You're emerging into a new phase of your life, one where you'll be taking more risks and be more vulnerable, yet you can be well protected.

Do more of the kinds of activities that bring passion into your life.

You have a past-life connection to a time when Earth-based spiritual practices were predominant.

You're entering into a period of considerable prosperity.

Spend some time regularly in meditation or contemplation and you'll receive some valuable insights and inspiration.

Call on DRAGON when:

You're attracted to the study and practice of any of the ancient mystical arts.

You've become enmeshed in the more mundane aspects of your life and are yearning for adventure.

You're faced with a number of obstacles in a project or business venture.

There's a situation you have to deal with that triggers a lot of fear for you, yet you know that you need to confront it and clear it.

If DRAGON is your POWER ANIMAL:

You practice Earth-based spirituality and mystical arts from the Wiccan, Pagan, Druidic, or shamanic traditions.

You're a contemporary wizard, quite evolved spiritually, and the more you mature, the more refined your wisdom and skills become.

You have a very commanding presence and carry yourself with an air of dignity and regality.

You're very open-minded and accepting of other's spiritual paths and of new ideas and possibilities.

You have a lot of enthusiasm and vitality, and it's contagious.

DRAGONFLY

If DRAGONFLY shows up, it means:

Be on the lookout for any falsehoods, deceit, or illusions that are clouding a current situation or relationship.

You're being entirely too rational about everything and really need to tap in to your deeper emotions, whatever they may be.

This is a time when the magic and mystery of life is reawakening for you.

It's important now to recharge your psychic energy, which you can do so by regularly meditating.

More than simply a change, you're going through a major transformation, so enjoy the process!

Call on DRAGONFLY when:

You feel emotionally shut down and want to free up your energy and expressiveness.

Your life feels stagnant and you need a change of pace.

A situation or relationship seems clouded with illusion or falsehood, and you want to get to the truth of what's going on.

You're feeling drawn to study any mystical arts or ancient mystery schools.

If DRAGONFLY is your POWER ANIMAL:

You're a very emotionally intense and passionate individual, although as you've matured you've learned the art of detachment and emotional containment.

You have a lot of nervous energy, flitting here and there a lot, and must balance this energy by getting grounded from time to time.

You have a strong connection to the nature spirits and love gardening and working with plants.

You're a master of seeing through illusions, whether others' or your own.

DUCK

If DUCK shows up, it means:

This is a time of fertility, either literally or metaphorically.

It's time to have fun and maybe even get a little silly.

The time of turmoil has passed, so now you can release any pent-up emotions that have been suppressed.

Do whatever is necessary to find emotional comfort rather than trying to deny your need for this.

— If MALLARD:

- Whatever project you're engaged in, this is a time for great productivity.
- Whatever new idea comes to you, develop and pursue its manifestation.

— If WOOD DUCK:

- The more you accept yourself just as you are,
  the more it opens you to your true spiritual path.
- Do whatever it takes to regain your sense of
  humor and play.

Call on DUCK when:

You're at the beginning of a new cycle with either work or a relationship.

You need help moving through some difficult emotional entanglements.

Your life has become too dull and monotonous and you want to loosen things up and have some fun.

You've realized that you're taking yourself way too seriously and need to lighten up.

If DUCK is your POWER ANIMAL:

You're a homebody and have a strong nesting instinct.

You're very generous and have a big heart, willing to give to anybody.

You enjoy the company of others, particularly those of like mind and spirit.

You're very amiable, accessible, and quite emotionally expressive.

You're a very resilient individual, able to bounce back very easily.

DUGONG
(see Manatee)

EAGLE

If EAGLE shows up, it means:

There's an opportunity for you that you're considering, and it would be best if you take advantage of it soon.

There will be a new beginning in a positive direction following a recent period of strife, one in which you've gained a great deal of stamina and resilience.

Detach and rise above the mundane so that you're able to see your life and circumstances with a broader perspective and greater vision.

It's a time for a great spiritual awakening, one where you experience a greater connection to the divine.

This is an important time to get creative inspiration from the divine, so heed any guidance you receive.

Whatever you put out, positive or negative, will now return to you in some form, more quickly than ever.

— If BALD EAGLE:

- You have an increasing ability to walk between the material world and that of spirit.
- Dive into your inner depths, paying close attention to any visions or inspirations that arise.

— If GOLDEN EAGLE:

- Go on a spiritual adventure, a pilgrimage to a holy and sacred spot.
- Find your passion and a means to express it.

Call on EAGLE when:

You're caught up in the little details of life and have lost sight of the big picture.

You've recently had some spiritual insights or revelations and want to integrate them into your daily life.

You have to face some major challenge as a result of a massive life change.

You're in a period of struggle or difficulty, one where you get completely caught up in the mundane aspects of your life's drama.

When an opportunity presents itself and you're not sure whether to act on it or not.

If EAGLE is your POWER ANIMAL:

You're a very spiritually evolved individual and a born leader, and people gravitate quite naturally to you.

You're willing to endure challenges and struggles because you're confident that you can meet them, and you trust that they're necessary for your spiritual development.

Even though you're an old soul, you must still go through various initiations throughout your life that will ultimately lead you to living a completely spiritually directed life.

You're passionate, and have a bit of a temper that you have to watch.

One of your main life lessons is learning to conserve your energy and apply your focus to what's truly important.

You take advantage of opportunities without hesitation and with a strong faith that there will be lessons or gifts that you'll discover in doing so.

Pay attention to the sensations in your backbone as an instinctual trigger to be more alert to what's going on around you.

ECHIDNA

If ECHIDNA shows up, it means:

This is a time to be vigilant and cautious in unfamiliar or uncomfortable situations.

You'll find yourself more easily accessing the nonvisible worlds, so pay close attention to any forms of communication with spirit helpers and ancestors.

Be more discerning about letting others into your personal space, but don't keep everyone at a distance in order to do so.

Whatever you've been curious about exploring or studying, dig in and learn more about it.

Call on ECHIDNA when:

You're in a harsh and challenging environment, whether literally or figuratively.

You want to keep a secret for someone else.

You feel the need for gentle but effective protection.

You'd like to be more discriminating as to whom to trust and whom to allow in your personal space.

You're close to the completion of a cycle of transition or transformation and ready to birth a new you.

If ECHIDNA is your POWER ANIMAL:

You feel very comfortable and completely at home wherever you are.

Your home shows a very creative although rather unusual décor, both inside and out.

You're very inquisitive, with a hunger for knowing the "why" of things and willing to go to great lengths to understand the causes of various matters.

You're very sensitive to energies from the realm of spirit such that you can communicate with spiritual beings rather readily.

EEL

If EEL shows up, it means:

Others, both male and female, will be increasingly attracted to you, and some of this attraction will be sexual.

Take several classes in kundalini yoga and continue the practice at home.

You're going to embark on a spiritual pilgrimage in the near future, one that will so profoundly alter your sense of who you are that others may not recognize you.

You'll soon get to the bottom of the question or puzzle that's been bothering you.

Call on EEL when:

You're preparing for a spiritual journey, one you sense will deeply impact you.

You want to enhance your sexual attractiveness to prospective mates.

You've been mired in some situation that's draining your energy and want to get out of it.

You've been thinking and analyzing too much and want to take a break.

There's a recurring dream that has you puzzled.

If EEL is your POWER ANIMAL:

Every so often you need to take a voyage or journey to a familiar destination, even though you don't know why you feel compelled to repeat this journey.

You love to live near water and enjoy quite a few water sports and activities.

You have considerable depth, yet this isn't always immediately apparent to others until they get to know you.

You carry a natural and guileless aura of sexuality about you without even trying.

You're attractive to others, both male and female.

EGRET

(Also see <u>Heron</u>*)*

If EGRET shows up, it means:

Patience, patience, patience—you'll soon get your reward.

This is a time to rely more on yourself than on others to provide what you need.

Although it's useful to be aware of what you're feeling, it's better to rely on your intelligence and wit in this situation.

Keep your head above water so you can see what's going on around you.

Stay alert to unusual movements or shifts that are taking place by using your vision and by paying attention to the vibrations you feel in your body.

Go under the surface of your feelings, and allow whatever emotions are there to flow through you easily and without inhibition.

Call on EGRET when:

You require the cooperation of others in order to get done whatever you need to.

You want to investigate and understand some feelings that are just below the surface.

You're assisting someone in their passage to the spirit world.

You're feeling nervous about getting a task done, yet your anxiety is interfering with doing so efficiently and effectively.

You're caught up in your emotions and need to detach yourself somewhat and rise above them.

If EGRET is your POWER ANIMAL:

Although you're very confident and self-reliant, you enjoy being with the people you're closest to.

You're a shy, gentle person; although you feel things deeply, you tend to be very intellectual and relatively detached from your emotions.

You have the gift of vision and use it to help provide for yourself and your family.

Once in a while you like to gently stir things up with others just to see what emerges.

Even though you tend to stay in the background, others notice you and feel your presence strongly.

ELEPHANT

If ELEPHANT shows up, it means:

Make it a point to be of service in some way to the young, elderly, or those less fortunate than yourself.

Do not let *anything* stand in the way of attaining this goal that is so integral to your purpose.

You have the determination and persistence required to overcome the current challenges you're faced with.

Trust your senses, and if something in your life "smells" bad, take the necessary action to do away with it.

Remain loyal to those closest to you in spite of anyone questioning their integrity.

It's a good time to renew your sense of connectedness to the divine.

Call on ELEPHANT when:

You're feeling alone and isolated from any sense of family or community.

There are mental, emotional, or physical obstacles in your path that seem to block you from achieving your goals or following your mission.

You're feeling tired, weak, or depressed and want more energy and vitality.

You want to feel more confident.

You want to increase your libido and encourage romantic feelings.

You find yourself in a position of power and responsibility, one that requires you to be a strong and effective leader.

If ELEPHANT is your POWER ANIMAL:

You have an insatiable hunger for knowledge and continually seek to understand things.

You're at your best doing some kind of political or social work, or otherwise being in a responsible position of public service.

You have an innate capacity for drawing on ancient wisdom and communicating this whenever appropriate.

You're a passionate and uninhibited lover who's quite able to please and satisfy your partner.

Once you set your mind to something, there's nothing that will stop you from obtaining it.

ELK

(Wapiti)

(Also see Deer)

If ELK shows up, it means:

Seek out the company and friendship of others of your same gender.

You're entering into a time of plenty, one where you'll have everything and anything you need.

Eat vegetarian for a few days and note the difference in how you feel.

Your inner child requires considerable nurturing and protection right now.

Pace yourself, and eat energy foods so that you can maintain your stamina.

Call on ELK when:

You feel that someone has treated you disrespectfully.

You're involved in a project that requires considerable stamina and durability to see it through to completion.

You're overly involved with members of the opposite sex and need to find the type of validation that comes only from same-sex friendships.

You need extra strength to handle an inordinate number of demands for your time and energy.

You're needing some "love magic" to attract romance into your life.

If ELK is your POWER ANIMAL:

You're fiercely independent and prefer to rely on your own strengths rather than seek help from anyone.

You carry yourself with an air of nobility and regalness.

Even though you value your independence, you also value being part of a group.

You prefer the companionship of people of your same gender (whether straight or gay).

You're a very determined individual and can stick with any project to its completion.

EMU

If EMU shows up, it means:

You've been longing for adventurous travel or a spiritual pilgrimage, so make a plan and put it into action.

Allow yourself to fully explore whatever has been the object of your curiosity lately.

You'll soon be noticing a strong, balanced, and nurturing masculine energy emerging in yourself.

This is a period of increased activity and movement, one where you'll find yourself wandering about quite a bit.

Maintain openness to new ideas and possibilities, and be willing to put aside judgments or preconceived notions about these.

Do your best to keep a sense of playfulness and lightheartedness as you go about your life.

Call on EMU when:

You've been feeling tied down, bored with your routines, and yearning to venture out and explore new places.

You're a single father or single mother and you want to keep the masculine and feminine energies in proper balance so you can remain grounded while responsibly raising your children.

You're in a relationship that continues out of habit, and although you want to remain with this person, you also want to stir things up a bit.

You're eager to find some like-minded folks who share your passion for spiritual exploration.

Everything feels rather heavy and burdensome to you, and you want to let go of that feeling.

If EMU is your POWER ANIMAL:

You're a wanderer and a nomad, and are quite happy with this lifestyle.

You like to stay in one place for only brief periods and have no desire to settle down.

You're very active, always moving about, and because you're naturally curious, you're willing to try just about anything once.

In a relationship, you have a tendency to get restless and dissatisfied even though you're faithful and enjoy the stability of having a partner.

You enjoy joining with others of a similar nature in making your spiritual journeys.

FALCON

(Also see <u>Kite</u>)

If FALCON shows up, it means:

Before making a decision, step back from it and consider it from a broader perspective.

There's an opportunity before you; however, be patient and trust your instincts to know when the time is right to act on it.

Pay close attention to the natural rhythms of your body and your surroundings and see what this can teach you.

Whatever choice you make at this time, once you've made your choice, commit to it fully and take the plunge.

— If KESTREL:

- Use your mental capacities and your wits to resolve the situation you're dealing with.
- Focus on what you want rather than what you don't want, and develop your strategy accordingly.

—— If PEREGRINE FALCON:

- This is a time to act swiftly in the pursuit of your goal.
- Be courageous, willing to face whatever it is that intimidates or frightens you.
- Be especially guarded with your health at this time, sticking with healthy, organic foods, and healthy environments.

Call on FALCON when:

You're too close to the situation to make sense of it and need to distance yourself from it in order to see more clearly.

You're devising a plan and a strategy for an important piece of work and need some support and guidance.

You're not sure whether to move ahead, pull back, or stand still, and you're waiting for a clear signal as to what to do.

You're in a situation where speed, agility, and precision is called for.

If FALCON is your POWER ANIMAL:

You have a strong need to reside or rest in places that offer a panoramic view.

You're independent and require a lot of time alone.

You're tactful, diplomatic, and a sharp strategist, and gravitate naturally to (and love) any work that utilizes these talents.

You're a very intense individual with an awesome ability to mentally focus and concentrate without distracting yourself.

You have considerable agility, and you're able to stop on a dime and change directions quickly—all with very fluid, flowing, and natural movements.

Although you're very patient, when you set your mind on something you want, you go for it decisively and unequivocally.

FERRET

(Also see <u>Weasel</u>)

If FERRET shows up, it means:

Don't hesitate to take advantage of any opportunities that show up for you.

Stock up on any provisions you might need in the near future.

Have a playful attitude, be light-hearted, and take everything with a grain of salt.

Sit in silence and stillness, simply observing, and you'll discover what's secret or hidden around you that others don't see.

Pay particularly close attention to your instincts at this time, as they'll give you clues about what to do or what not to do.

Call on FERRET when:

Whatever you're doing requires you to stay focused on what's right in front of you without distractions.

You're puzzled and confused about some events in your life and you want to understand them.

You feel that something is amiss or out of place but you're not sure what it is.

You're in a tight spot and need the strength and wherewithal to squeeze through it.

If FERRET is your POWER ANIMAL:

You're a generally happy and playful individual, with a voracious curiosity.

You're always well prepared for just about any situation that arises.

You've managed to create a safe haven with your home, one where you feel comfortable, secure, and nourished.

You're very athletic, quick and agile, enjoying a variety of athletic activities.

You're highly intuitive and very sensitive to whatever is going on around you, both what is obvious and what is concealed.

FLAMINGO

If FLAMINGO shows up, it means:

Avoid loud, noisy events and any chaotic or frenzied situations.

Be ruthlessly honest with yourself as you check in and see if you're following your inner truth.

Significantly increase the amount of vegetables in your diet that contain beta-carotene, such as carrots, broccoli, and spinach.

Before taking action on the question before you, balance the information you're getting psychically or intuitively by thinking it through carefully and logically.

You've been isolating yourself too long, so it's now time to seek out the company and companionship of others.

Call on FLAMINGO when:

You've been called to do any sort of performance or audition and want to do your best.

You're involved in any activity with a large group of people, and you're nervous about it.

You want to sort and sift through those people and elements in your life that are either compatible with your philosophy and sensibilities or not.

You're courting or attracted to someone whom you're quite serious about, and are willing to move slowly toward a possible intimate relationship with this person.

You need a healing of the heart, either emotionally or physically.

If FLAMINGO is your POWER ANIMAL:

You love to socialize, and enjoy living with large groups of people such that you have difficulty living on your own or spending time alone.

You're more of a follower than a leader, so you have to be careful about whom or what you follow.

Because of your ability to shape-shift, you make an excellent actor or performer.

You have a refined ability to filter out things and people in your life and maintain a connection with anything that has a lot of heart.

FOX

If FOX shows up, it means:

Trust your intuition, and be wary of someone you're involved with who's attempting to trick you in some way.

Your intelligence and ingenuity are more useful right now than confrontation and righteousness.

It's better for you to remain in the background and exert influence from that position than to take an active leadership role.

It's best to blend into your surroundings, move with stealth, and keep your intentions to yourself.

It's important at this time to break out of your social conditioning and express yourself more freely.

Listen and hear, look and see, sense and feel—trust your senses to guide you.

— If ARCTIC FOX:

- Don't let the negative things that others say about you affect you adversely.
- Plan for the future by storing up some of your supplies.
- Welcome the changes of season with the behavior and attitude appropriate to that season.

—— If GRAY FOX:

- Right now it's best to keep to yourself and not stand out.

—— If KIT FOX:

- Speak your truth directly, without explanation or qualification.
- Constancy, courage, and integrity are important for you to display right now.

—— If RED FOX:

- It's important to be flexible and adaptable, using the resources you have immediately available.

Call on FOX when:

You're faced with a seemingly insurmountable problem, and so far, confronting it head-on hasn't worked.

You're being scrutinized or observed in some way that's uncomfortable for you, and you want to blend in without drawing any attention to yourself.

You find yourself in a situation that requires quick thinking and action.

Tact, diplomacy, and wisdom are called for.

You need to defend yourself but don't want to fight; and instead want to use cunning, camouflage, and your innate intelligence.

If FOX is your POWER ANIMAL:

You're a night person and often are most productive and creative at night while others sleep.

You're a keen observer, always watching others, noticing what's being said as well as what's not, and because of this you can usually anticipate what's about to happen.

You're an excellent parent or parental figure—very nurturing, protective, and conscientious.

You're capable of blending into the environment so as to be nearly invisible; and by adjusting your body language, vocal characteristics, and what you wear, others who know you may not recognize you at first.

You sometimes surprise everyone by coming up with obscure yet creative solutions to problems.

FROG

If FROG shows up, it means:

If you hear a frog during the daytime, it will rain very soon.

Do a physical cleanse to detoxify your body.

Do an emotional cleanse by letting yourself really feel your emotions, and cry as much as you need to in order to clear and release any emotional toxicity.

Singing or chanting out loud will help you feel more balanced, at peace, and connected to the divine.

You're entering into a time of plenty and abundance.

This is the start of a slow and steady transformational process for you, a movement from an old life to a new.

Call on FROG when:

It's time to cleanse your life of people, places, or things that no longer fit in with your present lifestyle and who you are.

You're in the midst of any life change, whether small or large, and you need the emotional sustenance and strength to go through it in a fluid and graceful way.

You're planning to do a clearing and blessing ceremony for your home, office, or a specific space.

You feel intimidated or hesitant about honestly stating your thoughts, feelings, or opinions to someone.

You simply feel overwhelmed with negativity and want to clear it up.

If FROG is your POWER ANIMAL:

You're a very sensitive and compassionate person, and readily express deep feelings in words and actions.

Your voice, and especially your singing, can at times arouse deep emotions, yet at the same time soothe anyone within its range.

To others you initially seem rather remote and self-absorbed, yet once they get past their first impressions of you, they discover the depth and nobility of your character.

In your work, you seem to plod along very slowly and have trouble getting started, but you stay with it and get the job done.

You enjoy the study of ancient mysteries and particularly the art of magic.

GAZELLE

(Also see <u>Antelope</u>)

If GAZELLE shows up, it means:

Trust your instincts to determine how you respond in the situation you're concerned about, and do so quickly.

This is not the time to stand out or be the center of attention, but instead to be demure and stay in the background.

To manifest your vision, you must be willing to tolerate and endure dry spells when it doesn't appear that much is happening.

Your spiritual growth will accelerate now in leaps and bounds.

Your path at this time will take a few twists and turns, zigzagging here and there, yet every turn will be in alignment with your soul's purpose.

Call on GAZELLE when:

You need the stamina and determination to withstand a period of emotional or material drought.

You're seeking a vision or inspiration of some kind that will suggest the next direction your life should take.

You've been hiding out for some time, and now you're ready to go out in public and be more social and outgoing.

Your life has meandered quite a bit lately and you want to make sense of these wanderings.

If GAZELLE is your POWER ANIMAL:

Rather than eating three large meals a day, you tend to graze throughout the day on lighter fare.

You're slow, easy, and graceful in your movements, but quick to react when you need to.

At times you have some incredibly powerful and detailed visions or dreams that are also a call to manifesting them.

Sometimes you have a tendency to leave things partially done or incomplete, which results in more work for you.

Your life path is one of periodically wandering rather aimlessly, followed by stretches where you're moving more steadily in a particular direction.

GECKO

(Also see <u>Lizard</u>*)*

If GECKO shows up, it means:

Pay close attention to your dreams, record them in a dream journal, and spend a few minutes each morning contemplating and writing about their meaning.

When you're in the midst of a conflict, be clear with your communication and strong about what you are and are not willing to do.

When you've tried and tried to get through to someone or resolve a problem and it's not working, it's best to detach and move away from the situation.

Don't hesitate to speak up if you have something to say, and don't automatically hold back for fear of others' disapproval.

Regarding the task or project you're involved in, stick with it to completion no matter how you're feeling; you'll reap rewards when you're done.

Singing or chanting will be very healing for you.

Seek your spiritual nourishment by going inside yourself and dwelling there for a while.

Call on GECKO when:

You want to gain a different perspective on the current situation.

You've had a recurring dream or one that was vivid and seemed very real at the time, and you want to understand it.

You're in the midst of conflict and nothing is getting resolved.

You feel intimidated or fearful about speaking up, yet you have something important to say.

If GECKO is your POWER ANIMAL:

You're a very perceptive and insightful individual, able to interpret and understand both your own and others' dreams and visions.

You're amiable and likable, able to get along with just about everyone; however, if someone crosses you, you react quickly and rather sharply.

You're most active and get your best work done after the sun goes down.

You're an effective negotiator in any situations where there's dissension or disagreement.

You definitely prefer to live or stay where the weather is warm.

You have the ability to understand and have empathy for the viewpoints of others.

GIBBON

If GIBBON shows up, it means:

It's time to extend your reach to new areas, so be willing to explore in depth anything that piques your interest, even if you think it might be challenging.

Your family needs you and your undivided attention now, whether it's obvious to you or not.

Be bold and attempt to accomplish something that you'd always thought would be impossible for you to do.

Take some time out soon and go for a stroll through the woods, pausing here and there to appreciate the trees, and perhaps even climbing one just for fun.

Try singing or whistling first thing in the morning to get your day started in a different way.

Give some of your time, money, or energy to a reputable organization that contributes to saving animals that are in danger of becoming extinct.

Call on GIBBON when:

You're taking on a new project that's a stretch for you and you feel some uncertainty about it.

You have a fear that you don't want to confront, but instead want to work around it.

You feel lonely and want some companionship.

You have a variety of things and activities that interest you but have a hard time knowing which one to choose.

You've been swinging from relationship to relationship, but now you want to either settle down or abstain from dating for a while.

If GIBBON is your POWER ANIMAL:

You have this amazing and enviable ability to leap at opportunities that come your way and make the most of them.

You're a family man or woman, immensely enjoying the associations and activities of your family, whether they're your biological family or a close-knit group of friends that you consider to be family members.

There are cycles in your life when you swing from one interest to another, not pausing for too long on any one thing.

You often announce your presence by singing or talking loudly before you actually show up.

GILA MONSTER

(Also see <u>Lizard</u>)

If GILA MONSTER shows up, it means:

If you're in doubt at all, be patient and wait.

Be conservative with your energy and resources rather than giving them away so readily.

Don't start any new major projects or expand your present business until the timing is more appropriate.

Pay close attention to your natural biorhythms and coordinate your activity cycle to those as best you can.

In order to succeed, be sure that you're completely prepared before you move ahead.

This is a good time for a cleansing fast over a few days, or if you're physically able to do so, a complete fast with only water.

Call on GILA MONSTER when:

You have a long stretch ahead of you requiring that you pace yourself in order to get the job done.

Someone is verbally attacking you and you want to defend yourself.

You're dealing with someone who's very opinionated and self-righteous.

Resources are sparse and you need to sustain yourself.

You're not sure if the time is right for you to bring out your latest creation to share with others.

If GILA MONSTER is your POWER ANIMAL:

You're at your best in the earliest part of the morning and in the late afternoon.

You move slowly and carefully most of the time and are cautious about taking on too much all at once.

You're able to accomplish a lot with very little and can go a long time with very little nourishment.

You don't let much bother you or get to you, and you can easily deflect criticism and harsh or negative energies.

Seasonally, your most active and creative time is in the spring, which is typically when you begin long-range projects.

GIRAFFE

If GIRAFFE shows up, it means:

Keep your head up, have faith, and trust your gut regarding the situation you're dealing with at present.

You'll have to reach a bit, but you will achieve your goal.

Keep your eye on the possibilities that are just on the horizon.

It's better to not act too hastily in this situation.

Spend some social time with friends and family.

Make it a point to be a better listener and to be clearer in your communication in both professional and personal relationships.

Call on GIRAFFE when:

You're concerned about the outcome of an event or a relationship and want a glimpse of what's down the road.

You're tense and short-tempered with other people and want to be more relaxed and friendly.

You have a clearly defined goal in mind but are hesitant to take steps toward that goal.

You find yourself feeling stagnant and complacent and have lost sight of where you're going in life.

You feel too involved with the material world and what's immediately in front of you at the expense of your spirituality and ability to see ahead.

If GIRAFFE is your POWER ANIMAL:

You have the gift of foresight, being able to see ahead through dreams, visions, ideas, or signs from the environment.

You enjoy casual socializing with friends more than formal affairs.

You're a very effective communicator, mainly because you listen so well.

You strike an easy balance between spirituality and the fact of living in the material world.

You're willing to stick your neck out if something appeals to you in spite of any risks.

GNU

(Wildebeest; *also see* <u>Antelope</u>)

If GNU shows up, it means:

There are some significant changes you want to make, so start with the top two on the list and go for it!

Whether you already know it or not, you're going on a spiritual pilgrimage, one that will feed your soul.

Use your senses and your instinctual pulse to determine when to move ahead and when to retreat.

Shape-shift by changing your body language, such as gestures, posture, voice, and the way you move.

Your life is about to make a dramatic and unexpected change, toward one of even greater abundance and clarity about your mission.

Know that you're abundant, and be willing to share this abundance generously with others.

Join a group that's compatible and congruent with your interests, or participate in a group activity on a regular basis and get to know the people involved in it.

Call on GNU when:

Your life has been feeling rather stagnant and you want to change some things, but you're not sure what.

You want to step back and review whatever has just happened.

You're in any sort of public performance.

You want to create more abundance and prosperity in your life.

If GNU is your POWER ANIMAL:

You're very often looking for new adventures and places to explore.

You're an observer, continually ingesting the sights, sounds, and sensations from your surroundings.

You're very effective at using your entire self to convey clear messages.

You're involved in any of the performing arts, whether as a sidelight or a profession.

GOAT
(Mountain)

If GOAT shows up, it means:

Be very discerning regarding your relationships, trusting your senses and intuition over your rational and logical mind.

Stop butting your head against the wall, trying to get through to someone who isn't accessible.

Ask for the support you need in spite of any fear of being vulnerable.

Keep moving forward step by step toward whatever goal you're after, trusting that you'll be able to climb over any obstacles, and knowing that if you slip, you'll always land on your feet.

It's critical that you spend time outdoors and immerse yourself in Nature.

Your libido is strong right now, so allow its expression in a variety of creative and harmless ways.

Call on GOAT when:

Someone is criticizing or being negative toward you and you want to disarm them.

You feel out of balance emotionally, physically, psychologically, or spiritually, and want to regain your equilibrium.

You're taking your work and relationships much too seriously.

You're starting out on a new project that feels somewhat overwhelming to initiate and follow through on.

Stretch yourself and reach for that goal that you've been thinking about, with the assurance that whatever obstacles appear, you'll be able to overcome them.

If GOAT is your POWER ANIMAL:

You're a very industrious individual with a strong work ethic.

When you set out for a goal, you show great determination and endurance in achieving that aim.

You're very serious, focused, and willing to take on tasks that others are intimidated by.

You're quite able to ride the natural fluctuations and cycles of life, moving through the various valleys and peaks with ease.

Even though you're rather materialistic, you maintain a continual sense of the divine.

GOOSE

If GOOSE shows up, it means:

This is a time of good fortune, so be receptive to and appreciative of all the good things that come to you.

Call on your ancestors for their guidance and protection, and once you do so, you'll notice a significant increase in your spiritual awareness.

Reread some of your favorite fairy tales and legends and see what new meanings you can get from them now as an adult.

Write creative and imaginative stories, either about actual experiences you've had or those that are made up.

Even though it may not always appear to be so, you're very well protected.

— If CANADIAN GOOSE:

- Lose your inhibitions and sing or chant as loudly as you can.

— If SNOW GOOSE:

- You're about to travel to a familiar place, one you haven't been to for a while, but this time you'll view it with fresh eyes.

Call on GOOSE when:

You want to renew the magical and wondrous nature of childhood through the eyes of your inner child.

You're planning a spiritual pilgrimage to any sacred land or area.

You're about to be married or enter into a new relationship and want to solidify your commitment.

You and your partner want to make a baby.

You need some inspiration for a creative project.

If GOOSE is your POWER ANIMAL:

Traditional values and your ancestral heritage are important to you, and you make it a point to honor your ancestors regularly.

The majority of your activities are centered on your home, community, school, or church.

You love to travel, mainly to familiar places, but not more often than once a year.

You're highly protective of your young and your territory, and if threatened, you will lash out.

You possess an innate wisdom about life here on Earth and know how to make the best of most situations.

GOPHER

If GOPHER shows up, it means:

Look under the surface and behind the obvious of whatever you initially see, particularly when it's another person.

It's a good idea to stock up on groceries and water, mainly to provide a sense of security and comfort, even when your cupboards are full.

More than ever, it's time to take full responsibility for your own growth—your achievements, your errors, and most important, the choices you make.

In order to move forward, you may have to take a few steps backward from time to time, but know that overall you're always moving toward your goal.

Have your eyes checked soon if you haven't in the last two years.

Call on GOPHER when:

You feel rather cut off and somewhat numb and want to awaken your senses.

You're involved in a very intricate, complex project that requires you to be both quick and agile.

You're trying to solve a problem or puzzle by understanding the connection between the various pieces.

You need to get away from all the noise and find a place where you can relax and enjoy the peace and quiet.

You're growing a garden and you don't want it to be disturbed.

If GOPHER is your POWER ANIMAL:

Like a good Boy or Girl Scout, you always seem to be prepared for any eventuality.

You're very sensitive to vibrations, registering these as sensations in your body, which then become a fount of intuitive guidance and wisdom upon which to base your choices.

You love building things with your hands, and the more elaborate and detailed, the better.

You're hypersensitive to loud, harsh noises, so you try to live and work in areas where that's not a problem.

You like to dig around for various tidbits of information and save them in case they may be of some practical use someday.

GORILLA

If GORILLA shows up, it means:

Clear and concise communication is very important at this time, so listen carefully and speak sparingly and articulately.

More than ever, it's important to respect yourself and extend that respect to everyone you come in contact with.

An important teacher is about to come into your life—one who is wise and knowledgeable, yet unpretentious.

You'll be experiencing a heightened sense of clairaudience, so listen closely for messages and signs that come through hearing.

Take some action about your environmental concerns, whether recycling or otherwise actively participating in cleaning up the environment.

Call on GORILLA when:

You're in a situation that calls for you to be strong and protective toward someone else.

You're feeling lonely and isolated and want to socialize more with people with whom there's mutual caring.

You've been spending a great deal of time indoors and feeling the lack of direct contact with Nature.

You're feeling fragmented and ungrounded from being either too much in your intellect or dissociated from your body.

If GORILLA is your POWER ANIMAL:

Although others may perceive you as rather intimidating, you're very gentle, tender, and compassionate, and would only become aggressive if someone seriously threatened you or your family.

You're loyal and extremely protective toward your family and loved ones.

You carry yourself with an air of dignity and nobility, yet without a trace of arrogance.

You're quite social, to the point of feeling lost without the company of others.

You're very observant and have an excellent memory for what you see and hear.

GOSHAWK

(Also see <u>Hawk</u>)

If GOSHAWK shows up, it means:

This is a time to take the lead and not wait for someone else to do it.

You'll feel the presence of spirit even more powerfully and in many different ways.

Keep your focus steady even through the twists and the turns that you have to negotiate.

Don't get stuck on your agenda, as the present situation calls for flexibility and grace, and requires you to heed the direction of spirit for everything to work out.

If you can visualize what you want, you can obtain it.

Seek variety and purity in whatever you ingest—physically, mentally, or spiritually.

Call on GOSHAWK when:

You're faced with a challenge that will require considerable dexterity and flexibility.

There's something or someone you need to keep an eye on and you don't want to be distracted.

Your plans either don't make sense or are not working out, so you've decided instead to go with your gut feelings about what to do.

You're strongly motivated to have and enjoy the simple comforts of life.

You can see that the path ahead is full of twists and turns.

If GOSHAWK is your POWER ANIMAL:

You're very charismatic and have an air of mystery, and others are readily attracted to you.

You probably have a past-life connection to royalty, the higher clergy, or some other form of leadership.

You have the gift of clairvoyance and can see what most others don't.

Whatever tasks you take on, you do them with care, precision, and a desire for perfection.

You're able to focus whenever you need to, and you're conscientious in doing what has to be done.

GREAT HORNED OWL
(Also see <u>Owl</u>)

If GREAT HORNED OWL shows up, it means:

Be more insistent that others treat you with the kind of respect you deserve.

Whatever project is in front of you, go for it with enthusiasm, fearlessness, and ferocity.

When others are communicating with you, stay attuned to what's not being said by observing their body language and vocal characteristics, such as volume, pitch, and inflection.

Once you've identified your goal clearly, be persistent and focused in your pursuit of it.

Be courageous and undaunted by anything that you've previously been fearful of.

Call on GREAT HORNED OWL when:

You're suspecting that someone is being deceitful with you, but you're not sure.

You're in a situation that requires you to be assertive and speak up for yourself.

You're feeling that others are encroaching on your personal space or territory.

You have a tendency to speak in a monotone and want to practice varying your speech pattern.

If GREAT HORNED OWL is your POWER ANIMAL:

You carry yourself with dignity and aloofness, which some may judge as arrogance.

Although you don't intend it and haven't given cause, others sometimes feel intimidated by you.

You're a powerful person with a strong sense of purpose, and when you want something, you don't hesitate to go for it wholeheartedly.

You're able to adapt readily and without complaint to any situation you're in or wherever you happen to live.

Both your hearing and vision are excellent—in fact, so good that you're able to see behind any masks or personas someone wears and hear what they're not saying.

GREBE

If GREBE shows up, it means:

Go ahead and follow your urge to create an artistic piece for the pure joy of expressing rather than impressing.

Immerse yourself in a creative project, but be sure to come up for air from time to time.

Your dreams will be more vivid and perhaps you'll even do some lucid dreaming, so be sure to record these in a dream journal.

Your psychic and intuitive powers are on the increase, so be receptive to visitations and messages from your helping spirits.

Be confident that whenever you're having strong feelings, you'll be able to manage them.

Call on GREBE when:

Your emotions feel out of control and you're losing your temper a lot.

You've been suppressing your creativity, and now you're ready to let it loose.

You feel out of place and you need a change of environment.

You're having some trouble with indigestion and suspect that it has something to do with either your emotions being out of balance or your creativity being suppressed.

If GREBE is your POWER ANIMAL:

To feel comfortable and relaxed, you have to be in a place that's supportive of your personality and soul.

You're creative and artistic, and love to get in the flow of your dreams and your subconscious meanderings.

You're a very caring, compassionate, and attentive parent or caregiver for children.

You love living near water and you enjoy any and all water sports.

You're a sensitive and emotional individual, sometimes temperamental, yet you always seem to know when to express your feelings and when to contain them.

GROUNDHOG
(Woodchuck)

If GROUNDHOG shows up, it means:

You're about to investigate a new area of study that will require intensive effort on your part, but will be well worth it.

Pay close attention to your dreams at this time and see if you can discern their meaning.

You're going through an initiation, one where you'll experience a cycle of death-rebirth, and emerge with a new sense of self.

As you experiment with altered states of consciousness, you'll find these experiences becoming more intense and stronger.

Communicate your boundaries and limits clearly and straight-forwardly.

Call on GROUNDHOG when:

You're going to retreat for a period of time to rest and recuperate.

You're drawn to a study of death and dying, perhaps even considering some type of hospice work.

You want to explore any mystical or shamanic arts and practices.

You're interested in using breathwork of any sort to slow down your metabolic processes in order to enter the deepest states of meditation possible.

You're dreaming a great deal and need some support in understanding the meanings of these dreams.

If GROUNDHOG is your POWER ANIMAL:

You're very adept at lucid dreaming, where you consciously direct the dream as you're sleeping.

You have a keen interest in studying and learning as much as possible about death and the dying process without being morbid about it.

You have a very organized and clean household and are extremely careful about sharing it with anyone else.

Your cycle of energy is naturally the strongest in the spring and summer.

GROUSE

If GROUSE shows up, it means:

Close the curtains, turn on some music, lose your inhibitions, and allow your body to do freeform, spontaneous movement to the rhythm of the music.

Study the sacred spiral and its relationship to higher states of consciousness, and see what meaning it has in your life at present.

You're increasingly coming into your personal power, which draws from Source and expresses through you and as you.

Create a sacred ceremony, one with lots of drumming and dancing as a way of honoring Spirit.

— If RUFFED GROUSE:
- Working with rhythm and movement will open a new flow of energy in your life.
- While dancing and/or drumming, focus on something you want to change or manifest, be clear on your intention to do so, then watch for results over the next few days.

— If SAGE GROUSE:
- Find a place in your home that you designate as sacred space; create an altar there and use this area for meditation, ceremony, dancing, and drumming.

- For a few minutes, do a circle dance—one in which you dance around in a circle, or a spiral dance, where you rotate clockwise or counterclockwise like a whirling dervish.

Call on GROUSE when:

You feel sluggish in your physical movements and need to loosen up a bit.

You find that your vitality and libido are waning and want to increase your desire and performance.

You want to revitalize and renew your sense of the sacred by embodying it through movement and rhythm.

You feel crowded and want to establish your own personal space or territory.

If GROUSE is your POWER ANIMAL:

You're a natural shaman and need only to tune in to this innate capacity.

You're quite independent, and in fact somewhat of a loner, preferring solitude to the company of others.

You have a keen sense of the natural life cycles and Earth rhythms, such as solar and lunar cycles, and often construct ceremonies to honor these.

You're a very protective parent, or if you don't have your own children, you're very protective of others'.

As you mature, you become more and more familiar with other dimensions and realities.

GULL
(See Seagull)

HARE
(Also see <u>Rabbit</u>)

If HARE shows up, it means:

Whatever project you're working on, move quickly and remain flexible.

Beware of anyone trying to trick or deceive you.

You may be fooling yourself about some venture or relationship and not be paying attention to the obvious signs.

Pay closer attention to the cycles of the moon, and coordinate your activity so that it corresponds with the moon's waxing (active/dynamic) and waning (release/receptive) stages.

You'll be required to make some unexpected and rapid changes in direction in the coming days.

Call on HARE when:

You're in a situation that requires speed, finesse, and making your choices quickly and intelligently.

You need to plan for several contingencies and at the same time not communicate your possible moves in advance.

There's an opportunity that presents itself that you know in your gut is a good one, but you have to move fast in order to take advantage of it.

There's someone in your life whom you're not sure whether you can trust.

If HARE is your POWER ANIMAL:

You're quite sensitive, with a flair for artistic endeavors.

You tend to be a loner, enjoying your solitude, and you get so anxious around others that you avoid socializing.

You're ambitious and tend to achieve results in leaps and bounds.

You're quite the trickster, and often use your natural wit to fool others.

You're very resolute about defending your territory and maintaining your personal space.

HAWK
(Also see Goshawk; Osprey)

If HAWK shows up, it means:

You're caught up in too many details, so step back so you can get a greater perspective on the situation.

Stay alert and focused on the task before you, eliminating as many distractions as possible.

Spend some time observing and studying the situation, and when it's time for action, make it quick and decisive.

Pay close attention to your surroundings, as you're about to receive an important message.

Be aware of any personal or psychic attacks and be prepared to defend yourself.

Stop trying to change others or the situation and work instead on accepting things as they are.

Call on HAWK when:

You've been caught up in an emotional turmoil and have lost your perspective.

Your plans haven't gone as you'd expected, they're taking a lot of twists and turns, and you're having difficulty accepting this.

You're in the midst of an intense project that requires vigilance and focus for extended periods of time.

You're being harshly criticized or psychically assaulted and need to defend yourself.

You're feeling depressed and rather helpless and want to lift your spirits.

There are distinct messages from your environment and you want to discern their meaning.

If HAWK is your POWER ANIMAL:

You're very good at interpreting signs and omens from the natural world, whether these come as a blessing or a warning,

You easily flow with the movements of life and don't typically get your feathers ruffled, unless you need to defend yourself in some way.

You're very effective at taking care of and protecting your home and family.

You're a freedom-loving individual and difficult to tie down, but when you do mate you're very faithful and dependable.

You're very insightful; people come to you for your sage counsel and advice.

HEDGEHOG

If HEDGEHOG shows up, it means:

No matter what is going on for you right now, do your absolute best to enjoy your life.

Retreat from your usual routines for a day or two as a way of refreshing your body and spirit.

This is a very fertile and creative time for you, so express yourself artistically in some enjoyable way.

You have a powerful connection with ancient goddess energy, whether you're male or female.

Work directly with the earth by doing some planting and gardening at your first opportunity.

This is a good time to honor your natural curiosity and satisfy it by following any whims, intuitive leads, or inner promptings that occur.

Call on HEDGEHOG when:

You want a clear and accurate prediction of the weather and the climate for the next couple of weeks.

You want shielding and protection from any harsh criticism that you're subject to or negativity that's around you.

You were in a bad mood recently and took it out on someone dear to you, and now you want to apologize to this person and be more sensitive.

You want to do some exploring of your neighborhood and community to get to know the territory better.

If HEDGEHOG is your POWER ANIMAL:

You're very gentle, wise, and nurturing.

People look to you for sage advice, and if you're a woman, you're a model of graceful maturity and humility.

Other people often don't understand who you are and what you're all about, which at times makes you feel like an outcast until you remember your uniqueness and accept it lovingly.

You do your best living in an area where you have enough land to do some gardening and planting.

When you make an entrance, others sense your presence whether they're aware of you or not.

Your essence subtly and gradually charms those you're with whether you ever say a word or not.

HERON

(Also see <u>Egret</u>)

If HERON shows up, it means:

You've approached the opportunity before you at a leisurely pace, but now it's time to grab it and go for it with gusto.

By meeting this challenging situation head-on, you'll discover that you have some powerful gifts and skills that you were unaware of.

If one way isn't working, try another; don't get stuck in any single approach.

Spend a day or two with no plans or agenda, guided only by your intuition—whether a day of activity, quiet reflection, or a combination.

Take full responsibility for your thoughts, feelings, and actions, rather than blaming others or life circumstances.

— If GREAT BLUE HERON:

- Take some time for self-examination, reflecting dispassionately on your goals, motivations, actions, feelings, strengths, and limiting beliefs.
- Only you know what's best for you, so follow your inner wisdom and guidance rather than the dictates and pressures of others.

Call on HERON when:

You've studied an opportunity that has presented itself, it looks good and feels right, but you're still hesitant to act on it.

You feel bored with your routines or the way your life is structured, so you want to reevaluate things, make some decisions, and take action.

You're feeling an inner urge toward greater autonomy and need to stand on your own two feet.

You've been trying and trying to make something work, but it's not, so you're ready to explore other options.

If HERON is your POWER ANIMAL:

You're a dabbler, a jack-of-all-trades, have many varied interests, and love exploration for its own sake.

You're always willing to look at yourself with detachment in order to see the truth of your inner workings.

You're a nontraditionalist and feel no pressure to conform or keep up with everyone else.

You know how to take advantage of events and circumstances that most people would overlook or ignore.

You live your life in a relatively unstructured way, seemingly without stability and security, because you enjoy the novelty that's reflected in each day's new adventure.

HIPPOPOTAMUS

If HIPPOPOTAMUS shows up, it means:

Trust your intuition and act on it, yet stay grounded at the same time.

Your skin is especially sensitive right now, so moisturize with lotion as needed and use sunscreen when exposed to the sun for any length of time.

It's critical that you don't deviate from your path at this time, so stay true to yourself and don't let anything distract you.

Now is the time to immerse yourself in whatever artistic or creative endeavor you want to accomplish and stay with it to completion.

Be protective of any of your artistic creations and don't let anyone demean or criticize your work.

Call on HIPPOPOTAMUS when:

You're feeling suspicious that there's something deceptive going on, and you want to get to the truth that's under the façade.

You're preparing to throw yourself into a challenging but gratifying project that will allow you to express your artistic side.

You're entering a period of intense self-examination and spiritual exploration.

You've been engrossed in some form of deep internal experience and need to emerge and get yourself grounded.

If HIPPOPOTAMUS is your POWER ANIMAL:

You're able to know what's beneath the surface of things and people and can get to the truth quickly.

You honor your truth, speak it readily, and expect others to do the same.

You tend to follow routines and habits religiously and feel upset if any of these are disturbed or changed.

You can be temperamental, so you have to work on controlling your temper and focusing that energy on your creative pursuits.

HORSE

If HORSE shows up, it means:

You're about to embark on an unexpected adventure and will have to move very quickly once it's initiated.

It's time to free yourself from those physically and emotionally constricting aspects of your life.

You need to call upon reserves of stamina and strength to get you through this ordeal.

You're much more powerful than you think you are.

This situation requires strong warrior energy, balanced with sensitivity, patience, and compassion.

Teamwork with your family, friends, or community is important right now.

— If WHITE HORSE:

- You're very well protected from any negative or harsh psychic attacks.
- You're being called to investigate other spiritual realms and dimensions through meditation, a vision quest, or shamanic journeying.

Call on HORSE when:

You're feeling held back by external circumstances or by conditioned beliefs about your supposed limitations.

You're feeling victimized and are blaming others for your current situation.

You're getting the urge to travel and explore new territories, yet have doubts and fears about acting on it.

Your energy is low, and you need a boost of strength and endurance to handle the tasks before you.

You're being prompted to expand and deepen your spiritual practice, but you're not sure how to go about it.

If HORSE is your POWER ANIMAL:

Your personal freedom is of the highest priority—sometimes at the expense of others' approval—and you buck whenever someone tries to stifle you in any way.

Even though you know how to travel to other dimensions and realities, you still deal well with mundane issues and concerns.

You're very loyal to others once they've earned your trust.

You love to wander about just for the sake of exploring, with no particular goal or agenda in mind.

You're a natural leader and evoke confidence in others.

HUMMINGBIRD

If HUMMINGBIRD shows up, it means:

You need to be very flexible with the twists and turns your life will take in the next days.

Put more emotional sweetness in your life—you need it.

You're going through some very heart-opening kinds of experiences, and you'll quite naturally draw more and more love into your life.

Openly express the love you have and feel for those important people in your life.

Give yourself the gift of as many flowers as you can, spread them around your home, and enjoy their sight and fragrance throughout the days to come.

Call on HUMMINGBIRD when:

You're feeling down and sullen and want to lighten up, have more fun, and experience more joy.

You find yourself around any negativity or harshness and want to protect yourself and lift your spirits.

You're feeling fragmented and distracted, ruminating about the past or future, and want to be more present in the moment.

You're feeling guilt or shame about some perceived transgression in the past and want to clear yourself of these feelings.

If HUMMINGBIRD is your POWER ANIMAL:

You're fiercely independent, and if anyone threatens that independence, you're prepared to take flight.

You're full of joy, generally have a positive outlook, and affect others in this way.

It's crucial for your health and sanity to find work that allows you to be outdoors as much as possible.

You're extremely sensitive, drawn to those who are light and positive, while shying away from anyone with harsh or negative energies.

You confound others with your ability to go from being passionate to cool, or intimate to emotionally distant, in the blink of an eye.

HUMPBACK WHALE

(Also see <u>Whale</u>)

If HUMPBACK WHALE shows up, it means:

Take this next year to explore the use of sound and vocalization for healing.

Both playing and listening to music is an absolute necessity for you right now.

There's someone in your life, a significant ally, who nudges and encourages you to reach higher and express your creativity in a fashion that's most suitable for you.

Take some voice lessons, as they'll not only help you with your singing, but also with your self-confidence.

Allow yourself to surface more and reveal yourself to others—and don't let fear get in the way of doing so.

Call on HUMPBACK WHALE when:

You feel urged to do something to keep the oceans clean and unpolluted.

You're about to make a long voyage or spiritual pilgrimage, especially one over water.

You're considering singing as a hobby or a career.

You need to come up for air after you've been immersed in a complex project for too long.

If HUMPBACK WHALE is your POWER ANIMAL:

You enjoy and are especially good at vocal musical expression, either singing or chanting.

You enjoy socializing with others, yet after a certain amount of time you like to break away and go off on your own.

You're a master communicator, combining the elements of body language and vocal expressions to express even the most complex ideas or notions clearly and coherently.

You like to move from one place to another over a year's time, preferring warmer climates in the winter and cooler ones in the summer.

You're very comfortable with your emotions and have learned to manage them well.

HYENA

If HYENA shows up, it means:

When you're pursuing a particular goal, solicit the support of your friends and family.

Make it a point to have some one-on-one time with each of your children.

You're quite ready and capable to take on more than you're presently handling, even though you have doubts about how much you can handle.

Be extra sensitive and attentive to the words you choose and how you express them, as whatever you verbalize will be amplified considerably.

Your powers of discernment and discrimination are strong right now, so pay attention to your intuition and trust what you get, no matter what.

It's a good time to do something silly that makes you laugh.

Call on HYENA when:

You're participating in a business venture with a group and you want it to be a success.

You're in a course of study where you want to learn as much as possible and digest it all.

Something "smells" funny, and you want to determine what it is.

You've been alone for a while and feel the need for companionship and support from your friends and family.

You've been in the doldrums and you need a good laugh to lift your spirits.

If HYENA is your POWER ANIMAL:

You prefer to live in an area that has a lot of land around you, and are particularly fond of more arid areas.

You're a strong survivor, having been through a difficult childhood filled with derision, yet now you thrive and shine.

You have an extended network of friends and family that you like to call your clan, and you enjoy doing just about anything with them rather than on your own.

Due to your highly developed ability to heed your instincts, you're able to consistently discern what to do and when, and whom to either trust or not trust.

IBIS

If IBIS shows up, it means:

Every day pause for a few moments at least a couple times and think the thought, *Everything is sacred,* and observe what happens as you do.

Call on the Egyptian god Thoth or goddess Isis for guidance and protection.

Follow your heart and trust in its wisdom.

You're going to be introduced to some ancient and sacred healing techniques and the wisdom that accompanies them.

This is a very magical time, so keep your eyes, ears, and heart open in order to notice the miracles and wonders around you each and every day.

You're about to experience a very deep and profound healing, one that will cause your life to shift into a different direction.

Call on IBIS when:

You're pursuing an investigation of the metaphysical or magical arts and sciences.

You're interested in learning more about ancient wisdom, particularly that which emanates from Egypt.

You're a healer, and you want to expand your repertoire of sacred healing techniques.

You've experienced a recent spiritual revelation or insight and want to assimilate it.

If IBIS is your POWER ANIMAL:

You're a romantic, and enjoy showing your love for your partner in time-tested ways, such as courtship and flowers.

You have a past-life connection to the gods and goddesses of ancient Egypt, particularly Thoth and Isis.

You're an old soul with a profound understanding of the mysteries of life and death, yet you keep this wisdom to yourself unless you're invited to bring it forth.

You're always ready to adventure into new mysteries and new philosophies.

You're a subtle catalyst for others of spiritual investigation and transformation.

IGUANA

(Also see <u>Lizard</u>)

If IGUANA shows up, it means:

In planning a project, be sure to break down the details step by step in order to accomplish it successfully.

There are a lot of complications in your life right now, yet with intention and effort you can simplify them a great deal.

Even though you feel mired in the mundane circumstances of your life, make the choice to climb out of them and view them from a different perspective.

This is a good time to take action on something you've dreamed about doing or having but had forgotten or dismissed sometime ago because you thought it was unrealistic.

Although you've had a hard fall recently, you have to get up and keep going.

Call on IGUANA when:

You're reviewing some of your past errors and mistakes as a way to avoid repeating them.

You've been having a recurring dream and want to understand its meaning and significance.

You've been having some skin problems, such as dermatitis, and want to be cured quickly and easily.

You've suffered a loss in a business deal or have lost a significant number of your material possessions.

If IGUANA is your POWER ANIMAL:

You're able to find useful treasures in what others view as junk or throwaways.

When you're upset with others, you may snap at them, but you'd never hurt anyone.

You're able to look back on any mistakes in judgment or choices you've made and learn from them in order to plan for the future.

You have the ability to break down complex questions and ideas into their simplest components to make them more easily understood.

You prefer to live alone, but enjoy getting together with friends from time to time.

IMPALA
(Also see <u>Antelope</u>)

If IMPALA shows up, it means:

There are going to be some quick and unexpected changes in your life, ones that will cause your path to zigzag a bit for the next few weeks.

Yes, take the leap with this opportunity or relationship that has presented itself recently.

There's a situation or relationship that's been feeling rather negative and oppressive, and you need to retreat from it to restore your balance.

Your hearing will be particularly acute for a while, so in any communication with another person, listen for what's not being said more than the content of what's being said.

Go ahead and jump a little higher in your aspirations, and adjust your thinking to correspond with these aspirations.

Call on IMPALA when:

Your rational mind dictates that you should do one thing but your instincts tell you otherwise.

You're getting mixed messages from a partner or friend and want to get clear on what's being communicated.

You're in a position of responsibility for a group of people, whether you volunteered for it or it was thrust upon you.

You feel a lack of social contact and friendly affection and you're tired of trying to go it alone.

If IMPALA is your POWER ANIMAL:

You enjoy the companionship and camaraderie of friends of the same gender, and sometimes get together for group activities.

You're very graceful and poised and move through most days with considerable ease.

You prefer to live near water, ideally with the forest or bush near your back door.

You love to dance, particularly any free-form and unstructured types of movement.

JACKAL

If JACKAL shows up, it means:

In any travels you take physically, mentally, or spiritually, you're very well protected and will be guided along the way.

Be alert to any opportunity that shows up in the next few days and be willing to act on it.

You have a past-life connection to ancient Egypt.

You'll be clearly forewarned psychically or intuitively of any impending adversity or danger so you can avoid it.

You have strong and enthusiastic protection no matter where you are or what you're doing.

Call on JACKAL when:

You have a goal in mind that will require the cooperation of your family or close friends.

You have a number of items that you want to recycle so that they will find good use in other hands.

Someone has recently passed into spirit world, or someone is dying and is about to cross over.

You're getting an urge to experiment with astral travel or lucid dreaming.

If JACKAL is your POWER ANIMAL:

You may find very satisfying work either as a hospice worker or someone who deals directly with death and dying, helping the soul to transport to the spirit world (psychopomp work).

You're a scavenger, someone who can find the most useful and practical things in the midst of larger collections of items.

You're very clever and intelligent, using your wits to elicit what you want and need.

You enjoy working on projects with a group of people and are often the instigator of such projects.

When you've found someone you love and want to be with, you're very loyal and committed and see this person as a lifelong mate and partner.

JAGUAR

If JAGUAR shows up, it means:

Focus on what you want with clear and unequivocal intention, and stay with it to its successful conclusion.

You're going to experience an awakening or a deepening of your psychic vision.

You've been very patient, and you're just about to manifest the key to prosperity and beneficial outcomes, so as soon as the next opportunity appears, take the leap and go for it.

Keep your plans and intentions to yourself, not to be secretive, but so they will gain power and your intention and purpose will become even clearer.

No need for striving or ambition at this time, so relax and enjoy the fruits of your labor until the next quest.

Let go of whatever isn't working anymore in your life; by doing so you'll reclaim your power.

— If BLACK JAGUAR:

- Express and enjoy your sensuality and your passion in as many ways as possible and as much as you can.
- For your personal and spiritual growth, it's time to face your fears squarely and let them go.
- Stop worrying about everything, surrender to what is, and let the future take care of itself.

Call on JAGUAR when:

You're feeling unbalanced and off center.

You're experiencing night fears or scary dreams, ones that are so vivid and real that you wake up greatly relieved that it was only a dream.

You know there's an opportunity in front of you that feels right, but you hesitate to act on it for one reason or another.

You have any doubts, fears, or hesitation about claiming your power and standing fully in it.

You're in a situation that requires you to be assertive, clear, and direct with your communication.

If JAGUAR is your POWER ANIMAL:

You're very clear and straightforward in your communications, sometimes to the point of bluntness.

You're a strong and natural leader with a great deal of charisma coupled with humility, and you carry yourself with relaxed authority.

Your presence tends to dominate the room, even if you're not the center of attention at any given moment.

You have a great deal of respect for Mother Earth and always try to step softly on her belly.

Sometimes you have to work to contain your temper or you may unintentionally wound others.

JELLYFISH

If JELLYFISH shows up, it means:

Keep your faith strong and know that life will supply everything you need.

Practice the art of nonresistance, going with the currents and movements of life rather than fighting them.

Be a little more cautious at this time with any work you're doing in the spirit realm.

Be sure that you're getting enough water throughout the day.

Organize your work and your home so that you're more efficient and effective, doing a little bit each day.

Call on JELLYFISH when:

You've been struggling with something that hasn't yielded much progress or any results.

The group you're with, or your family, is out of sync with each other, causing unnecessary disturbances and upsets.

There's considerable disarray and fragmentation at work or at home.

You're involved in a conflict with someone where there seems to be no resolution because each of you is being stubborn and intractable.

If JELLYFISH is your POWER ANIMAL:

You have absolute faith that you'll be provided for no matter what.

You're very sensitive and responsive to the natural rhythms of the earth and easily flow with them.

You prefer living with a group of people or within a harmonious community, one where everyone tries to be cooperative.

You're very organized and like to manage and coordinate events that require these kinds of skills.

KANGAROO

If KANGAROO shows up, it means:

There's nothing to worry about, as you will always have all your needs met.

It's important to stay connected to your family right now and receive your emotional sustenance through them.

Once you've gotten some momentum, keep moving forward and don't look back.

Progress will happen in leaps and bounds.

A new idea will need slow and careful nurturing over the next several months, so it's best to keep it to yourself until then.

— If RED KANGAROO:

- It's time to take full responsibility for your actions and do the right thing.
- Your family needs your attention right now.
- A sacrifice may be called for that will benefit the greater good.

— If GRAY KANGAROO:

- This is a particularly abundant and prosperous time.
- Express your appreciation for what you have and for those you love.

— If WALLABY:

- Even if you have doubts and feel uncertain, stay the course that you've begun.
- This is a good time to stretch out of your comfort zone in some way.

Call on KANGAROO when:

You find yourself indulging in poverty thinking or a belief in lack and want to trust the abundance of life.

You've moved into a position of greater responsibility with family, friends, or co-workers, and want to increase your confidence in dealing with these new circumstances.

You know that it's time to take the leap with your new project or phase of your life, but you're afraid to do so.

You feel out of balance in your relationship with work, play, and family, and want to regain equilibrium.

You're obsessing and ruminating so much about the past that you're feeling stuck and finding it difficult to move forward.

If KANGAROO is your POWER ANIMAL:

You start off slowly, but once you get moving, nothing can stop you.

You have little or no attachment to the past, and instead focus on the present and what lies ahead.

You live in a continual state of abundance and find that what you need typically shows up for you readily.

You're a very caring, sociable individual, especially with your family and friends, and you balance this with periods of solitude.

When necessary, you willingly put your desires on hold when you see that others have more pressing needs to be fulfilled.

KESTREL
(See Falcon)

KINGFISHER

If KINGFISHER shows up, it means:

Make it a point to express yourself clearly and concisely with everyone you communicate with.

For the next seven days, set aside a few minutes in a quiet place where there's no chance of intrusions to simply contemplate, without any particular structure or restrictions on your thinking.

Take the plunge into this project or relationship with confidence and alacrity, and let go of all doubt and fear, because it will be successful.

Get daily physical exercise that involves both cardiovascular and muscular elements.

You're at the initial stages of a cycle of abundance and prosperity, so welcome and receive it.

Call on KINGFISHER when:

You're starting on a new project or task and feel somewhat intimidated by the scope of it.

You're yearning for a stretch of peace and quiet after a tumultuous, nerve-racking cycle.

You're worrying a lot about money and how you're going to provide for yourself and your family.

Your instinct says to go ahead with a project or a relationship, but you're feeling afraid to jump in.

You're searching for new and stimulating opportunities to take advantage of that will be both fun and prosperous.

If KINGFISHER is your POWER ANIMAL:

Your verbal communication is articulate and songlike.

You value your meditation time and the sacred space you've created in your home to meditate.

You must live near a body of water in order to thrive, preferably in a northern climate.

You're very willing to sacrifice your own needs for those you love.

KINKAJOU

If KINKAJOU shows up, it means:

Remain calm and be aware of overreacting to others if someone criticizes you or says something you don't agree with.

Do a walking meditation through the forest or the bush, where your pace is slower than usual and you can pause from time to time to take in the sights, sounds, and smells.

You're going to be attuned to subtle vibrations that announce earth changes, so do your best to discern whether what you're feeling is personal or prescient.

You may be required to take a leap of faith soon, so trust your instincts when the opportunity appears, and if it feels right in your gut, go for it without hesitation or qualification.

Consider changing your diet to one of primarily organic whole grains, fruits, and vegetables for a few days.

Call on KINKAJOU when:

You've recently received or purchased an item that appears rather complicated to operate or put together.

You're entering into any sort of major new cycle in your life.

You sense that something is off in your body, but are not sure if it's personal or something greater that you're registering intuitively.

You're entering into a fertile and creative time and want to make the most of it.

You're interested in exploring the use of sound as a healing tool.

If KINKAJOU is your POWER ANIMAL:

You have a keen ability to comprehend fairly complex ideas and concepts.

You have a great deal of curiosity and you love to explore things.

You're rather shy, yet do enjoy the company of your family members or close friends.

You have to retreat to a space in Nature—woods, bush, mountains, or seashore—regularly to maintain your health and sanity.

You have a strong connection to the plant kingdom—particularly trees—and to the Nature spirits.

KITE

(Also see Falcon)

If KITE shows up, it means:

Take off your mask and let the world know who you really are.

Trust that none of what you have to deal with in the next few days will be a crisis, so do your best to remain calm and centered, no matter what.

Take either a Tai Chi or a yoga class that emphasizes breathing and slow, gentle movements.

The next few days will take adaptability and flexibility on your part as you maneuver around any twists and turns that your life takes.

Make sure you're eating healthy and organic foods as much as possible.

A few times each day, take several slow, deep breaths and count to ten as you inhale, and ten as you exhale.

Call on KITE when:

You're going through an identity crisis as a result of dramatic changes in your life.

Life has been challenging, and you've had to face a few obstacles lately.

You're doing any kind of mediumship or psychopomp work (helping transport the soul of a deceased person to the spirit world).

You've been feeling tense and anxious and would like to replace these emotions with calmness and peace of mind.

You're having trouble adjusting and adapting to a situation.

If KITE is your POWER ANIMAL:

You're at your best in warmer climates and don't do at all well with the cold.

You seem to glide through life without getting your feathers ruffled about much of anything.

You're a master at taking any opportunity that appears before you, large or small, and making the most of it.

You consistently respond to other people with respect, gentleness, grace, and kindness.

You have a natural gift of being able to make contact with the spirit world and the helping spirits there.

KIWI

© Mark Jones / Oxford Scientific / JupiterImages

If KIWI shows up, it means:

Spend some time in the forest or woods enjoying the sights, smells, and feel of this environment.

Working with your hands doing clay sculpture will bring out the artist in you.

You're faced with an opportunity to surrender something of yourself for the greater good of your family or community.

You have the choice of dramatically changing your lifestyle, so make that choice from love rather than from fear.

Do a walking meditation outside 15 minutes each day for the next few days, walking more slowly and consciously than usual, synchronizing your breath with your pace.

Call on KIWI when:

You've been feeling a bit flighty or spaced out and need to get grounded.

You're in a situation where you have the choice to sacrifice something of yourself—your desires, preferences, needs, or material goods—out of your love for someone else.

You feel stymied about making an important decision because you're imagining all sorts of catastrophic consequences, and you want to release your fears and doubts so you can make a clear choice.

You've experienced a significant loss of lifestyle or material goods and want to put it into perspective.

If KIWI is your POWER ANIMAL:

You're very practical and down-to-earth.

You do your best work at night and structure the day so that you're able to do so.

You're very courageous in your willingness to give of yourself wherever needed, out of love for other beings.

Most everyone you know loves and appreciates you, and you return this in kind.

KOALA

If KOALA shows up, it means:

Watch your diet, and make sure that it primarily contains foods that are easily digested, with a particular emphasis on green vegetables, herbs, and herbal supplements.

The next time you have a glass of water, before you drink it, say a prayer of gratitude for the gift of the water you're about to imbibe, and include a prayer for all the waters of the earth.

You need a relaxing retreat from daily life for a few days, so plan one soon and get away.

Be aware of your emotions, yet remain somewhat detached from them and keep them contained.

Practice a slow breathing meditation (with music, if you desire) twice a day for at least ten minutes, and notice what it's like to be in a state of deep relaxation.

Explore your interest in shamanic arts and practices, and if you're inspired to do so, learn how to do a shamanic journey.

Call on KOALA when:

You need to retreat from your regular routines for a while, so do so and enjoy your own company.

You're preparing to do a physical and/or emotional detoxification and cleanse and need some additional support.

You're feeling the need to have more personal space, even though you're not clear how to go about getting it.

You want to learn how to access deeper stratas of consciousness in your formal meditations.

You've been working hard and need a rest, either an afternoon nap or a longer spell.

If KOALA is your POWER ANIMAL:

You're a very solitary individual, and even in the company of others you tend to be rather detached.

One of your assignments while you're on the planet is to do whatever you can to care for and clean up the waters.

You have a remarkable ability for observing your feelings dispassionately, yet you can be completely empathetic with others without hooking into their drama.

You do your best work in the late evening and early morning hours.

You need frequent and regular periods of rest, even if it's only a few minutes each time.

KOMODO DRAGON

(Also see <u>Lizard</u>)

If KOMODO DRAGON shows up, it means:

Some fiery energy is about to be awakened in your life, so be prepared to direct that energy constructively.

Whatever changes you make in your life at this time will last for a long time.

You'll be feeling an extra dose of power now, so be sensitive to how you use and express it.

Be especially aware of how you're affecting others with your words, being careful to choose those that are gentle and loving.

This is a time of great passion, so enjoy expressing this in all that you do.

Call on KOMODO DRAGON when:

You've been feeling listless and cut off from your feelings.

You have evidence that someone is overtly or covertly trying to undermine your efforts.

You're having some difficulty getting going on a project that you know you need to get moving on.

You see an opportunity that will be challenging yet has the potential for immense benefits.

If KOMODO DRAGON is your POWER ANIMAL:

You value your privacy and generally don't care for the company of others.

You're a very powerful and imposing individual and people take notice when you walk by.

Although most of the time you move at a leisurely pace, when necessary you can be very quick and fast.

Your words carry great force and weight, so you do your best to choose them carefully lest they be inappropriate or hurtful.

KOOKABURRA

If KOOKABURRA shows up, it means:

To manifest your dreams, stay centered, maintain your focus and determination, and let nothing deter you.

Be compassionate, yet don't be fooled by anyone who acts casual and lighthearted when you sense that they're covering up some other unpleasant feelings.

The best way to overcome your fear is to face it and do whatever you need to do in order to accomplish your objective.

Take a break from your worries and cares by participating in something that makes you laugh out loud.

You're spending too much time daydreaming and fantasizing rather than taking steps toward manifesting your actual dreams and visions.

Call on KOOKABURRA when:

You've been called to serve your community in some capacity and provide wise leadership and guidance for others.

You're very clear and certain about a particular goal and you want to go for it.

You're feeling heavy and way too serious, to the point that you've lost your sense of humor.

You know that it's time to release some of your outworn values, beliefs, and behavior patterns that no longer serve you.

If KOOKABURRA is your POWER ANIMAL:

You're a very determined individual and you aggressively go after what you want when you want it.

You easily command respect from everyone you come into contact with and enjoy the recognition that your role as a leader provides.

For you to do your best, it's critical that you have a stable and secure home life.

You have a tendency to laugh away your true feelings and pretend that everything's fine, when in fact, it isn't.

You come across as a very casual and easygoing person most of the time, with a consistent air of indifference about you, even though inside you may be feeling very intense.

LADYBUG

If LADYBUG shows up, it means:

If it alights on you, make a wish and your wish will be granted.

Structure a time each day where you can pray or meditate in silence and solitude.

Something you thought was lost will be making its way back into your life.

Mother Mary is with you to guide you and console you, no matter what your religious or spiritual orientation.

You're shielded and protected from irritations, pestering thoughts, or annoying behaviors from others.

Call on LADYBUG when:

You're being called upon to increase your spiritual or devotional practices.

You want to release your fears and anxieties and return to feeling trusting and happy.

You've felt disillusioned, and you want to find your faith and joy again.

You've planted your garden and want to keep pests to a minimum or eliminate them altogether.

If LADYBUG is your POWER ANIMAL:

You're family oriented and traditional in values and morals.

You have a very delicate, loving, and inoffensive quality to your being.

You have a natural flow of abundance and never worry about where the next meal is coming from—or anything else for that matter.

You approach the world with innocence and guilelessness, as you have a variety of ways to protect yourself both physically and spiritually.

LARK

If LARK shows up, it means:

You're entering a cycle where you'll be completely happy and free of worry.

Rather than looking to others, go inside to find the answers you're seeking.

Whatever you're doing, try singing softly or whistling as you do.

The words you use and how you use them will take on greater power, so be aware of whether you're speaking lovingly or harshly, as your words will have greater impact either way.

Find your own power song by sitting in nature, and ask your helping spirit to give you a song, then let the melody and the words come to you as you sing them.

Call on LARK when:

You feel dispirited or discouraged.

You're thinking about taking singing lessons to improve your voice.

You're a professional singer and are about to give a performance.

You're curious about the use of sound, singing, and storytelling as healing techniques.

You want to discover your own sacred music or song.

If LARK is your POWER ANIMAL:

You're generally happy and carefree, with few or no concerns or worries about the future.

You love to sing and do so at each and every opportunity.

You're not only a singer but also a storyteller, and people love to hear you tell your tales.

Your words, whether spoken or sung, have an incredible power and an aura of mystery.

LEMUR

If LEMUR shows up, it means:

Your powers of clairvoyance will increase to the point where you'll be seeing your helping spirits more clearly.

Spend some time in a forest, the woods, or the bush; find a tree, then sit and meditate with your back against it to see what messages or impressions you get.

Explore the use of incense and aromatherapy for various purposes.

Donate your time, energy, or money to a reputable organization that contributes to reforestation and is dedicated to halting deforestation.

You may want to investigate any past-life links to Africa, particularly Madagascar.

Call on LEMUR when:

You're studying evolution and are particularly interested in the evolutionary relationship and connections among various primates, including humans.

You've recently developed an interest in psychic and metaphysical phenomena and want to expand upon what you've learned so far.

You're curious about a piece of your past that feels unsettled, and you want to review those memories and find a place for them in the context of your life now.

You're not sure whether you need to expand on your socializing or retreat from the usual world for a while.

If LEMUR is your POWER ANIMAL:

Whether you're female or male, you have a strong feminine essence.

You're very adaptable, with a diversity of interests and talents that others tend to underestimate.

What others first notice about you are your captivating and penetrating eyes.

You have a strong sense of smell, both literally and metaphorically, and you're able to sniff out whether something is good for you or not.

You're unique in many ways, so much so that you sometimes feel out of place with others and need to seek out the comfort of solitude.

LEOPARD

(*Also see* <u>Ocelot</u>; <u>Snow Leopard</u>)

If LEOPARD shows up, it means:

Take some time in solitude, preferably in Nature, for a full day.

Be sure to pace yourself by providing times of rest and play during any intense cycles.

Whatever goal you're pursuing, do not reveal too much about it until it's completed, or this may interfere with its achievement.

You'll be able to foresee events very vividly and accurately through dreams, visions, or feelings.

A secret that's been kept from you will soon be revealed.

This is a time for expressing yourself passionately in whatever you do.

With persistence and steadiness, you'll attain your goal.

Your intuition is heightened at this time, so pay close attention to your feelings, and trust them.

Call on LEOPARD when:

You feel the need for extra protection.

You want to pursue your goals and need the strength and vitality to leap over any obstacles.

You've just been through a challenging period in which you've lost or let go of a significant part of your life that wasn't working and are ready for rebirth into the next cycle.

You've been confronted with some aspect of yourself that has been in shadow and are ready to face this part of you and release its hold on you.

You need to reawaken your passion and sensuality.

If LEOPARD is your POWER ANIMAL:

You were born with an extraordinary gift of awareness of your inner realm and seem to have considerable insight into your own makeup, as well as others.

You're a sprinter, not a long-distance runner, and accomplish much more with short-term goals punctuated with periods of rest and play.

You have an air of mystery about you, rarely talking about your dreams or plans, but just quietly pursuing them without a lot of fanfare.

You're a very sensitive person, enjoying anything that's tactile and sensual, yet are also prone to react strongly to irritating touch and annoying people.

You're a sensual and giving lover and make a great romantic partner.

LION

If LION shows up, it means:

Hold your head up high and keep your dignity, no matter what you're faced with.

You're much stronger than you think you are and need to use your emotional strength in this situation.

Call upon the well of courage that's available to you to confront this uncomfortable situation.

Listen closely and discern carefully before acting, rather than moving ahead impulsively and recklessly.

When faced with a tough decision, follow your heart rather than what you think you should do.

Call on LION when:

You feel particularly stressed or beaten down by any situation and want to boost your sense of power and self-confidence to deal with these circumstances.

Your dignity and integrity have been called into question and you want to recapture your self-respect.

You've been called upon to assume a position of authority and leadership.

You've taken on a project that at first seems overwhelming, even though you know you have the necessary skills and intelligence to complete it.

If LION is your POWER ANIMAL:

You have a strong presence and a dignified manner, such that people always notice when you walk into a room.

Although your anger can sometimes be triggered rather easily, you generally have a great deal of compassion for others.

You're a natural leader and have great organizational skills.

You're at your best when you function as part of a group or community rather than being alone.

You like to stretch your capabilities and are always seeking to learn more.

LIZARD

(*Also see* <u>Chameleon</u>; <u>Gecko</u>; <u>Gila Monster</u>; <u>Iguana</u>; <u>Komodo Dragon</u>)

If LIZARD shows up, it means:

Pay close attention to your dreams—especially recurring themes and images—by keeping a dream journal and meditating on your dreams' meanings and their messages.

The situation calls for quiet and stillness until it's time to make your move, but when you do, you need to do so quickly and efficiently.

This is an especially sensitive time right now, one where you're acutely aware of sights, sounds, and vibrations, so be extra careful about who and what you surround yourself with.

Meditate and call upon a deep and ancient part of you, asking to be shown a vision of your life path.

Listen to your own intuition over anyone else's.

Call on LIZARD when:

You're in circumstances that require you to endure emotional or physical hardships and a seeming lack of resources.

You're having trouble remembering your dreams, or if you do remember them, it's difficult for you to decipher their meanings.

You're obsessing about your past, a past situation, or an old part of yourself that's no longer useful, and you want to detach and release it.

You've been depressed or shut down and want to reawaken your senses and increase your vitality and responsiveness.

It has become difficult to hear and honor your own intuition due to others' opinions and advice.

If LIZARD is your POWER ANIMAL:

You're a very relaxed individual to the point of appearing lethargic to others, yet you're acutely aware of what's going on around you and alert to the subtlest of changes in your surroundings.

You're a dreamer and a visionary, both clairvoyant and clairsentient, and you pay close attention to the visual and kinesthetic information you receive in determining your path.

You intuitively know when to remain still and quiet and when to take action; when you do, it's effortless, quick, and purposeful.

You have an instinct for knowing the right thing to do and rarely make your choices impulsively or emotionally.

You're very quick and accurate at sizing up the character and motivations of others.

LLAMA

If LLAMA shows up, it means:

It's been a long haul, but you're just about there, so hang in there.

Volunteer some of your time by being in service to someone or by working with a service-type organization.

Move slowly and steadily toward your goal and be assured that you're on solid footing.

Take time for yourself, which may require that you turn down requests from others for your time or assistance.

Seek out the company of others who share similar interests and activities rather than spending so much time alone.

Call on LLAMA when:

You're about to go on a challenging journey or pilgrimage, one that at times looks to be quite demanding.

People are coming to you with their problems, and you want to help them without feeling overwhelmed or overburdened.

You're about to enter into a position or role of service to another person or organization.

You're engaged in a task that requires considerable physical work over a long period of time, particularly one where you'll be carrying or transporting heavy loads.

If LLAMA is your POWER ANIMAL:

You're easygoing, gentle, and a great companion in any relationship or friendship as long as you're treated fairly.

You're very persistent, adaptable, and able to endure considerable stress and challenging environmental situations with no ill effects.

You're very willing to sacrifice your own needs to be in service to others, yet you sometimes feel the weight of the world on your shoulders and tend to forget about yourself.

You have a tendency to compromise more than makes you comfortable in order to please others.

LOBSTER

If LOBSTER shows up, it means:

You're in the midst of a powerful process of transformation in which you'll find yourself trying out different expressions of who you are throughout each phase.

One of your big lessons right now is patience, particularly in learning to wait for whatever you need to come to you rather than pursuing it.

You'll find a number of useful things by rummaging through some of the items you've had in storage for a while.

Your best work will be done in the evening after the sun goes down.

Call on LOBSTER when:

You're going through some major life changes such that your old self no longer serves you.

It's necessary for you to submerge yourself in your work and stay there for a considerable length of time.

You're feeling impatient about something you want to achieve or have, feeling confident that it will happen, yet stressing out over the delay.

You've been around a lot of people for quite a while and need to find some privacy and solitude.

If LOBSTER is your POWER ANIMAL:

You have amazing powers of concentration, and once you set an objective, you stay focused on it.

You're very resourceful and able to find what you need in your immediate environment, often by just foraging around.

Your appearance is such that others are fooled into thinking you're something you're not, until they get to know you.

You're a solitary person, and although you can tolerate other people for short periods of time, you get irritable and snappy if you're around others for too long.

You acquire greater and greater depth of wisdom and understanding as you mature.

LOON

If LOON shows up, it means:

Do regular exercises that strengthen your muscles, bones, and joints, and especially your legs and feet.

Dreamwork, journaling, or meditation will be beneficial for you in helping you explore your subconscious, which will in turn help you understand yourself better.

Be especially tender and nourishing with your throat chakra at this time.

Pay particular attention to vivid and dynamic dreams, such as those that stay with you through the day, as these are powerful messages and teachings.

Call on LOON when:

You're having visions or dreams that are hard to interpret or understand.

There's an opportunity that has presented itself and you're considering taking the plunge and acting on it.

You're experimenting with various altered states of consciousness, particularly those that employ slow, deep breathing as a means of inducing these deeper states.

You're interested in working with lucid dreaming, where you become aware as you're dreaming and can alter the course of the dream.

If LOON is your POWER ANIMAL:

One of your challenges in this lifetime is keeping a balance between the physical, emotional, and mental aspects of yourself.

You're a powerful communicator—eloquent, coherent, and articulate.

You maintain a careful equilibrium between your masculine and feminine energies.

You're keenly interested in dreamwork and consider the information in your dreams to be of utmost value in guiding and teaching you.

You're unconventional in your beliefs and lifestyle, uncomfortable in more traditional settings and around other people who fit the norm for your society or culture.

LYNX
(Also see <u>Bobcat</u>)

If LYNX shows up, it means:

Spend some time in silence, whether a day with no speaking or a visit to a quiet area in Nature.

Someone will tell you a secret and it's critical that you keep it strictly in confidence.

Be alert to anyone trying to deceive or take advantage of you at this time, and trust your instincts about this.

Acknowledge others' hidden talents and abilities that they don't recognize, and encourage them to bring out these gifts.

Your clairvoyance and clairaudience are particularly acute at this time, so pay close attention to what you see and hear that's beyond the immediate realm of your usual senses.

The very worthwhile goal you've set for yourself will require clear intention, patience, and the willingness to stick with it even if it means waiting for a long period of time to achieve it.

Call on LYNX when:

You're feeling uncertain and have a gut feeling about the honesty or integrity of someone you're involved with professionally or personally.

You've been feeling distressed and overwhelmed by all the hustle and bustle and noise of your surroundings and want to find some stillness and silence.

You're aware that you've been doing a lot of talking and need to quiet down and listen more than talk.

You're feeling vulnerable and need protection from any psychic attacks or emotional assaults.

If LYNX is your POWER ANIMAL:

You have the gift of being able to see in others what they've kept hidden or aren't aware of, including fears, falsehoods, secrets, and untapped abilities.

You find that your path has led you to shamanic practices and want to explore these more.

Others feel uncomfortable around you at times because they sense that you know more about them than they care to reveal, even though you'd never say anything about what you perceive in them.

You treasure your independence and have to spend considerable time in solitude, even though the cost can be loneliness and isolation.

People trust you and will often disclose things about themselves that their best friends don't know.

MACAW

If MACAW shows up, it means:

You'll benefit from getting out in the sunlight for at least a few minutes each day.

You're at the beginning stages of heightened spiritual perception and an increased creative pulse.

You're going to notice a shift in your communication abilities that prompts people to pay attention and listen more closely to what you have to say.

Trust your perceptions, no matter how outlandish and bizarre they seem.

Wear brighter and more colorful clothing, no matter what season it is.

Call on MACAW when:

You need to take advantage of the warmth and healing powers of sunlight.

You've been overly reactive and emotional and want to manage your feelings more effectively.

You want to enhance your communication skills to be a more effective and colorful speaker.

You're seeking a physical or emotional healing, one that requires you to be outdoors more to partake of the sun's healing powers.

Things are a bit dull and gray, and you want to add some color to your life, literally and figuratively.

If MACAW is your POWER ANIMAL:

You're alert and perceptive and don't miss a thing that's going on around you.

You're a very sensitive, emotional individual, willing to express your feelings freely and openly.

Others tend to seek you out for advice and counsel, as you're very insightful, compassionate, and understanding.

You're a loyal and faithful mate or partner, and you enjoy socializing with your partner by your side.

You're a talented voice mimic, able to duplicate just about anyone's inflections and intonations.

MAGPIE

If MAGPIE shows up, it means:

Act on any and all opportunities that present themselves to you without hesitation.

Pay attention to any signs or omens, as they will serve to guide you—whether they're visual, auditory, or kinesthetic.

Be especially clear and straightforward in your verbal communication, saying what you mean while at the same time listening carefully to what the other person is saying.

Make certain you're using your intuitive and psychic gifts with pure intention and egoless service.

It's important now to bring yourself to balance if you're polarized too much in one direction or another, such as with masculine-feminine, intellect-emotions, or spiritual-mundane polarities.

Call on MAGPIE when:

An opportunity has come to you, but you're not sure whether to take advantage of it or not.

You know that you're getting signs from your environment, but are not sure of their meaning.

You're investigating or studying metaphysics or the occult and want some support, guidance, and protection, especially if you're new to these areas.

You're involved in a project that requires you to use your ingenuity and resourcefulness, one where what you need to do isn't always obvious.

If MAGPIE is your POWER ANIMAL:

You're very resourceful, intelligent, and adaptable, drawing on whatever's available to achieve your objectives.

Your interests are broad and varied and your curiosity leads you to explore anything that comes across your path.

You're very wise with respect to the spiritual powers available to you and use considerable discretion when you work with these powers.

You're intelligent, have a great deal of ingenuity, and are a bit of a dabbler.

You're quite willful, and once you set your mind to something, very little can stop you.

MANATEE
(Dugong)

If MANATEE shows up, it means:

Adjust your diet to include a lot of green leafy vegetables and by grazing (eating very small portions a few times a day) rather than eating two or three larger meals each day.

Slow down to about 80 percent of your usual pace and you'll find that you can still make steady and consistent progress.

Stop procrastinating, focus on what you need to be attending to, and move forward with courage and confidence.

This is a very nurturing time, both for receiving and giving comfort to others emotionally and physically.

This is a time to put others' needs before your own, not so that you martyr yourself, but so you willingly and lovingly give your time, attention, and energy where needed.

Call on MANATEE when:

Life has been hectic and fast-paced, and you want to reduce or even eliminate the stress and intensity.

You need more nourishment and nurturing for your body and your soul.

You don't feel as healthy as you like and know that you need to adjust your diet in order to feel better.

You're in a situation or role where you're in charge of children, either as a parent figure or a caretaker.

You're pregnant and have decided to have a water birth.

If MANATEE is your POWER ANIMAL:

For group activities you prefer smaller groups with closer and more casual interactions with the members.

You function much more positively and effectively when you're in an intimate relationship or have a close friend to share things with.

No matter what your physical age is, you're an old soul, at times surprising yourself and others with your depth and wisdom.

You move at your own pace, generally slower than others, but you get the job done.

You're very open, trusting, and willing to be vulnerable with nearly everyone you meet.

MEADOWLARK

(Also see <u>Lark</u>)

If MEADOWLARK shows up, it means:

Expect some good news or a pleasant surprise very soon.

Sing out loud any song of your choosing, putting any and all inhibitions or self-consciousness aside.

It's time for some form of inward journey, whether through contemplation, meditation, or a Nature quest, and it's important to do so cheerfully and enthusiastically.

Doors are about to open upon a new opportunity that will bring you considerable abundance.

Whatever project you've been working on is about to come to fruition.

Call on MEADOWLARK when:

You sing professionally or want to do so for your own enjoyment.

You're involved in a wedding ceremony, either as the bride, groom, or the ministerial official.

There are obstacles in the way of your progress, and you'd like them to just disappear.

You're involved in a new relationship or you want to reaffirm your love and faithfulness with your present spouse or romantic partner.

You wake up in a bad mood and want to cheer up.

If MEADOWLARK is your POWER ANIMAL:

You have a sunny disposition and definitely brighten things up wherever you go.

You have a musical voice, whether talking or singing, and you love to sing.

You enjoy each day, seeing the best in everything and everyone, while at the same time staying grounded and levelheaded.

You're a warm, gentle individual, and attract others quite easily because you accept people for who they are and don't judge.

MEERKAT

(Also see <u>Mongoose</u>)

If MEERKAT shows up, it means:

You may have to do some digging to get to the solution or answers you're seeking.

Sometime in the next few days, go to a place where you can greet the sunrise.

Seek out the companionship and support of your family or a group of close friends.

Trust that others who love and care about you are always watching out for you.

Once you've identified what you want, keep your plans to yourself until you've achieved your goal.

Call on MEERKAT when:

You're doing research and want to dig around for the appropriate information or resources.

You've been engrossed in your work for far too long and need to get outdoors in the sun.

You're studying for an exam.

You've been isolating yourself and need to get involved with other people.

If MEERKAT is your POWER ANIMAL:

You're a very grounded individual, with a strong connection to Mother Earth.

You're at your best when you're surrounded by close family members or friends.

You love to network with others and stay consistently involved and in contact with those you connect with.

You're intelligent, able to learn things and assimilate information very quickly.

MOCKINGBIRD

If MOCKINGBIRD shows up, it means:

Sing, whether by yourself or with others, and don't worry about how it sounds.

It's time to bring forth one of your inner talents and share it with others rather than being clandestine about it.

You need to pay attention to people's body language and see if you can determine what they're communicating by their postures, gestures, and facial expressions.

At this time, others will be paying much more attention to what you do and not so much to your appearance.

Other people you encounter will reflect back to you both pleasing and not-so-pleasing aspects of yourself.

Call on MOCKINGBIRD when:

You're called on to give a speech or performance and want to enhance your voice so you can easily project without stress or strain.

You're trying to learn a new language and want to be able to speak it fluently, as if it were your original language.

You have a good idea of your life purpose—what you know you're supposed to be doing—yet you feel afraid of going forward with it, or you're not sure how to.

You want to improve on your ability to understand communication in order to express yourself even more effectively.

You're feeling intimidated or threatened and want extra protection.

If MOCKINGBIRD is your POWER ANIMAL:

You're an excellent mimic and do great impressions.

You have a naturally resonant singing voice and enjoy singing by yourself or in groups.

You have a subtle but powerful presence, and when you're around, other people lighten up and seem friendlier.

You're very attuned to others and the kind of energy they give off, leading you to either keep them at a distance or bring them closer as possible friends.

You're very protective of your home and your family and will go to great lengths to keep them safe.

MOLE

If MOLE shows up, it means:

Trust in what you feel more than what you see or hear.

Seek to physically touch others and to be touched, such as by showing affection to your romantic partner with caresses and hugs and by bestowing gentle and appropriate physical gestures upon others.

You'll find yourself getting psychic impressions whenever you do touch others, so trust those impressions.

You're entering a period of self-examination, one where you're unearthing information about yourself without judging it in any way that triggers guilt or shame.

You need to be more grounded in order to maintain your vitality and health.

Call on MOLE when:

You need to dig yourself out of an overwhelming amount of work or responsibility.

You're feeling spacey and ungrounded.

You're feeling touch deprived and need to be physically nurtured.

You've been holed up too long, such as at home or an office; and you need to get out and enjoy the beauty of the earth, fresh air, and sunshine.

You keep getting psychic impressions through your feelings but are not sure you trust them.

If MOLE is your POWER ANIMAL:

You're a hermit, and quite content to stay that way.

You're clairsentient—you feel things psychically through your emotions and physical sensations.

You're attracted to alternative therapies, particularly those using plant-based methods, such as herbology or aromatherapy.

You have the gift of healing touch, whether or not you consider yourself to be a healer.

Your intuition is so strong at times that you can predict the future with uncanny accuracy.

MONGOOSE

(Also see <u>Meerkat</u>)

If MONGOOSE shows up, it means:

When it's necessary to defend yourself, do so with absolute courage, honesty, and openness, and the outcome will be beneficial to you and to all parties concerned.

Pursue your goals actively and with passion and you'll get the results you want.

This is a good time to clear up and clear out any annoying or distracting problems or situations that interfere with your well-being.

Clean up the clutter that subtly or overtly bugs you, and which interferes with your productivity or your ability to relax.

Call on MONGOOSE when:

You're being verbally assaulted and want to shield yourself in defense.

You're feeling pestered and bugged by a lot of little interruptions and want to reduce or eliminate them.

There are insect or reptile intruders in or around your home and you want to get rid of them.

You have a friendship or relationship that isn't good for you or which brings you down, and you want to distance yourself from that person.

If MONGOOSE is your POWER ANIMAL:

You're very agile and quick, with lightning-fast reflexes, of great use when you need them.

You're intelligent, witty, and enjoy performing for others when called upon to do so.

You're very clear about your purpose and relish the opportunity to express that purpose each and every day.

You have a high tolerance for (and a great deal of patience with) people whom others find annoying and toxic.

MONKEY

If MONKEY shows up, it means:

First accept things as they are, and once you do, you'll be able to generate creative solutions for any problems you're having and put them into action.

Be willing to adjust your course quickly and as necessary when fresh information, whether intuitive or logical, comes your way.

Be open to new perspectives and approaches rather than getting bogged down in rigid thinking or acting.

At this time, it's especially important that your communication is clear, congruent, and distinct, conveyed through words, body language, and action.

You're in close communication with the Nature spirits, particularly fairies and sprites, so seek their help.

Call on MONKEY when:

You need a dose of ingenuity and innovation to tackle the situation before you.

You're involved in a study of the origin of the human species and an examination of ancient wisdom.

There's a situation where communication has broken down and you want to correct it.

You've been feeling somewhat depressed and negative and need to surround yourself with uplifting, positive people and situations.

If MONKEY is your POWER ANIMAL:

You're able to move through life with grace and fluidity, rarely getting stuck in old habits and routines.

You're intelligent, clever, and adaptable, and you use these skills for creative problem solving.

You're an excellent communicator, straightforward and concise in words and deed.

You're very sociable, and you get recharged when you have a chance to be around others.

You're very curious and inquisitive, eager to learn more about anything that crosses your path.

MOOSE

If MOOSE shows up, it means:

You can feel proud of your recent accomplishment and share it enthusiastically with others, not to be boastful or competitive, but for the simple joy of sharing.

It's important to encourage others with their dreams and visions and by supporting their triumphs.

You have the strength and ability to endure this emotionally turbulent period.

Others will soon be looking to you for direction, inspiration, and guidance.

This is a time to explore new depths of awareness and be prepared for increasing sensitivities.

Call on MOOSE when:

You're being excessively self-critical, putting yourself down in thought or word, and need to remind yourself of your positive characteristics.

It's a time of conflict or turmoil and you need extra strength and endurance to cope with it.

You have children, and it's time to encourage their autonomy and discourage their dependence on you.

Something doesn't smell right or sound right and you want to be clear about how to respond to it.

You're in a position of authority or leadership and want others to respect you and heed your direction.

If MOOSE is your POWER ANIMAL:

You're very discerning about what to say, when to say it, and whom to say it to.

You pride yourself in your independence and generally don't have a need for strong bonds with your family or community.

As you age you'll find yourself imparting the wisdom you've gathered to future generations.

Sometimes you can be very patient, such as when you're teaching youngsters new skills, while at other times you're quite belligerent, particularly with those you find annoying.

You're unpredictable and contradictory; others aren't always sure which side of you will show up at any given time.

You came into this world with a strong intuition and psychic sensitivity.

MOTH

If MOTH shows up, it means:

A letter, e-mail, or package will be coming shortly bringing important news.

Trust your sense of smell and avoid anything that "smells" bad.

Whatever has been hidden or veiled is about to be revealed.

If you're single, focus your intention of attracting a romantic partner, and once you do, trust your senses as to whether or not it's a good match.

If you're in a romantic or intimate relationship, enhance the attraction by using essential oils as aromatherapy rather than perfumes or colognes.

Call on MOTH when:

You're involved in a creative project that you need to be very discreet or even secretive about.

There's an increase in your level of activity, such that you find yourself flitting from one thing to another.

You're in a cloud of confusion and need somehow to clear things up.

You're involved in a conflict or you're feeling attacked and want to defend yourself with discretion and stealth.

If MOTH is your POWER ANIMAL:

You keep your creative ideas and projects to yourself until they're completed.

You can be rather fickle, flitting from one idea or relationship to another.

You do your best work after the sun has set and tend to be wide awake long past when others have gone to sleep.

You're a very kinesthetic and sensual lover, enjoying the aromas and affection of lovemaking as much as any other aspects.

MOUNTAIN LION
(See Cougar)

MOUSE

If MOUSE shows up, it means:

Pay close attention to details so as not to let anything important escape your attention.

It's a time of plenty for you, yet one that requires vigilance in order to avoid any diminishment or significant losses.

You may be missing something that is obvious and right in front of you.

It's an appropriate time for closer scrutiny of all that's going on in your life and to sort out that which no longer fits.

Make a dispassionate assessment of your strengths and your limitations without judgment, and be completely honest with yourself.

You're missing an opportunity by narrowly focusing your attention on only one or two activities.

Call on MOUSE when:

You feel overwhelmed and disorganized and want to get things in some kind of order.

You're involved in a contractual transaction where it's critical to pay close attention to the fine print.

You're feeling unproductive and want to get motivated to pursue some project or task.

You feel like your attention and your energies are scattered and you need to get focused.

If MOUSE is your POWER ANIMAL:

You're very detail oriented, so much so that you sometimes lose track of the big picture.

You're very organized, always putting things in their proper place and able to keep track of things easily.

You're a paradox in that you're clean and fastidious in many areas of your life, but neglectful in others.

You like to warehouse supplies, keeping enough around so that you don't have to worry.

MUSK OX
(Also see <u>Ox</u>)

If MUSK OX shows up, it means:

No matter how harsh the emotional climate or physical environment, you will endure.

You're discovering a primal strength and fortitude inside you that is increasingly available to you for your protection.

Right now it's important to provide extra guidance and protection for any children in your domain.

Meet any challenges head-on with courage and persistence.

Look to your family or group of friends for support, comfort, and protection.

Call on MUSK OX when:

You're in an environment that is physically challenging.

You're studying what the prehistoric earth was like, with a particular interest in mammals of that time.

There's an intense emotional drama that's occurring around you, and you want to stay on an even keel and remain detached from it.

Someone who's very competitive is challenging you and you want to meet that challenge head-on.

If MUSK OX is your POWER ANIMAL:

You find strength in numbers and enjoy being surrounded by friends and family.

You maintain a primal connection with the ancient earth.

You're very protective of your children and any others who are in your charge and expect friends and others in your family to support you in your staunch protectiveness.

You're a smaller, stocky individual with big shoulders and short legs.

You never back down from a challenge.

MUSKRAT

If MUSKRAT shows up, it means:

Clean out your home and get rid of the clutter, starting with one room at a time.

This is a time to go inside yourself through meditation or contemplation as a restorative and regenerative measure.

Keep a dream journal for the next few days, spending a few minutes each morning when you first wake up recording your dreams and reflecting on their meaning.

Don't be surprised or alarmed if you have a few out-of-body experiences in the next few days.

Rely much more on what you hear and what you "smell" rather than what you see in your communications, as doing so will help you pick up on more subtle meanings or contradictory messages.

Call on MUSKRAT when:

You've been so busy with your various responsibilities and obligations that you need some quiet, contemplative time to regain your balance.

You've had a vivid dream, one that seemed very real, and you want to understand its meaning.

You've been feeling some disturbing and unfamiliar emotions and want to feel comfortable with them.

Something is gnawing at you and you want to pinpoint what it is.

If MUSKRAT is your POWER ANIMAL:

You're fastidiously clean and well organized, never letting things get into disarray.

You have to live near a body of water for the sake of your health and vitality.

When you're involved with an intense and personal creative effort, you get so obsessed with it that you lose track of anything else that's going on around you.

You like living with your family in spite of occasional flare-ups, most of which are related to boundary violations.

You're an excellent swimmer and enjoy a variety of water sports.

OCELOT

(Also see <u>Leopard</u>)

If OCELOT shows up, it means:

Channel your nervous energy or tension into artistic expression.

Keep that important goal you're pursuing to yourself rather than talking about it, as doing so will support its achievement, whereas discussing it will rob the goal of its energy.

Be choosy in picking your next creative project, and only go for the one that stirs your passions.

Someone close to you will soon share something that he or she wants you to keep confidential.

Call on OCELOT when:

You're going on an open-ended shopping excursion, one with no specific items or goals in mind.

You want to discern another person's feelings or motives that aren't obvious.

Secrecy and confidentiality are required, whether in a relationship or a project.

You have a feeling that someone close to you is holding something back from you, and you want to find out what it is.

If OCELOT is your POWER ANIMAL:

You're very agile, both mentally and physically.

You don't care for team sports, but you do like to compete with yourself and strive to do better.

You have a knack for finding real bargains and treasures without having to expend a lot of energy searching.

You have a powerful intellect and know a lot about a wide range of topics.

You do your best when you're in a committed relationship, and you're a very loyal and dedicated partner.

You're a night person and do your best work then.

OCTOPUS

If OCTOPUS shows up, it means:

Explore the possibility of somehow working with those who are transitioning into the spirit world.

It's time to take those yoga classes you've been thinking about to help your body become more flexible.

Get a thorough physical, ideally from an M.D. who practices integrative medicine, paying particular attention to your heart and lungs.

Use your mental agility to get whatever it is you're seeking, and be surreptitious and guarded about your objective as you pursue it.

You'll soon find your clairvoyant sensitivities and abilities increasing.

Call on OCTOPUS when:

You've had an out-of-body or near-death experience.

You're in a social situation where you want to blend in and be relatively obscure to others.

You've experienced any sort of loss and you want to recover and regenerate as quickly as possible.

You realize that you've been so immersed in a task or project that you've forgotten to take care of yourself.

If OCTOPUS is your POWER ANIMAL:

You're very comfortable with the life-death cycle, perhaps even working in a hospice or as a therapist dealing with death and dying.

You're very flexible and agile in body, mind, and spirit.

You're quite adept at moving with the currents of life, rarely getting upset about things and continually adjusting and adapting as needed to make life easier.

You're an expert at camouflage, blending in with your background and being able to seem invisible in the middle of a crowd.

You're a natural clairvoyant, especially when you don't try so hard and instead simply relax and allow the visions to show up.

You're nocturnal, having a lot more energy and getting a lot more done at night.

OPOSSUM

If OPOSSUM shows up, it means:

In order to accomplish whatever you've been striving to achieve, it will be necessary to stretch yourself a bit further than you think you can.

The situation you find yourself in will require that you be a good actor, in that you'll have to exhibit behavior that's the opposite of what you're actually thinking or feeling.

Do some planning and develop an effective strategy for the object of your concern, with back-up plans in place in case your first effort doesn't work out.

If you're in a tight corner, rely on your instincts to determine the best way out.

Study either Aikido or Tai Chi in order to learn to use dynamic and receptive forces as useful approaches in challenging situations.

Call on OPOSSUM when:

You're feeling stressed out or overwhelmed, and you're not sure of the best way to deal with these emotions.

You find yourself using habitual, self-defeating strategies to deal with challenging situations, and you want to develop more effective tactics.

The circumstances you're in call for tact and diplomacy, requiring you to act differently than you actually feel.

You're not sure if someone you're with is trying to create a false impression or deceive you in some way.

You need to quickly come up with a strategy that's the most appropriate for the particular situation you find yourself in.

If OPOSSUM is your POWER ANIMAL:

You have a natural gift as an actor, whether you've used this talent professionally, as a hobby, or in some social situations.

You're very nurturing and extremely protective of those you love, especially your children.

You can assess and understand an event immediately and know how best to cope with it.

You're a very flexible individual with considerable dexterity, both physical and mental.

You're a master at disguising your feelings and pretending, so much so that you can easily fool others into accepting your false front.

You readily see through others' masks and façades, yet you accept them for who they are and deal with them accordingly.

ORANGUTAN

If ORANGUTAN shows up, it means:

To accomplish what you have set out to do, put on your best face in order to get the job done.

Pay closer attention to the expressions on the faces of those you deal with, and trust what you see more than what you hear.

Whatever your needs are, do your best to be creative and use the available resources you find in your immediate surroundings.

It's best to have more fruit in your diet on a regular basis in order to create a healthier physical balance.

Call on ORANGUTAN when:

Ingenuity and cleverness are required to solve the problem before you.

You need to get a broader perspective on the situation you're dealing with.

You're feeling overwhelmed by a number of social commitments and obligations and want to spend some time on your own away from everyone else.

You feel the need for some compassionate and tender nurturing.

If ORANGUTAN is your POWER ANIMAL:

You have considerable ingenuity and resourcefulness in dealing with problems you have to face.

You're very expressive when you communicate, particularly with your body language, and especially with your facial expressions.

You have a knack for finding some usefulness in whatever is available to you.

Whether you're male or female, you're very gentle and have a well-developed capacity for nurturing others, particularly children.

You're very connected to the nature spirits, such as fairies, elves, and sprites.

You enjoy being on your own and especially value your periods of solitude.

ORCA
(Killer Whale)
(Also see Whale)

If ORCA shows up, it means:

Solicit the cooperation of friends and family to support you in pursuit of the goal you're targeting.

You can be confident that you're well protected, so there's no need to fear anything or anyone at this time.

You'll find yourself being more cued in to others who belong to your soul group, so trust your intuition with those you know and those you meet in the next few weeks to see who belongs.

Pay extra attention to the subtleties of communication, such as body language and especially vocal inflections, even more so than words.

It's time to fearlessly take your creative pursuits out of the box and bring them into the public eye, without concern for criticism or rejection.

Call on ORCA when:

You feel out of balance and pulled in opposite directions.

You're going through any sort of crisis and you need support and nourishment from others.

You're feeling depleted and worn out and you need a boost of energy and vitality.

You're participating in a project or venture that requires the coordination and cooperation of a number of different people.

If ORCA is your POWER ANIMAL:

You're very social and gregarious, and the bonds you form will last a lifetime.

You're good at camouflaging yourself, choosing whether to be seen or not in any given situation.

You're well organized and systematic, and enjoy cooperative ventures with others, whether play or work.

You're quite creative; however, you tend to keep that creativity under wraps or obscured.

OSPREY

(Also see <u>Hawk</u>)

If OSPREY shows up, it means:

Once you've surveyed the possibilities before you and one grabs your interest, dive in and go for it.

Your body is calling for the kind of nutrients that fish can provide, so include seafood in your diet at least twice a week.

Eat certifiably organic foods as much as possible, as your system is delicate right now.

This is an opportune time to immerse yourself in your creative energy, channeling it into a form of artistic expression that suits you.

Call on OSPREY when:

You want to impress your mate/partner with a loving, romantic time together.

You're ready for an intimate relationship and want to attract the perfect mate.

You've been feeling somewhat isolated and emotionally and socially undernourished.

You're ready to immerse yourself in a project that you're confident will be a huge success.

If OSPREY is your POWER ANIMAL:

You like living in a place with a vantage point that allows you to see all around you.

You like a sturdy, insulated, and well-built home, one that you can feel completely safe and secure in.

You're very committed to your family, your work, and your friends, and always place your family first on the list of priorities.

You're very protective of your home and your family and will defend them whatever it takes.

You're a caretaker and guardian (probably the oldest sibling in your family), and you're great at taking care of children.

OSTRICH

If OSTRICH shows up, it means:

Sort out whatever is no longer useful to you and let it go to make room for the new.

You're completely protected from any harmful psychic or spiritual intrusions.

Find some practical uses for whatever inspirations and ideas have come to you recently.

Be courageous in exploring and gathering information from new metaphysical and spiritual areas, trusting that you'll be able to stay grounded in the physical world.

This is a great time to satisfy your hunger for knowledge by pursuing a course of study, whether through an informal or formal education process.

Call on OSTRICH when:

You're feeling very spacey and out of touch with your body and the sensate world.

You're feeling so fragmented and distracted that it's difficult to focus on the task at hand.

You need to get something done swiftly and efficiently.

You've been entirely too visible and in the public eye and you want to lay low for a while and enjoy some privacy.

If OSTRICH is your POWER ANIMAL:

You're capable of accessing other dimensions of the spiritual realm while at the same time staying grounded.

You do not tolerate any intimidation or threats and will either choose to leave or fiercely defend yourself.

You're a very practical person, and once you've gathered enough intellectual and intuitive information, you make very sensible choices.

You know when to stand tall and let yourself be seen and known . . . and when to lay low and be less visible.

You have a strong digestive system and can eat just about anything.

OTTER

If OTTER shows up, it means:

It's time to relax and be more playful, spontaneous, and creative.

Clean up that area in your home that's needed organizing for some time.

Whatever struggles you're up against right now, confront them head-on with courage, determination, and tenacity.

Make your family a top priority at this time.

You're going to experience a surge of energy and vitality.

Call on OTTER when:

You find yourself worrying obsessively, picturing all sorts of catastrophic outcomes.

You've been feeling lethargic, keeping yourself indoors too much, and taking it all too seriously.

You're in need of some gentle and tender healing and nurturing.

You've done your best to avoid conflict in a situation, but now see the need to be fiercely assertive and stand your ground.

You've been feeling stressed out, caught up in work, and wearing a frown much of the time, and you know you need to have more fun.

If OTTER is your POWER ANIMAL:

You have a knack for fun, possess a great sense of humor, and you approach almost everything you do with an attitude of playfulness and joy.

When you do have a task to complete, you go at it with determination and steadfastness until it's done.

You're very friendly, have a great deal of curiosity, and love being around other people, trusting others to be safe until and unless they prove otherwise.

You're very easy to get along with, never seeking disagreements or disputes, but if you're confronted with anyone challenging you, you're very willing to take them on.

You're very energetic, active, and adventurous, finding it hard to sit still for very long.

OWL

(Also see <u>Barn Owl</u>; <u>Barred Owl</u>; <u>Great Horned Owl</u>)

If OWL shows up, it means:

Meditate in silence and in darkness for a few minutes each evening for the next few days and see what is revealed to you.

Be alert to any deception on the part of others, whether they're aware of it or not, and look closely behind any guises that they may wear.

This is a particularly ripe period to tap in to the fount of intuitive wisdom that's available to you.

Quietly observe your environment, watching and listening for signs and omens that will give you answers to any questions you may have.

Now is a particularly significant time for prophecy, and you will see, hear, or feel events before they actually happen.

Your most creative cycle now is the night, so set aside time in the evening to work on any projects.

— If SCREECH OWL:

- You're able to retain a strong sense of autonomy even though the task at hand requires cooperation with and from others.
- You're being called to do something that seems overwhelming, but be assured that you have the courage and tenacity to handle it.

— If SHORT-EARED OWL:

- Be fearless and courageous in responding to any perceived criticism or obstacles.
- You'll need to be quite versatile and imaginative in approaching the situation of your inquiry.
- It's a fiery and passionate time for you right now, so find ways to express these aspects.
- You'll soon find yourself in the right place at the right time, so take advantage of the opportunity that will be presented to you.

— If SNOWY OWL:

- Be sure to have a strategy for approaching the current situation.
- Be patient and wait until the right opportunity shows up, then go for it 100 percent.
- This is a time when you'll know in advance what's needed and be able to manifest it quickly.

Call on OWL when:

You're facing a difficult decision, one that has considerable consequences, and you want to make the decision that will reap the best benefits for all concerned.

You want to be more discerning about someone as to what is true and what is illusion or deception.

You're going through a rather dark period in your life and need some help navigating through it.

You've undertaken a new and challenging course of study and want to increase your confidence in your ability to learn this new material.

You want to uncover the hidden qualities, talents, and aspects in yourself and bring them into the light.

If OWL is your POWER ANIMAL:

You typically see what others don't see, hear what others don't hear, and are able to discern the truth behind any falsehoods.

You're an old soul and have an inherent wisdom that continues to expand as you mature.

You have a very finely tuned awareness and sensitivity to others.

One of your greatest gifts is being able to foresee the future.

You're able to contact the spirit world through your clairvoyance and clairaudience.

OX

(Also see [Bull](#) or [Musk Ox](#))

PANDA

(Also see [Red Panda](#))

If PANDA shows up, it means:

Your thinking is much too polarized into black/white and right/wrong, so try to broaden your perspective.

You can do anything you want once you set your mind to it, especially if the desire originates in your heart.

Take yourself somewhere up high where you can view the world below and meditate from this vantage point, observing how you feel as you do so.

Rather than juggling a whole bunch of projects, take one at a time and finish it before moving on to the next.

Incorporate the goddess Kwan Yin in your panoply of spiritual consultants.

Rely on your intuitive voice for guidance rather than input from others.

Call on PANDA when:

You're reconsidering a commitment you made as to whether you should break it, keep it, or renegotiate it.

You're having difficulty staying focused on the task at hand, as you're tempted to distract yourself with other things.

You're getting hung up on all-or-nothing type of thinking, rather than considering other alternatives.

You're considering a change of diet due to some persistent digestive disturbances.

If PANDA is your POWER ANIMAL:

You're a solitary individual, so if you live with a partner, you'll have to create some private and sacred space just for yourself.

You have a very sensitive digestive system, so be attentive and careful about what you eat.

You're modest and unassuming, yet at the same time very strong.

You like to do things in sequence, completing one thing and enjoying the satisfaction of a job well done before taking on another job.

PANTHER

(See <u>Leopard</u>; <u>Jaguar</u>; <u>Ocelot</u>)

PARROT

If PARROT shows up, it means:

Be discerning about when to speak and when to stay silent, and stay clear of gossip.

It would be a good time to study the power and effects of light and color.

Be alert to any new ideas that pop into your head, as these may give you some ideas for new growth or a new direction for yourself.

It's time to revisit and renew something you've always dreamed of doing, as now is the perfect time to act on it.

Call on PARROT when:

You've felt rather depressed for a while and want some relief from your mood.

You want to be a more effective communicator both in speaking and listening.

You want to invoke the powers of the sun for any kind of healing ceremony.

You've been too agreeable and easy and want to be more discerning and careful about what you agree to.

If PARROT is your POWER ANIMAL:

You're easygoing, have a good temperament, and get along with just about everyone you come in contact with.

You're very tactful and diplomatic and make a good mediator in times of crisis or conflict.

When you walk into a room, you have the effect of brightening things up.

You work with color and light as a means of healing others.

You're an excellent vocal mimic, so good that you can fool people quite often.

PEACOCK

If PEACOCK shows up, it means:

You're about to experience a vision that will greatly affect your life and the direction you're going in.

More than a time to take action, this is a time to be watchful, observing what goes on inside and around you.

You're safe and very well protected, so there's no need to worry.

It's important now to take a risk and speak your truth rather than holding back, as there will be ample opportunities to do so soon.

Your dignity and integrity are particularly called for right now, so make it a point to walk your talk and to hold your head up.

Call on PEACOCK when:

You're on the verge of making an important decision and you want to anticipate as many ramifications as possible before doing so.

You're questioning the truth of what someone has told you and need help discerning this.

You're entering new and unfamiliar territory, whether emotional or geographical, and need a guardian who will give you more than adequate warning of any danger.

Your self-esteem is rather low and you want to feel better about yourself.

There's an opportunity for you to perform in some kind of show, particularly one that calls for you to dress up in colorful costumes.

If PEACOCK is your POWER ANIMAL:

You're very showy and flashy and love to display yourself in colorful garb.

You're able to access deep inner wisdom, and when asked, readily communicate this knowledge.

You carry yourself with a very regal air, exuding confidence and warmth.

You're incredibly lucky, protected at all times, and always seem to be able to avoid any misfortunes.

PELICAN

If PELICAN shows up, it means:

This is an opportunity to forgive either yourself or someone else and release any built-up guilt or resentment.

It's time to free yourself from whatever is weighing you down—whether possessions, emotions, or mental strife.

Go ahead and take the plunge with respect to the opportunity that has recently presented itself.

Focus on cooperating with others rather than competing, particularly concerning any project you're involved with right now.

Call on PELICAN when:

You're feeling resentful or angry toward someone and you want to release it and lighten up.

You're feeling overcome with heavy emotions and want to rise above them.

There's an opportunity before you that looks, sounds, and feels right, but you need to move on it soon and trust that it's the right choice.

You're faced with some trials and tribulations and need to keep your head held high.

If PELICAN is your POWER ANIMAL:

You're able to remain light and relatively cheerful no matter what is going on in your life or around you.

You're unselfish, willing to share your space and material possessions.

You're very sociable and enjoy having others around you most of the time.

You're highly intuitive and able to catch subtle nuances and meanings that others miss.

PENGUIN

If PENGUIN shows up, it means:

You're much more powerful and durable than you think you are.

You have everything you need inside you and in front of you to have a good life, so always keep that in mind.

You'll soon be able to experience lucid dreaming, where you become fully aware while dreaming and can change the details of the dream.

This is an excellent time to explore altered states of consciousness, especially out-of-body experiences such as astral travel.

Whatever you feel like you're suffering through or simply enduring, be as loving, compassionate, and patient with yourself and others as you can be through the remainder of this cycle.

You'll soon face a test of your will, and as long as your will and purpose are aligned with Spirit's, you'll sail through it.

Call on PENGUIN when:

You're facing a task that will require considerable endurance and fortitude.

You feel remorseful and regretful about something in the past and you want to let it go.

You're in an environment that feels emotionally or physically harsh, whether you're in that environment temporarily or for a longer period of time.

You're feeling alone and alienated from your friends and want to establish a greater connection, sense of caring, and intimacy.

If PENGUIN is your POWER ANIMAL:

You have a remarkable capacity to endure even the harshest of conditions.

You're a very caring, protective, and patient parent with your own children or with those who are in some manner in your care.

No matter what challenges you go through, you always end up landing on your feet.

You're a well-balanced individual, comfortable with your inner masculine and inner feminine aspects, whether you're male or female.

You have a gift of being able to feel comfortable and function effectively in different states of consciousness.

PHEASANT
(Ring-Necked)

If PHEASANT shows up, it means:

This spring plant a garden, whether indoors or outdoors, growing whatever suits your fancy.

You may want to investigate a possible past-life connection to Asia, particularly China or India.

You're at your best when you stay grounded, because then you can decipher esoteric or spiritual information for practical use.

Just for fun, dress up a bit in playful and colorful clothes, and take yourself out or go with friends to a public place.

Your libido and vitality are at a peak right now, so enjoy yourself as much as you can.

Call on PHEASANT when:

You're going through a tough time and need to keep your head up and trust that it will pass.

There's a creative seed inside you that's begging to be expressed in some way.

You want to set a romantic mood for an intimate evening with your partner.

Things are pretty much black, white, and gray, and you want to add some color to your life, literally or metaphorically.

If PHEASANT is your POWER ANIMAL:

When things aren't going well for you, you're very patient and able to endure the situation for as long as it takes, quietly confident that it will change for the better.

You like open spaces without boundaries and just enough foliage to make it interesting, where you can roam around to your heart's content.

You love to shop at garage or rummage sales where you can poke around in boxes of stuff looking for hidden treasures.

You're open to new experiences, particularly meeting new people and making new friends.

You enjoy variety in places, people, and things.

PIGEON

If PIGEON shows up, it means:

You're about to receive an important message from an unexpected source in an unexpected way.

Keep your mind on the goal that's just ahead, stay with it, and you will get there.

No matter where you are in the world, you can draw on the feeling of home by closing your eyes, remembering what it was like, and breathing in the feeling.

If you're going through any kind of a struggle, look to your family and close friends for support and compassion.

Call on PIGEON when:

You feel alone and lost and need to find your way home, wherever that is and whatever that means to you.

You've had a volatile and disturbing childhood and want to experience greater stability, peace, and a sense of place as an adult.

You have a long way to go with a project, and you need the endurance and perseverance to complete it.

You're trying to conceive a baby.

You're trying to get an important message to someone and are having trouble getting it to this person by the usual means.

If PIGEON is your POWER ANIMAL:

You enjoy being at home so much that you rarely venture out unless necessary.

Whether male or female, you have strong maternal instincts.

You're family oriented, and when you do spend time with others, your family members are your first choice.

You have very clear and distinct morals and values, although you don't try to push them on others.

You're proud of your accomplishments, but rather than resting on your laurels, you continue to aspire to other goals.

PLATYPUS

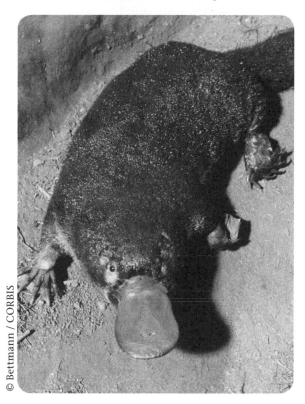

© Bettmann / CORBIS

If PLATYPUS shows up, it means:

This is a time of heightened sensitivity, so pay close attention to the cues that your body gives you.

Take time to discover the layers of meaning behind any significant encounters.

Rather than trying to adapt to others' demands or their pace, stay in tune to your own internal rhythms and move with those accordingly.

The situation before you requires you to have absolute faith in the process and to go with the flow, neither resisting nor being passive and nonresponsive.

Your clairvoyance is increasing and you'll find that you more readily trust your inner vision.

Include food in your diet that's grown underground, such as potatoes or carrots.

Call on PLATYPUS when:

You're trying to make sense of something that seems rather odd or strange.

You've experienced a recent shock or trauma, and although you're still somewhat numb, you're ready to do some healing and reawaken your physical senses.

You've been having difficulty getting back to and finishing an important project.

You're having difficulty understanding the meaning of a recent experience and you want to put it into its proper perspective.

If PLATYPUS is your POWER ANIMAL:

You're very kinesthetic, able to detect and move energy currents through your body.

You're naturally clairsentient and would do well as an energy healer.

You're a very sensitive individual, yet able to be lighthearted and spontaneous much of the time.

You're very inquisitive, constantly probing for the hidden or deeper meanings of your experiences.

Although you're rather unusual looking, you're charming and affable, and almost everyone likes you.

POLAR BEAR

(Also see <u>Bear</u>)

If POLAR BEAR shows up, it means:

Be assertive and strong in both your communications and your actions, yet be willing to yield as necessary.

Treat yourself with respect and maintain your dignity at all times.

Before you take action, pause and observe the situation; then when you're ready to make your move, commit to it fully and without hesitation.

Use only the amount of energy needed for the task before you rather than diverting it to unrelated matters.

This is a time to nourish and replenish your body, mind, and spirit, so prepare the means to do so.

You're about to embark on a spiritual adventure, one that will awaken some of your innate gifts and qualities that have been dormant until now.

Call on POLAR BEAR when:

You're faced with an important change in your life, but you're having trouble accepting it.

You're feeling afraid or threatened in any situation, no matter the trigger; and you want to feel safe, strong, and protected from any and all harm.

You're feeling pent-up emotionally and want to unfreeze these feelings a little bit at a time so you can release their hold on you.

You've been expending a tremendous amount of energy, your reserves are down, and you want to manage this energy more effectively.

You're doing any kind of work between the spirit world and this one and need a good, strong guide.

If POLAR BEAR is your POWER ANIMAL:

You're a skilled survivor, highly adaptable, and incredibly strong physically and emotionally.

You're confident yet cautious when approaching novel situations, but when you determine that the time is right to do so, you're willing to move forward to investigate.

Your spirit is very pure and you know who you are.

You have unquestioning faith in the Power that governs all, which is expressing itself as you and through you.

You're a powerful individual and readily command respect wherever you go and from whomever you meet.

PORCUPINE

If PORCUPINE shows up, it means:

Make sure your diet includes nutritious and organic vegetables, especially green ones.

It's important for you to move along at your own pace rather than hurrying because of pressure from others or external circumstances.

There's no need to worry because you're well protected, so relax and enjoy whatever you're doing.

Trust that you'll be respected as long as you respect others.

Know that you have magical abilities as long as you maintain faith in yourself.

Call on PORCUPINE when:

Someone is being mean-spirited toward you and you want to protect yourself.

You're feeling caught up in schedules and busy-ness and miss having more open-ended time to explore and wander.

You're taking life too seriously and need to loosen up and be more casual about everything.

There's a possible threat of some sort and you need adequate warning to deal with it.

If PORCUPINE Is your POWER ANIMAL:

You're good-natured, gentle, and loving, and enjoy just about anything that you're involved with.

You're an explorer, curious about a number of things, and you enthusiastically pursue these interests.

It takes a while to reach a boiling point when others aggravate you, but when you do reach that point, you're capable of sticking it to them so that it hurts.

You live and let live, respecting everyone without being intimidated by anyone.

You handle crises very well, without getting terribly alarmed, and are ready to deal with them as necessary.

PORPOISE

(See <u>Dolphin</u>)

PRAIRIE DOG

If PRAIRIE DOG shows up, it means:

Get involved in your immediate community in some way, through volunteer work or civic activity.

Take some time for yourself, such as a retreat or a day of silence, in order to recharge your batteries and get a fresh look at the situation at hand.

Increase the amount of vegetables in your diet or try a vegetarian diet for a few days, and note any differences you feel.

You've been pushing too hard in the situation and meeting resistance all the way, so step back from it and give it a rest so you can get a fresh perspective.

Discernment is called for in this situation as to when to push forward or when to retreat.

Call on PRAIRIE DOG when:

You're feeling isolated and in need of some companionship.

You've been burning the candle at both ends and need to take a break from it all before becoming completely exhausted.

You're feeling overwhelmed with responsibilities or beleaguered by the task at hand and don't seem to be making any progress.

There's something bugging you, but you have no clue what, so you need some time to dig in and analyze it in order to understand what it is.

If PRAIRIE DOG is your POWER ANIMAL:

You're a very sociable individual with strong ties to your community.

You know when and how to pull back from situations and relationships that could potentially drain your energy.

You're able to go with the flow and rarely get rattled about anything.

Although you love the outdoors, you're extra sensitive to sunlight and need to protect yourself by wearing sunglasses and sunscreen.

PRAYING MANTIS

If PRAYING MANTIS shows up, it means:

You could benefit from studying and practicing a martial-arts discipline such as Kung Fu, Chi Gong, or Tai Chi, which has a strong meditative and spiritual component.

Make prayer, meditation, or contemplation part of your daily regimen, even if only for a few minutes each day.

Listen to your instincts as to when to move forward and when to retreat.

Spend some time in the natural world, and practice being as still as you can for as long as you can, with nothing else to attend to except your breathing.

Consider redirecting your energy by withdrawing it from whatever isn't working in your life and focusing greater attention on what is working.

Call on PRAYING MANTIS when:

You feel like your energy is blocked or obstructed in some way, zapping your vitality.

You feel trapped by the clock and schedules and want to operate for a period without having to think of time.

You're overwhelmed with the stimulation from your environment and want to have some peace and quiet.

You know you need to develop a practice of stillness of some sort, but you're not sure how to go about it or know what the best way for you to do so is.

If PRAYING MANTIS is your POWER ANIMAL:

You're centered and well balanced, and your movements are fluid and graceful.

You're attuned to your instincts and trust them to guide you in making the right moves.

You're very patient and perceptive and can maintain your focus for long periods of time.

Prayer and meditation are significant practices in your life.

You practice the art of stillness, and you're so good at it that you're able to quiet your outer mind and draw upon the internal and spiritual resources that become more available when this is done.

PUFFIN

If PUFFIN shows up, it means:

Action speaks louder than words, so pay closer attention to what you and others are conveying through their body language and vocal characteristics than through the spoken word.

Make it a point to pray every day for at least a few minutes, focusing on prayers of gratitude rather than those of supplication (requests).

It's better at this time to contain your true feelings rather than express them.

Look ahead and do your best to anticipate what's down the road before you make your move.

Do your best to avoid fights and conflicts as much as you can, as there wouldn't be any winners anyway if it were to come to that.

Lighten up and inject a healthy dose of fun and humor into your spiritual path.

Call on PUFFIN when:

Work has become somewhat of a drag and you want to create more fun and enjoyment in it.

You want to change any negative or limiting thoughts about abundance to those that are more positive and that will attract abundance into your life.

You've gotten rather monkish about your religion or spirituality and want to loosen up a bit and be able to play and laugh more within the context of your spirituality.

Your faith is being challenged, and this has been weighing on you heavily.

You're generally taking life much too seriously, to the point where you've become morose and withdrawn.

If PUFFIN is your POWER ANIMAL:

You have to live near a body of water in order to maintain balance in your life.

You have a powerful and accurate sense of intuition that would be invaluable in any work as a psychic or therapist.

Whatever work you're doing, you're generally playful and peaceful while you're at it.

You have an active and integrated spiritual life and are able to have fun and maintain a sense of humor with it rather than always taking it so seriously.

PUMA

(See <u>Cougar</u>)

PYTHON

(Also see <u>Snake</u>)

If PYTHON shows up, it means:

You'll soon embark on an educational process where you'll be required to assimilate a lot of knowledge very quickly.

There's an area in your life where you're feeling suffocated, and it's up to you to break out of it.

You're going through a major transformative process, one that will result in the next evolution of who you are.

You're about to shed something that has outgrown its usefulness and purpose.

With the opportunity that's presented itself to you, "Strike while the iron is hot" is an appropriate aphorism.

Call on PYTHON when:

You're going through any kind of difficult changes in your life.

You have a lot of information coming at you all at once and you want to be able to digest it.

You've just completed a project, and you're ready for some much-needed rest and relaxation.

You're in a tight squeeze financially.

If PYTHON is your POWER ANIMAL:

You're a very powerful individual, someone whom others treat with respect and deference.

You're a very dedicated parent, willing to always provide your children with warmth and nurturing.

You love to learn new things, and once you've found something that interests you, you gobble it up and digest it very quickly.

Once you've decided what you want, you go for it quickly and with considerable enthusiasm.

QUAIL

If QUAIL shows up, it means:

Stay away from junk food and fast food for a week, and instead eat nourishing and healthy foods, perhaps preparing some of these yourself.

You'll soon be starting a creative endeavor that will stretch you a bit, but will also allow you to expand the sense of who you are.

If you feel threatened or criticized, don't respond directly, but instead use distraction by changing the subject or excusing yourself for a couple of minutes, thereby redirecting the other person's energy and attention.

You're about to discover a greater sense of who you are and develop a stronger understanding of your soul's destiny and purpose.

Call on QUAIL when:

You receive any kind of gift that nurtures and nourishes you and you want to express your gratitude.

You're at the front end of a romantic and intimate relationship.

You want to know what your "soul name" is and how it sounds when spoken.

You're involved in a baby-naming or baby-blessing ceremony.

If QUAIL is your POWER ANIMAL:

You're happiest when you're surrounded by a number of people you're close to, such as family and friends, and when you're participating with them in group activities.

You give a lot, and in doing so, the people who receive what you have to give are nourished in body and soul.

You're a romantic and attentive partner, and you indulge consistently and frequently in the emotional and physical intimacy that you share.

Sometimes when others least expect it, you'll burst into song, a loud proclamation, or laughter, and lighten up the atmosphere in the group or person you're with.

RABBIT

(Also see <u>Hare</u>)

If RABBIT shows up, it means:

This is a very creative time for you, so it's important to quickly take advantage of any opportunity that comes your way unexpectedly.

Be extra vigilant for the next couple of days, and if anything threatening shows up, leave as quickly as possible.

Try a vegetarian diet for the next few days and pay attention to how you feel.

Rather than steady, step-by-step progress, you'll see it happen in leaps and bounds.

You're going to find yourself going through a period of quiet and stillness followed by a burst of intense activity.

Express your love freely and readily to those you're closest to.

Call on RABBIT when:

A great opportunity comes your way, but to take advantage of it you need to act quickly.

You want to have a baby, but there have been some challenges as you've strived to do so.

Progress has been moving much too slowly on a project, and the completion date is near.

Your creative energy has been low and you want to give it a boost.

You've been feeling sedate and lacking in vitality and want to perk yourself up.

If RABBIT is your POWER ANIMAL:

Your intelligence, common sense, and wit serve you well, especially by helping you out of scrapes and uncomfortable situations.

You're a great strategist, always ready with a back-up plan, and are quite agile and adept at shifting plans as the need demands, particularly in stressful situations.

You're an eternal optimist, generally so positive that you find it hard to tolerate gloominess and pessimism.

In both your personal and professional lives, you cycle through periods of relative calm and inactivity followed by phases of tremendous activity and busy-ness.

You're very sensitive, articulate, and artistic, with a depth of wisdom that often surprises others.

RACCOON

If RACCOON shows up, it means:

In spite of any doubts you may have, the resources you need for the current situation are readily available.

There's some sort of deception going on around you that you can discern by listening to and trusting your intuition.

Rather than being goal oriented, this is a time for indulging your curiosity in open-ended exploration.

Pay close attention to signs and omens that suggest you're getting messages from the ancestors or your deceased loved ones.

It's important to remain emotionally and mentally flexible for the next few days, as events will require you to adapt to rapidly changing circumstances.

Call on RACCOON when:

You're faced with a task that will require manual dexterity.

You're feeling stagnated and bored and are eager for adventure and exploration.

You're faced with a challenging situation that requires you to be flexible and adapt quickly.

An upcoming social event calls for you to put on a face that will help you feel more comfortable mixing with others.

You need to defend yourself using assertiveness, wit, agility, and perhaps even deception.

If RACCOON is your POWER ANIMAL:

You're gifted with an intuitive mechanical ability.

You express your creativity with your hands, whether through sculpting, painting, writing, or some other endeavor.

You're remarkably resourceful at finding whatever you need at any given moment.

You're quite adaptable and flexible, feeling at home just about anywhere you happen to be.

You have a number of different personas and are capable of presenting just the right one that is appropriate for the circumstances.

RAM
(Bighorn Sheep)

If RAM shows up, it means:

Whatever you've been considering starting, now is the time to go ahead and begin it.

There's something that is out of balance in your life, so determine what that is and take steps to correct it.

The timing is right for you to pursue intellectual or educational interests and activities, so make a plan to do so and put it into action.

You're ready for some new challenges, so be willing to charge ahead with whatever gets your attention.

You're going through or about to go through a spiritual initiation leading to an emergence of a different sense of yourself.

Call on RAM when:

Your energy is low and you need a boost so that you'll feel stronger and more powerful.

You're dealing with a very challenging or stressful situation and want to maintain a sense of balance.

You're at the beginning of a new project or relationship and want to leap ahead while at the same time keeping yourself grounded.

Your virility and vitality have declined and you want to restore these qualities.

If RAM is your POWER ANIMAL:

You're very confident, unquestionably believing in yourself and your abilities.

You're typically stoic, detached, and unemotional, relatively un-affected by the events around you.

You keep things to yourself and rarely communicate what you're thinking or feeling.

You're very imaginative and have a great deal of curiosity that increases as you mature, and you're willing to pursue whatever attracts your attention.

You're very spontaneous, even to the point of being impulsive, willing to move quickly when a new opportunity presents itself.

RAT

If RAT shows up, it means:

A project or investment is about to pay off.

You have plenty available to you at all times in spite of any thoughts or fears that this isn't so.

This is a good time to exercise caution, and to the best of your ability anticipate what lies ahead.

Take an inventory of the material goods you have and recycle or throw out what is no longer purposeful.

Call on RAT when:

You're involved with a venture that you want to succeed at, yet you're feeling some uncertainty about this happening.

You're feeling insecure about having enough supplies, making you want to acquire more and more even though you realistically don't need that much.

You have decided to do a major housecleaning and to sort and sift through your stuff and get rid of a whole lot of it.

You're involved in some dealings with someone who's very sharp and want to protect yourself by being just as clever and shrewd.

If RAT is your POWER ANIMAL:

You tend to hoard your belongings because they help you feel more secure.

You adapt very well to your surroundings and your environment and can live on whatever's available to you.

You enjoy the feeling of being successful whenever you've achieved something, and you use your cleverness and cunning to succeed.

You're rather shy, generally nervous, and you get restless very easily.

RATTLESNAKE

(Also see <u>Snake</u>)

If RATTLESNAKE shows up, it means:

Pay attention to any signs or omens that may be warning you to stay away or stay clear, especially any that you hear.

For your health, do a detoxification cleanse for three to seven days to release any toxins in your body.

Record your dreams in a journal for the next several nights, as they will offer clues and guidance to the passage you're going through.

Your sensitivity to others' auras will increase, such that you'll either see or feel them more strongly than ever, so trust what you're seeing or feeling when around other people.

Anything you do now to heal yourself physically or emotionally will be the start of a major transformative cycle for yourself, one that will lead to greater benefits for you and your family and friends.

Call on RATTLESNAKE when:

You've started on a course of healing your wounds and memories from a difficult childhood.

You need to release any physical, mental, emotional, or spiritual toxicity, or any toxic relationships that interfere with your complete health and your spiritual path.

You're going through some substantial changes in your life that require you to completely release some old habits, addictions, possessions, or some type of lifestyle.

You're going through a time of questioning your identity, since you're changing so much that the old you seems familiar yet obsolete.

If RATTLESNAKE is your POWER ANIMAL:

You're a powerful and compassionate healer whose gifts have come from healing your own wounds.

You're slow to anger, but before you reach your boiling point, you give ample warning; yet, if these warning signals are disregarded, you'll strike hard and fast verbally or physically in order to defend yourself.

You're nocturnal and enjoy activities that you can do at night.

You have a very active and profound dream life and have explored lucid dreaming.

RAVEN

(Also see Crow)

If RAVEN shows up, it means:

Magic is in the air, and something special is about to happen.

Pay attention to dreams and visions, especially colorful and powerful ones, as these are indicative of prophecy.

In any undertaking or in any relationship, be very clear as to what your intentions are because whatever they are, that's what will manifest.

You're gradually shape-shifting to a more confident, powerful, and spiritually based you that will continue to emerge the more you let go of your old self.

You'll observe an increasing number of synchronistic events over the next few days, so just notice these, appreciate them, and don't try to figure them out.

Call on RAVEN when:

You need to clarify your intention about a task, a relationship, or your spiritual path so that you can manifest that intention in third-dimensional reality.

You had an especially painful childhood and want to reclaim the lost innocence and joy.

You've lost touch with the magic of life and want to recapture that sense of awe and wonder, as well as manifest your desires.

You're in need of physical and/or emotional healing and want to augment whatever other treatment modalities you're using.

You have an ailing loved one who is some distance away, or there are others at some distance who are suffering and you want to send strong prayers and healing energy.

If RAVEN is your POWER ANIMAL:

You prefer solitude to the company of others.

As you mature, your spiritual awareness expands, while simultaneously your capacity for manifesting your preferences and desires increases.

You're a spiritual healer; when you're present, everyone around you can feel it.

You must be vigilant about any personal shadows that interfere with your true mission and that try to take you off the path.

You're able to communicate easily with animals.

You carry yourself with a reserved air of confidence and strength, remaining alert to all that's occurring around you.

You always know what to do, and when necessary, you do it quickly and decisively.

You're a natural shape-shifter, able to subtly disguise yourself as the occasion calls for, even to the point of seeming invisible to others.

RED PANDA

(Also see <u>Panda</u>)

If RED PANDA shows up, it means:

Do whatever is necessary in order to establish a home base for yourself that helps you feel safe and secure.

Meditate in the evening in a darkened room and keep a journal of what you experience each time.

You need to get more rest, so allow yourself to do so.

Investigate any past-life experiences in the Far East, such as Nepal, Tibet, Burma, or China.

Try a vegetarian diet for a while, and make sure to vary the types of foods you eat.

Worry less and play more.

Call on RED PANDA when:

What you've usually relied on to provide a sense of safety and security is no longer with you.

You're interested in exploring any Eastern spiritual beliefs and practices.

You want to make some positive changes in your diet and eating habits.

You're fretting and fussing over an imaginary future full of possible catastrophic events.

If RED PANDA is your POWER ANIMAL:

You feel most secure when you know that you have a solid foundation.

You're definitely a night person and get the best ideas and the most work done after sunset.

You do best by eating small amounts of food throughout the day rather than larger meals.

You have a very casual, carefree attitude toward almost everything you experience.

RHINOCEROS

If RHINOCEROS shows up, it means:

Experiment with doing things on your own, such as dining or going to a movie alone.

Do whatever you need to do to quiet your mind, such as setting aside some peaceful, relaxing time for yourself.

At this time be particularly discriminating in your choices, and don't make any major decisions without having gathered as much intuitive and intellectual information as possible.

Do whatever you can to stay clear of any dissension, conflict, or trouble of any kind and instead seek peace and harmony, even if you need to retreat to find them.

Rather than rushing ahead in the pursuit of your spiritual ideals, take one step at a time and be patient and persevering, staying present in the process rather than aiming for the goal.

— If WHITE RHINO:

- You'll soon be accessing ancient mysteries and wisdom; over time you will assimilate this into your life.
- You're about to come across a rare and precious item, something personally meaningful to you.

— If BLACK RHINO:

- You're completely protected from any and all harm, and any appearance otherwise is an illusion.

Call on RHINOCEROS when:

You're feeling a strong need for some alone time and need to take a break from your usual routines and the people you hang out with.

You feel the need to protect your personal space from any intrusions, including psychic ones.

Something "smells" funny, but you're not sure what it is or how to respond to it.

You're suspicious of what's behind the appearance of someone or something, sensing that there's more than meets the eye, and you want to dig in and find out what's there.

If RHINOCEROS is your POWER ANIMAL:

You're a solitary individual, preferring your own company.

You know how to create and enjoy your own personal space.

Sometimes others are intimidated by you, but once they get to know you they see that you're really a very gentle, peaceful, and rather timid soul.

You're a profoundly spiritual person with deep connections to the ancients, yet you keep this wisdom contained rather than wearing it on your sleeve.

You're a very solid individual and there's very little that could happen to you that would shake your foundation.

ROADRUNNER

If ROADRUNNER shows up, it means:

There are situations occurring in your life that require you to think on your feet, change direction quickly, and adapt to the new course—which you're quite capable of doing.

This is a great time to make some plans and put them into action so that you can manifest whatever it is you want.

Be willing to laugh at yourself and not take your quirks and idiosyncrasies too seriously.

Explore and experiment with different ways you can benefit yourself and others spiritually, emotionally, and physically through the use of sound.

Be sure to take care of yourself first before you attempt to take care of others; that way you can be completely present when you're in service to them.

Call on ROADRUNNER when:

You're involved in a project, task, or game that requires mental dexterity and quick reflexes.

You need some mental and intellectual stimulation that has been lacking recently.

You want to be more lighthearted and go with the flow so you can enjoy life that much more fully.

You need a good laugh.

You think someone is trying to trick you or play a practical joke on you.

If ROADRUNNER is your POWER ANIMAL:

You love the desert and spend as much time there as you can.

You're a doer and are happiest when you're busily involved with a project, whether for fun or profit.

You're very sharp and your mind is constantly at work, always thinking and analyzing.

When you try to communicate your thoughts to others, you have to remind yourself to slow down.

You're usually involved in several things at once, and often don't complete one thing before moving on to the next, yet you get the job done when you have to.

ROBIN

If ROBIN shows up, it means:

It's time to let go of anything in your life that's outmoded and stagnant and plant the seeds for the new by setting your goals and intentions for the coming year.

Let go of your attachment to drama and allow as much joy and laughter into your life as you possibly can.

Your spiritual path is steady and slow, with challenges along the way, yet it inevitably leads to your achieving your spiritual ideals.

You have a beautiful song inside you, so do whatever it takes to share it with the world.

Expect new growth in a number of areas in your life.

Make a wish, be patient, and watch how it comes true.

Call on ROBIN when:

You're starting on a new project or entering into a new relationship and you want to clear the decks for a successful venture.

You've experienced a surprising and profound spiritual revelation or awakening.

You're considering singing lessons as a professional enhancement, a confidence booster, or just for fun.

There's a potential conflict or confrontation, and you want to prevent it from becoming too aggressive or physical.

You recognize that you're at the end of a major cycle and beginning a fresh, new one, and want to enjoy both the ending and the beginning as you go through this transition.

If ROBIN is your POWER ANIMAL:

You're a happy person, often singing or whistling, and your joy affects others in a positive way.

You have a past-life connection to Christ, whether you're Christian or not, and you know that you're on a divine mission in life.

You're a dedicated spiritual seeker, using as many resources as possible to continue evolving as a spiritual being.

You like to be settled in one place more so than moving around a lot.

Your primary assignment while you're on the planet is, to the best of your ability, express the will of God in all you do and all you say.

SALAMANDER

If SALAMANDER shows up, it means:

You're about to go through a subtle transformation; however, don't try to hurry it along or dramatize it, but instead let it develop at its own pace.

You're about to receive help from an unexpected source with respect to the dilemma you're facing.

Cooperation with those around you and with the environment is key to your success right now.

If you're entering into a new personal or business relationship, check things out carefully before proceeding.

During this transition that you're going through, be emotionally contained so that you don't get burned out or consumed by the changes.

Call on SALAMANDER when:

You need some fresh inspiration for a project and need to look outside yourself for it.

Your life has become stale and routine and you need to get unstuck, but you're not sure how to go about doing so.

You're going through a life change, one that requires considerable vitality and energy.

You're feeling overwhelmed emotionally and need to ground yourself in order to gain some insight about what you're feeling.

If SALAMANDER is your POWER ANIMAL:

You're very sensitive to your environment and do your best when you live in an area that's nontoxic.

It's necessary for your health and sanity to be working and living in a creative and supportive atmosphere with like-minded people.

You come across as rather cool and aloof, and are very careful about what you confide to others.

You tend not to get involved with or get too close to others, even though you have considerable wisdom that you could impart.

You can get rather fiery with others if you get riled up.

SALMON

If SALMON shows up, it means:

In spite of any challenges or discouragement, persevere toward your goal and you'll reach it.

It's critical that you trust your gut feelings and inner knowing at this time and avoid the influence of anyone who may have hidden agendas.

You may experience some sort of loss such as a relationship or a move, yet this will precede a new beginning.

Through some sacrifice you willingly make, you'll experience a rebirth into a new "you."

This signals a time of plenty, where you'll have more than enough for yourself and to share with others.

Call on SALMON when:

You feel lost and unsure of what direction your life is taking and need some help navigating.

You're seeking to find a sense of purpose and meaning in your life, particularly at the beginning of any new developmental era.

You're uncertain as to whether to trust some outside influence in determining any major decisions.

You're trying to understand the life lessons to glean from any particular experiences, whether those experiences seem positive or negative.

If SALMON is your POWER ANIMAL:

You're very wise for your years, and others often look to you for counsel.

You always know where you're going and how to get there, and whatever you begin, you finish.

To others you may seem rather distant and aloof, even a bit odd or different, yet people are attracted to you.

Although you'll listen to others' advice and counsel, you ultimately trust in your own inner wisdom for your decision-making.

SANDPIPER

If SANDPIPER shows up, it means:

Set aside some time each day to select some of your favorite music . . . and dance.

You're going to experience a lot more masculine or yang energy, which will stimulate you to be more physically active.

Do what you need to in order to stay grounded, even through a challenging emotional time.

An appropriate diet for you at this time is one of eating very small portions of light food and healthy snacks throughout the day.

If you're a man, participate as much as you possibly can in your children's lives—from pregnancy, birth, and on into adolescence.

Call on SANDPIPER when:

You're going through a very emotional time and want to stay centered throughout the process.

You're feeling passive and lethargic and need a boost of energy to get going.

You want to devise some practical steps for getting a project or task done.

You're seeking spiritual sustenance that's compatible with your beliefs.

If SANDPIPER is your POWER ANIMAL:

You love spending time at the seashore, feeling very much at home there.

You're a very good scavenger, and much to others' surprise, you find things that others easily overlook.

Your masculine and feminine energies are very well balanced.

You're very nurturing and enjoy affectionate encounters with those you're closest to.

You can be quite flirtatious and seductive when you want to be.

You're very quick, witty, and can make others laugh—or at least smile broadly.

SCORPION

If SCORPION shows up, it means:

In order for these changes that you're going through to go smoothly, contain and control your temper and passions at this time.

You'll soon be asked by a close friend or family member to keep something confidential.

Sex with someone you love will move to even greater heights of intensity and passion.

Show those you're closest to plenty of nonsexual physical affection such as hugs and gentle caresses.

This is a period of transformation for you, one where you'll be releasing a lot of toxic habits and a few toxic relationships.

Call on SCORPION when:

You need protection and shielding from the negativity or psychic assaults of others.

Someone you know is dying or has passed on and you're charged with praying or otherwise helping to transport their soul to the spirit world.

You're going through a transformational cycle that stings a bit and is rather chaotic, and you want to make the process easier and smoother.

You're pondering the mysteries of life and death and trying to develop an understanding of these.

If SCORPION is your POWER ANIMAL:

You'd be very satisfied working with death and dying in some way, such as being a hospice worker or a therapist dealing with these issues.

You're very powerful and influential, with considerable strength of character, yet you must be careful about misusing your psychic and spiritual capacities.

You naturally inspire others by your presence and by what you express and how you express it.

You have periods of being solitary followed by those of intense and fiery relationships with others.

If anyone crosses you, beware, as you can sting with your words.

SEAGULL

If SEAGULL shows up, it means:

You're opening up communication with the realm of the Nature spirits, particularly fairies and water sprites.

It's time to clean up your home environment and let go of and recycle as much as you possibly can.

It's important to clear up any misunderstandings you've had with someone you're close to that resulted from poor communication.

Pay close attention to those you interact with, particularly noticing any nonverbal cues and voice intonations, and trust what your senses are picking up.

Spend a significant amount of time at the seashore meditating, allowing the rhythms of the waves and the wind to be your guiding pulse.

Call on SEAGULL when:

You find yourself in a social situation where you feel out of place or uncomfortable.

There has been a recent situation with someone where the communication has gotten garbled or unclear.

You're feeling called to do more to help clean up the environment, particularly the oceans or seashores.

You're required to teach others, particularly younger people, about proper behavior in social situations.

You're feeling uptight and in a bind about your responsibilities and obligations and want to relax and not take it all so seriously.

If SEAGULL is your POWER ANIMAL:

You're a very gifted communicator, both articulate and a good listener.

You maintain a comfortable balance between your emotions and your rational side.

You're quite attentive to the decorum that's necessary in any social situation, and you're well mannered and courteous to all.

You're committed to doing things that help the environment, such as picking up trash and recycling whatever can be recycled.

You're casual about most things in life and don't get alarmed about much.

SEA HORSE

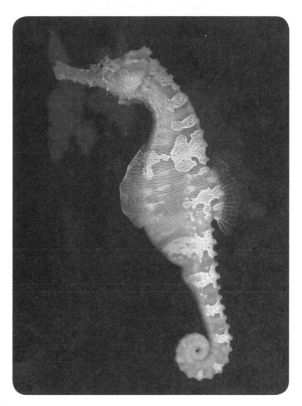

If SEA HORSE shows up, it means:

You're being called upon to sacrifice your own needs at this time to be in service to another person or a cause.

This is a good time to experiment switching gender roles, doing things that you ordinarily think of as belonging to the domain of the opposite sex.

Volunteer some of your time to a service organization.

You're about to go on a quest or spiritual pilgrimage of some sort, so prepare yourself by being open to the opportunity when it surfaces.

Call on SEA HORSE when:

You want to feel a more secure and stable foundation in your life.

You're a man and you want to participate more directly in the pregnancy, birth, and rearing of your child.

You're pregnant and want your man to be intimately involved in your pregnancy, the birth, and the rearing of your child.

You want to attract more romance and chivalry into your life.

You're seeking support for healing or preventing asthma, high cholesterol, impotency, thyroid or heart dysfunctions, and arteriosclerosis.

If SEA HORSE is your POWER ANIMAL:

You're good at blending in with your environment and not being seen if you don't want to be.

You have a gentle strength and serenity about you, and strike a balance with your masculine and feminine energies.

You have an unusual physical structure and distinctive features that are quite attractive to most people.

You're very gracious, polite, and courteous to all those in your life and all those you come across.

SEAL
(Sea Lion)

If SEAL shows up, it means:

Your creative imagination is active and fertile right now, so keep a journal nearby and write in it every day.

Your dreams will be very clear and vivid, so pay close attention to them for any messages from your subconscious.

The cycle of challenges and hardship is complete, and you're now moving into a time of plenty and abundance.

Although it's an emotional time for you, you're quite comfortable experiencing these feelings while at the same time staying grounded.

This is a time to stay attuned to your natural rhythms, such as sleeping when you're tired, eating only when you're hungry, and exercising when you feel the urge to do so.

— If SEA LION:

- This is a time to let yourself experience joy and be playful.
- Listening to all that's around you is important, especially to yours and others' feelings.
- Take the time to stretch or do yoga to keep your body flexible.

Call on SEAL when:

Your creativity seems blocked or stagnant and you need a dose of inspiration.

You're involved in a lot of right-brain activity to the point where you feel off balance and ungrounded, and want to get a bit more down-to-earth without losing touch with your creative side.

You know that there are emotions just below the surface that are tugging at you and that it would be useful to feel them, but you don't feel safe in allowing their expression.

You're going through a major life change and feel the need for some extra strength and protection.

This is an emotionally turbulent time and you need some help steering through these waters.

If SEAL is your POWER ANIMAL:

You're a creative and imaginative individual who can express these gifts through different channels, and you'll be happiest in a position where you can employ these talents.

You can live just about anywhere as long as it's close to a body of water.

You're very outgoing and easy to talk with and tend to brighten up any social gathering.

You're very adaptable and have always been able to meet any challenges head-on and rebound from them.

You're able to see behind the masks of others and intuitively and empathetically understand their emotions.

You're an emotionally expressive individual, yet you never let your feelings overwhelm you.

SHARK

If SHARK shows up, it means:

You're especially sensitive right now, so be careful what environments and situations you expose yourself to.

Allow yourself to swim through your emotions fluidly so as not to get stuck in any one feeling.

You're very well protected and can ward off any threats, negativity, or psychic attacks.

Notice how your mood shifts depending on what you've eaten, and if necessary, modify your eating habits to maintain your physical and emotional equilibrium.

Maintain your dignity and self-respect no matter who or what you encounter.

You'll notice a heightened ability for discernment and discrimination, sorting out what's right and what's not for yourself.

Call on SHARK when:

You're feeling overwhelmed by intense emotions and want to move through them more smoothly.

You sense that there's someone trying to manipulate or bully you and you need strong protection and support for asserting your boundaries.

You're faced with a lot of problems that otherwise could eat up your time, energy, and motivation.

You're finding it difficult to stay focused on the task before you.

There's an opportunity before you that you must act on immediately and with clear intention.

If SHARK is your POWER ANIMAL:

You need periods of time alone so that you avoid getting anxious and irritable.

Although others are intimidated by you at times, you're actually a very sensitive and peace-loving person.

You're very active, always staying busy with something or other, and you find it hard to rest for any length of time.

You do best in a role of authority, one where you have to maintain discipline and order.

SKUNK

If SKUNK shows up, it means:

Be assertive and stand your ground as necessary, and don't let yourself be manipulated or pushed around.

Make your self-respect and dignity a top priority, offering the same respect to others.

You're taking yourself far too seriously and need to relax, play, and trust that everything is all right.

It's a good time to deal directly and honestly with that person in your life whom you find so irritating and overbearing.

Your sensuality and sexuality are in a heightened state right now, so explore the uses of natural scents and essential oils.

Call on SKUNK when:

You're feeling the need to defend yourself, but don't want to be aggressive in doing so.

Your self-esteem and self-respect have hit a low and you want to regain good feelings about yourself.

You're missing a sense of playfulness and wonder, so you're exploring new avenues to recapture these elements in your life.

There's someone you need to confront about something that's uncomfortable; and you want to do so with courage and calmness, and without doing any harm.

You want to decide whom you can trust enough to let close and whom you should keep at a distance.

If SKUNK is your POWER ANIMAL:

You're very playful and nonchalant and not intimidated by anyone or anything.

You're your own best authority, preferring to discover possibilities for yourself rather than accepting information from someone else.

You're confident and charismatic without being cocky or arrogant, quite attractive to other like-minded people, while easily repelling those who would seek to drain your energy.

When it comes to defending yourself, you readily show courage to confront without being aggressive.

You exude calm and natural sexual energy without even trying.

SLOTH

If SLOTH shows up, it means:

Slow down your pace, as you miss so much by running around frantically.

It's healthier for you if you graze—eating small, light snacks throughout the day—rather than two or three larger meals.

It's important for you to exercise every day, a portion of which should be strengthening exercises, to help keep you grounded and in your body.

Whatever you're dealing with right now, try viewing it from a different perspective, putting aside any preconceived beliefs or notions that there's only one way to look at the situation.

You'll get where you want to go, but it's going to be slow and steady progress, one step at a time.

Do all the things you need to in order to maintain a healthy immune system.

Call on SLOTH when:

You need to camouflage or disguise yourself as a means of protection or as a way of concealing yourself when you don't want to be noticed.

Your psychic sight or vision is opening up and you want to channel it appropriately.

You're feeling frantic, hurried, and harried and want to slow the train down.

There's a piece that you're working on, whether personal or work related, that's gotten stuck, and you feel the need to step back and look at it from a different perspective.

If SLOTH is your POWER ANIMAL:

You move at a much slower pace than others, but you get the job done.

You give the impression to others that you're an easy mark, but appearances are deceiving, as you're quite perceptive and very capable of defending yourself.

In spite of your generally easygoing manner, if someone crosses you, you can strike out rather harshly.

There are times when you feel out of place on this earth and have had challenges trying to fit in various aspects of your society.

You're clairvoyant and a visionary, and have gifts that you have to hone and learn how to manage while still staying grounded.

You like your solitude and feel threatened whenever you feel that someone is trying to take away your independence, which makes for some interesting challenges when you're in a relationship.

SNAKE

(Also see Cobra; Python; Rattlesnake)

If SNAKE shows up, it means:

You're about to go through some significant personal changes, so intense and dramatic that an old self will metaphorically die as a new self emerges.

You're going to feel a surge of energy that will sharpen your senses, alert your mental faculties, and open up new channels of awareness.

You're about to resolve a long-standing issue, one that has required a great deal of your attention, by seeing things in a new light.

It would be a good time for you to start doing either tantric or kundalini yoga.

You'll experience a dramatic and unexpected physical or emotional healing very soon, coming from an unexpected source.

— If BOA CONSTRICTOR:

- Extricate yourself from the situation that's suffocating your growth.

Call on SNAKE when:

You're going through a major life or developmental transition, one so powerful that it requires you to shed a lot of attachments, especially to your old identity.

You're moving into unknown territory, a passage through darkness, and you're feeling afraid that you won't get through it and are anxious about what lies ahead.

You need a healing of any kind.

You need help in releasing any and all self-destructive or self-defeating tendencies or habits.

You want to increase your energy and vitality, including your libido.

If SNAKE is your POWER ANIMAL:

You're a healer, whether your focus is primarily on plants, animals, humans, or the earth.

You've gone through a series of initiations, including death and rebirth experiences and as a result have gained compassion, wisdom, and a powerful capacity for healing.

You've gained a deeper interest in ancient and indigenous cultures and spiritual practices and feel quite at home with these, along with other esoteric and metaphysical interests and pursuits.

You're very *sense-i-tive,* able to perceive subtle energies emanating from others and interpret them by trusting your gut feelings.

When you first meet people, you tend to be cool and distant, but once you warm up, you relax and become quite friendly.

SNOW LEOPARD

(Also see <u>Leopard</u>)

If SNOW LEOPARD shows up, it means:

Your path toward the completion of your goals will be one in which you'll easily leap over any obstacles you encounter.

It's best not to talk about any major goals you're pursuing or projects you're working on until they're accomplished or complete.

More than ever, it's important to trust your instincts and not be swayed by input from external sources, such as other people's opinions or perspectives.

Whatever it is you want, take your time and quietly but steadily do what you have to do to get it.

Investigate the possibility that you have past-life connections to Tibet or China.

Call on SNOW LEOPARD when:

You have a strong sense of something going on that's less than obvious, but you doubt your perceptions because nobody else seems to be picking up on the same thing.

You've been in a very noisy, chaotic situation and you need a break from it, preferably to go somewhere where there's peace and quiet.

You're living in a cold climate or through a very cold winter and you want to stay warm and cozy as much as possible.

You've been feeling rather awkward, either physically or emotionally and want to regain a sense of balance, ease of movement, and gracefulness.

If SNOW LEOPARD is your POWER ANIMAL:

You're able to see clearly into the hearts of others and love them no matter what.

You have strong intuitive capacities and pick up on what's going on by listening to the sensations in your body.

Throughout your life you've had to contend with others who wanted to negate or diminish the value of your highly accurate perceptions, but by now you've learned to trust what your inner guidance is telling you.

You're very athletic, with considerable agility, grace, speed, and flexibility.

Although you tend to be solitary, you're willing to share your home with guests from time to time.

SPARROW

If SPARROW shows up, it means:

This is a very productive and prolific time.

Look for the nobility in the most common of things and people, including yourself.

Walk with poise, your head held up, eyes straight ahead, showing the world your self-respect and dignity.

You're heart is opening more and more to the love you receive and you're more readily expressing love to others.

Your energy and vitality are awakening, and you find yourself whistling or singing without even being aware of it.

Call on SPARROW when:

Your dignity and self-worth are being demeaned or threatened in some way.

You're coming to the end of the hardships and travails you've faced lately.

External circumstances seem to be pinning you down in some way and you want to eliminate their grip on you.

Your willpower has dwindled to some extent and you want to renew it.

If SPARROW is your POWER ANIMAL:

You have little or no fear of anyone or anything and can hold your own if ever threatened.

You're assertive in asking and going for what you want and are clear in refusing what you don't want.

You're a survivor, and are quite comfortable wherever you happen to be and wherever you take up residence.

Within your considerable humility, you freely express love and joy, which positively affects others who are near.

Whenever you have to face a challenge, you do so courageously and never let yourself feel defeated.

SPIDER

(*Also see* <u>Black Widow Spider</u>; <u>Tarantula</u>)

If SPIDER shows up, it means:

This is an opportunity to access your deepest wisdom and assimilate it so that it becomes a part of your daily living.

Beware of any potential traps or ruses that you're tempted to get involved in.

Rather than staying stuck in this apparent impasse, open your mind to the infinite number of possibilities that are before you, and make a choice.

Don't limit yourself to the mundane world, but instead be willing to explore other dimensions and realities.

It's time to write creatively without limits of tradition or habit, allowing yourself to be inspired by Nature.

— If BROWN SPIDER:
- This is a time to eliminate as much toxicity in your life as possible, in your body and in your relationships.
- Honor your need for solitude.

Call on SPIDER when:

You feel trapped and don't see a way out.

You've had some negative experiences recently and you want to integrate them and discern the teachings from them as quickly as possible.

You're not happy with the way your life is right now and want to make some significant changes, but you feel stifled by your fears and beliefs in your limitations.

You feel out of balance in any way and want to recapture a sense of equilibrium physically—emotionally, mentally, and spiritually.

If SPIDER is your POWER ANIMAL:

You tend to have only two speeds: staying relatively still and motionless, or moving lightning fast.

It takes quite a bit to arouse your anger, but once that happens, your sting can hurt a lot.

You're in touch with and express a very powerful feminine creative force, whether you're male or female.

You have a knack for writing, with the ability to weave words together in new and creative ways, often affecting others profoundly with their magic.

SQUIRREL

If SQUIRREL shows up, it means:

Get ready for coming changes by lightening your load, clearing out and giving away any goods or material possessions that no longer serve you.

The best way to deal with the challenging situation that's before you is to confront it head-on and be totally honest with your feelings and thoughts.

Be extra vigilant and cautious right now, and be willing to avoid or escape any threatening situations.

Prepare for the future by gathering and storing extra food, water, clothing, candles, and money for possible later use.

Although you're actively and aggressively pursuing your goals right now, you need to balance this pursuit with more socializing and play.

Call on SQUIRREL when:

You're feeling scattered and fragmented, scurrying around a lot unproductively, and you want to focus your energies so that you're more purposeful and directed.

You find yourself so fearful and worried about the future that you feel blocked or even frozen into inaction.

You're feeling unsafe or in some way threatened and need a guardian who will tell you when to avoid certain situations or people.

You feel unprepared and anxious about an upcoming event and need to gather any and all available resources to get through it.

If SQUIRREL is your POWER ANIMAL:

You learn much more quickly with a hands-on approach or by someone showing you how to do something rather than by studying it in books.

You excel at organizing, strategizing, and implementing plans, although you'll typically delegate the follow-through to others so you can move on to other things.

You're quite sociable, although it takes you a while to warm up to strangers.

You're resourceful and prepared for just about any eventuality, and usually can find whatever's needed quickly and without a lot of stress.

You're typically straightforward and honest with others.

You have a keen sense of when to confront and when to avoid situations that are troublesome.

STAG

(Also see <u>Deer</u>)

If STAG shows up, it means:

There's an opportunity to release something that no longer fits your life so that room will be made for the new that's ready to be birthed and appear.

This is a particularly intuitive time, so pay close attention to information that comes through psychically.

You'll soon be invited to go on an adventure that will be fun and challenging at times, yet ultimately rewarding, as it will deepen your spirituality in ways you never expected.

Surrender, and allow the movement of life to move you and express through you in new and creative ways that will manifest in third-dimensional reality.

You'll soon have an experience with the fairy realm and spirits of the forest.

This is a time when your masculine self (or side) is in strong expression, so you'll be feeling especially virile and powerful.

Call on STAG when:

You're planning on doing some work, or you have a job, which requires you to move steadily and swiftly to completion.

You're ready for an adventure or a quest, one that would be both physical and spiritual in nature and requires you to follow the path of your truth with complete faith and trust.

You're setting fresh goals and intentions for the coming year through ceremony and want support for their actualization.

You need some additional male energy to help yourself feel more balanced, whether you're a man or a woman.

If STAG is your POWER ANIMAL:

You're adventurous and enjoy traveling, whether to other lands or to your inner dimensions.

You're a magnificent manifester, able to take your dreams and visions and bring them into physical reality.

You're gentle yet very powerful, respected by others for your grace and your strength of character.

You're a very stable and well-balanced individual, with a degree of masculine energy that is proportionate to your gender and your personal preferences.

You're very competent and enjoy guiding others, whether over physical or internal terrain.

STARFISH

If STARFISH shows up, it means:

Keep your senses open to the new opportunities that are about to appear, and trust your intuition about which are the right ones to take advantage of.

In spite of what others say, do things the way you want to even if it's unusual or different from how most people would do them.

There's no need to hurry, so take your time getting where you want to go.

In spite of any recent losses, trust that you'll recover fully and start anew.

Someone in your circle of friends or family is in need of your compassionate understanding.

Meditate on the felt connection to All-That-Is and your place on Earth and in the cosmos.

Call on STARFISH when:

There's an excellent opportunity before you, but you're not convinced that you should act on it.

You're not sure which direction to take your career.

A loved one is going through some troubling emotions but is trying to put on a happy face.

There's some new information or a course of study that you're trying to digest.

If STARFISH is your POWER ANIMAL:

You're quite sensitive and have a great deal of empathy for others, and are able to pick up on their emotional currents whether or not the other person shows it or knows it.

You have very definite ideas and opinions about things, yet also respect others' points of view.

You pride yourself in your adaptability and flexibility, and are willing and able to change direction in a moment's notice as necessity dictates.

You're very confident in knowing what is right for you because you completely trust and adhere to your inner guidance.

STORK

If STORK shows up, it means:

Get ready for a new birth into a different expression of yourself.

This is a good time to return to your original home or the place where you grew up and see it from your adult perspective, noticing how it feels the same but different.

Dedicate some extended and quality time to your home and family.

Do some drumming and rattling on your own or with a group with the intention of awakening some primal energy that can be channeled for creative purposes.

Seek out and participate in a group that is doing any kind of sacred dance that appeals to you.

Call on STORK when:

You're at the beginning stages of a new relationship, project, or job.

You've been alienated from your family and want to effect a reconciliation.

You're pregnant and about to give birth.

Your emotions are deep, strong, and disturbing, and you need some relief from their intensity.

If STORK is your POWER ANIMAL:

You're a very caring, nurturing, and dedicated parent.

You love to initiate new projects and see them through to their completion.

You enjoy doing movement and dance with others, particularly sacred practices such as Sufi dancing.

You're able to experience your emotions without becoming overwhelmed by them, remaining in control but not in denial.

You're able to communicate a lot with your body language in ways that allow others to clearly get your messages.

SWALLOW

If SWALLOW shows up, it means:

You're very caught up in the mundane aspects of life and need to step back and gain some perspective.

Your home is well protected from pests and intruders.

It's time to let go and move on rather than continuing to rehash old issues and wounds from the past.

It's best to keep some distance from, or let go completely of, the pesky people in your life.

You're going to find some unusual and creative solutions to familiar problems.

There will be some turbulence—which you're well equipped to ride out—prior to a surprising period of gain and abundance.

A journey back home to where you grew up will be a spiritual pilgrimage.

Call on SWALLOW when:

You're feeling a lack of emotional warmth in your life.

There are a lot of little irritations that are bugging you and you want relief from them.

You need to feel protected and guided during a period of darkness.

You're feeling a bit gloomy and out of sorts and want to cheer up.

You feel the need for extra protection for your home.

If SWALLOW is your POWER ANIMAL:

You're quite able to soar above any problems and keep your objectivity when difficulties and challenges arise.

You're a romantic and devoted partner to your loved one, expressing your affection in a number of creative ways.

You offer effective and wise guidance to others, some of it channeled from your ancestors.

You're an intelligent, positive, and radiant individual with graceful and quick movements, and you possess considerable humility.

SWAN

If SWAN shows up, it means:

No matter what is happening in your life right now, do whatever it takes to keep your faith strong.

It's important to accept your life circumstances and surrender to the will of Spirit, trusting that all will work out.

You'll soon find clarity and purpose in the confusion that you're experiencing.

Focus on the fact that life is a precious and sacred gift, and express your gratitude and appreciation in as many ways as possible.

Whatever changes you're going through, go with the flow.

— If TRUMPETER SWAN:

- Let others hear you by expressing yourself in a clear and concise way.
- Enhance your gracefulness through the study of yoga or Tai Chi.

— If WHISTLER SWAN:

- Make it a point to whistle a tune out loud at least once today and see how it feels.

—— If MUTE SWAN:

- Find a place where it's very quiet and meditate there for several minutes.
- For a couple of hours or a full day, be silent with no talking.

Call on SWAN when:

You have to deal with a variety of business and social situations that require you to be poised and confident.

You've been so focused on the mundane that you've forgotten about the magic and mystery of life and want to connect with it.

You're out of touch with the beauty in yourself, in others, and all around you, and want to appreciate this much more consistently.

You're ready emotionally and spiritually for your soul mate and want to manifest this person.

You need to defend or protect yourself, your mate, or your family, yet do so in a way where you maintain your composure and calmness.

If SWAN is your POWER ANIMAL:

You exude a sense of calm and gracefulness and are very much at ease with yourself and others.

You're very adept at gliding through the waters of change easily and effortlessly, moving smoothly with the daily rhythms of life.

You're highly intuitive, often to the point of foreseeing the future.

You shine with an inner beauty and walk through the world with humility and poise.

You're very powerful physically and spiritually and are highly protective of your loved ones.

TARANTULA

(Also see <u>Spider</u>)

If TARANTULA shows up, it means:

Trust your intuitive senses—what you feel in your body—more than what you see.

This is a time to shed anything that has served its purpose for the growth of your consciousness but now is no longer needed.

Your sensitivity is increasing, particularly to the vibrations you feel from your environment.

Be especially gentle to yourself in the next few days, doing whatever you can to provide comfort and self-nurturing.

In spite of your sturdiness and strength, this is a very sensitive and delicate time for you, so treat yourself accordingly.

Although you tend to stay in the background and by yourself, be willing to come forward as necessary for your own social and emotional nourishment.

Call on TARANTULA when:

You need to distract or redirect someone who's doing something that's irritating you.

You've outgrown some of your habits, patterns, and addictions and want to let them go.

You're feeling hypersensitive and vulnerable to any extreme sensory assaults and want to shield yourself.

You feel the need to get away from the day-to-day routines and demands and retreat for a while.

You feel strongly about what your senses are telling you, but others are trying to convince you otherwise.

If TARANTULA is your POWER ANIMAL:

You're basically a solitary person and like staying at home, venturing out only as needed.

Although you're gentle, shy, and tend to mind your own business, your presence can be initially intimidating to others until they get to know you.

You like to sleep in late whenever possible, since your most productive times occur after the sun goes down.

As you mature you become more defined and self-assured about your gender identity.

You'll bite back with your words when others get overbearing or aggressive with you, but not in a way that does any harm.

TASMANIAN DEVIL

If TASMANIAN DEVIL shows up, it means:

You'll find an increasing interest in either shamanism or Wiccan practices.

Take up yoga and pay particular attention to breathing more deeply and steadily, both in and out of your classes.

This is a time when you'll be getting some informal and surprising teachings on the proper use of power and the differences between power and force.

It's important to make your communications crisp, clear, and straightforward.

Call on TASMANIAN DEVIL when:

You have a task ahead that involves cleaning up some aspect of the environment.

You're preparing a sacred ceremony in honor of the winter solstice.

There's been a misunderstanding and you want to get to the core of it quickly so it can be resolved.

You've decided to clear out the clutter that creates a confusing and chaotic home or office arena.

If TASMANIAN DEVIL is your POWER ANIMAL:

You're a natural wizard and can manifest just about anything you desire.

You're a solitary individual, quite shy and preferring to live by yourself.

You're very resourceful in that you're able to utilize everything at your disposal, often in creative and unexpected ways.

You have a knack for getting to the heart of an issue by cutting through the extraneous verbiage that obscures the unbiased truth that's at the core.

TIGER

If TIGER shows up, it means:

Remain focused, be very patient, and you'll soon receive a surprise that will help you achieve your goal more quickly than expected.

You'll soon find a way of healing from a physical condition or an emotional disturbance very quickly, followed by a noticeable increase in vitality.

Create a sacred space in your home that is completely yours, one where others may enter only with your permission, and take the time to enjoy the solitude in this space.

You'll soon be experiencing a surge of passion and power that will remain with you for some time.

Get ready for a new adventure, one that may present some challenges, but will introduce some dramatic changes in your life.

— If SIBERIAN TIGER:

- You'll be taking a long journey soon, one that will be refreshing and restorative.
- Make it a point to enjoy your sensuality, and do a lot more touching.

Call on TIGER when:

You're aiming to accomplish something very important to you and only need to remain persistent and steadfast in your quest.

You're about to strike out on your own after being in a dependent relationship for some time.

You need to bolster your confidence and self-esteem.

You've been bored with the same old routine and want to experience something more adventurous.

You're studying mysticism or mythology, especially as it concerns tigers.

If TIGER is your POWER ANIMAL:

You're naturally clairvoyant, with the gift of prophecy that becomes stronger and more evident as you age.

You're a healer, and due to your strong tactile sensitivities, your best vehicle for healing is performing some kind of bodywork.

You're solitary and nocturnal and do your best work at night.

You're adventurous, powerful, and passionate, and enjoy life to the fullest.

You enjoy playing sports, particularly ones that are physically demanding.

TOAD

If TOAD shows up, it means:

It's a good time to withdraw into solitude and contemplate emotional or spiritual matters.

You'll have an opportunity to review and clear some uncomfortable emotional issues from the past.

This is an opportunity to contact your most primal, instinctual self—the part of you that's the seed of any new personal or spiritual growth.

This is a volatile period of personal change, one where you'll feel unsettled and fragmented, yet one in which a new "you" will emerge feeling more integrated and whole.

You have much more available to you in terms of skills, experience, and inner strength than you're aware of.

Call on TOAD when:

You feel overwhelmed with your emotions and want to purge them.

You're going through a rough transition and want to clear out anything that's no longer useful.

Something disturbing from your past is pulling on your attention and you want to release its hold.

You're not sure that you have the resources, skills, and fortitude to accomplish the task at hand.

If TOAD is your POWER ANIMAL:

You're very shy and secretive, keeping to yourself most of the time.

You're a hermit and generally do not enjoy socializing.

Because of your shyness and reticence to interact, others often mistrust you until they get to know you.

You have strength of character and are always able to rely on your inner resources to solve any problems.

TORTOISE

(Also see <u>Turtle</u>)

If TORTOISE shows up, it means:

You're taking on way too many of the problems and troubles of others.

Slow down, take your time, and enjoy the scenery, even if there's a detour.

Be patient, determined, and stick with it; before you know it, you'll achieve what you're after.

At this time, pay particular attention to the shifting sensations in your body, as these are energetically resonating with subtle changes in the vibrations of the earth.

It's a good time to change to a vegetarian diet, even if only for a few days.

By moving through your life more slowly and attentively, you'll discover a great deal of wisdom emerging from unexpected sources that you'd otherwise miss by being in a hurry.

Get out on the land and walk around a bit at about half your usual pace, using this as a meditation.

Call on TORTOISE when:

You feel caught up in a chaotic and hectic lifestyle, and you want to change it to a slower pace, but you're not sure how to do so.

You're feeling weighted down and overwhelmed by all of your responsibilities, even though you know you've created them by taking on too much.

You feel like giving up, but something inside you knows that you need to keep moving on.

You're trying to accomplish a particular task, but keep getting thrown off by various demands and distractions, such that you feel off center.

You've been feeling scattered and spacey and need to get yourself grounded by spending time in Nature.

If TORTOISE is your POWER ANIMAL:

People naturally turn to you to help them out because you're such a great listener and excellent problem solver, but your biggest challenge is to not let other people's problems weigh you down.

You need a stable environment and a strong connection to Mother Earth or else you'll find yourself prone to mood swings.

You move a lot slower than the world around you, but you still get the job done, sometimes to others' amazement.

You're self-reliant and self-determined, and have a remarkable ability to stay focused in spite of what's going on around you.

You're very wise and steadfast, and feel at home anywhere you are.

TOUCAN

If TOUCAN shows up, it means:

Consider stretching yourself by taking a class or workshop in acting, speech, or improvisational theater.

Be willing to speak up by both raising the volume of your voice and by letting your feelings, thoughts, and opinions be known.

Be aware of your words and communication style and how they affect others.

You'll benefit from doing some chanting or toning.

Take a chance and express the feelings that you've held back from someone.

Call on TOUCAN when:

You want your voice to be heard loud and clear.

You want to get involved in a group or class that will help you improve your communication or speaking skills.

You feel like holing up for a while and getting some much-needed rest.

You've gotten a message from Spirit in some manner, but you're afraid to hear it.

You have something you want to say to someone that's difficult to express.

If TOUCAN is your POWER ANIMAL:

You're an actor and enjoy acting as a hobby or avocation.

You're a colorful and effective speaker and communicator, with an excellent command of the language.

At times you speak too loudly when it's not appropriate, and this leads others to misunderstand you.

You're unpredictable, inclined to do what you want when you want to do it, sometimes to the point that others get annoyed with you.

You're a colorful person in more ways than one, and enjoy being seen and heard.

TURKEY

If TURKEY shows up, it means:

It's important to transcend the focus on your own needs to consider the greater needs of the whole, such as your family, community, or world.

You're about to receive a gift of some sort—material, spiritual, or intellectual—that could be anything from winning the lottery to a simple gift, such as witnessing a beautiful sunset.

Perform some act that honors the earth, whether a sacred ceremony or simply picking up trash.

Volunteer your time in selfless service for some organization that you want to support.

Call on TURKEY when:

You're feeling overwhelmed or disillusioned with materialism, your own and others', and want to break out of this way of thinking and acting.

You're feeling prompted to donate your time and energy to a worthwhile cause but are not sure how to go about it.

You're feeling some financial distress and need some additional supplies in order to meet your physical needs.

You're planning a giveaway ceremony with friends, one in which each person donates an item or items they're willing to give to others in the group.

If TURKEY is your POWER ANIMAL:

You do your best to help others in need and are willing to sublimate your own desires without playing the martyr in order to do so.

You're a very communal person, willing to share just about anything you possess.

Although you much prefer to be near forested areas, you're very adaptable, and are capable of living in many different environments.

You may appear somewhat awkward to others, but you're quick, alert, and capable when necessary.

TURTLE
(Also see <u>Tortoise</u>)

If TURTLE shows up, it means:

You've been going much too fast for too long, so slow down and pace yourself.

This is a time to be more self-reliant and less dependent on others.

Take time to nurture yourself and simply observe and feel your emotions.

This is a period of increased sensitivity to the earth's vibrations and those of the collective human consciousness, which you'll first feel as sensations in your body prior to the resultant emotions.

Spend a few hours or longer in solitude, away from other people and the usual noise that surrounds you.

This is a very creative, fertile time, and you need to shield yourself from interferences that threaten to distract you.

Call on TURTLE when:

You're feeling the need for emotional support and protection.

Your life has been so frenetic and fast-paced that you feel overwhelmed and know you need to pause, review, and assimilate what's been happening.

You have an important creative project to complete and are worried that you don't have enough time.

You're worried about not having enough money to obtain the things you'd like and want to develop trust in the abundance of life.

You find yourself in a new and unfamiliar situation and want to feel safe and more comfortable.

You need healing from any kind of physical wounds.

If TURTLE is your POWER ANIMAL:

You're an old soul with a strong sense of connection to the ancient and archetypal worlds, and have a great depth of understanding and compassion for the earth and all its inhabitants.

No matter where you are in the world, you have a very strong attachment to your home and always end up returning there.

You move at your own pace, typically slower than others, taking your time to make decisions and being very deliberate about it.

When feeling threatened or fearful, you tend to back away and retreat into your shell, not being terribly concerned about what others think of this way of dealing with disturbance.

You're incredibly compassionate and nurturing with others, willing to listen to their problems and able to do so without taking them on.

UNICORN

© Sue Dawe

If UNICORN shows up, it means:

It's vital that you pursue any creative or artistic interests that you've suppressed until now.

You'll notice more signs and visitations from the Nature spirits and elemental kingdom, such as the fairies and sprites.

Let go of your worries and responsibilities for a while and just play and have fun.

Suspend your disbelief and open yourself to perceiving any and all helping spirits from the nonvisible world.

You're going to meet some gifted children who have unusual artistic and creative talents, and you'll learn some important things from being around them.

You're going to experience a surge in your personal power, so use it wisely.

Call on UNICORN when:

You're feeling a call to get something artistic going, but you're not sure what to do or how to go about it.

You're a parent or caregiver of a child who has extraordinary creative gifts or talents, especially if they see, hear, or feel things from the spirit world.

You've been caught up in all of the responsibilities and intensities of the mundane and material world.

You're feeling cynical and disillusioned and want to recapture that sense of awe and magic that you've known before.

If UNICORN is your POWER ANIMAL:

You're a highly artistic and creative person and have to express yourself in this way or your life force becomes diminished.

You have an innocence and purity about you, retaining the childlike sense of wonder and awe.

You're going to work with children, particularly any highly sensitive children who have psychic or intuitive gifts.

You're attuned to Mother Nature and care deeply and passionately about the environment.

You work with the fairy realm and the Nature spirits.

VULTURE

(see <u>Condor</u>)

WALRUS

© Doug Allan / Oxford Scientific / JupiterImages

If WALRUS shows up, it means:

Be especially watchful for signs and omens from nature that will give you guidance.

Be willing to touch and hug those you love more than you usually do.

This is an important time to heal your relationship with money by understanding that it is simply a physical means of exchanging energy.

The going will be much easier if you move along the path of least resistance in all of your relationships and activities, rather than using force or being passive and static.

Join up with a group of like-minded people, or spend time with some close friends.

Call on WALRUS when:

You're feeling a lack of physical affection and want to enjoy mutual touch with someone.

You're feeling the need to migrate to a climate that's more suitable to your temperament and disposition.

You're faced with some financial woes and want to relax and think positively about the situation, as well as come up with solutions for your dilemma.

You have high blood pressure, clogged arteries, or need to improve your circulation.

If WALRUS is your POWER ANIMAL:

Your ingenuity and cleverness have served you well and in some instances have helped you survive.

You're very adept at intentionally shifting in and out of various states of consciousness.

You're an entrepreneur, enjoy the challenge of running your own business, and do so very well.

You have a genius for finding hidden treasures in the ordinary things surrounding you.

You look as if you would be a slow mover, but you're actually able to move with agility and speed when you need to.

WASP

If WASP shows up, it means:

Whatever task is before you, jump in and go for it with enthusiasm and determination.

Consider making a study of sacred geometry and how it applies to your life.

For the next few weeks, focus on fulfilling your responsibilities and personal obligations.

Break out of your routine and do something that's adventurous, unusual, and completely different from what you would ordinarily do.

Lead with your heart, not your mind.

Whatever you've dreamed of doing, put some plans into action that will help you realize them.

Call on WASP when:

You're going through a period of tangled emotions and mood swings and you want to stay as centered as possible throughout.

You're in a bit of a rut and want to break out of it.

You've been wishing and dreaming about something and now want to work toward its manifestation.

You feel the need for emotional and physical nourishment.

If WASP is your POWER ANIMAL:

You like to do things your own way rather than someone telling you how to do something.

You alternate between being independent, private, and irritable to being sociable, personable, and enjoying others' company—which can make for some challenges in a relationship.

As you age, you'll receive more and more recognition for being an innovator of new trends and new ideas.

You're a hard worker and are willing to do what it takes to get the job done.

Late summer and early fall are the seasons when you're the most active and dynamic.

WEASEL

(Also see <u>Ferret</u>)

If WEASEL shows up, it means:

Be somewhat cautious in any business deals with others and dig beneath the surface of what you're seeing and hearing.

For your dietary pattern during this period, eat small amounts of food throughout the day rather than your standard three larger meals per day.

Trust your senses about other people as to whom to trust or not trust.

Spend a day or two in silence, simply observing all that's going on around you, whether by yourself or in a crowd.

You're extremely protective and fearless when it comes to defending your family or home.

Call on WEASEL when:

You're feeling suspicious of the motives and intentions of someone you're doing a business transaction with.

You're in a tight spot and need to squeeze through to get out of it.

You're feeling unsure whether to trust your own senses about other people or about what's going on that's less than obvious.

You're pursuing a goal that's very important to you and you want to succeed in it.

If WEASEL is your POWER ANIMAL:

You're very analytical and tend to look for reasons behind any experience.

You're a solitary individual, enjoying the peacefulness of spending time alone.

You have the unique ability to maintain silence around others so well that you go unnoticed, and are often privy to things that are done or said by others without their being aware of your presence.

Although not easily angered, if you're provoked, you tend to go for the throat and don't let go easily.

WHALE

(Also see <u>Beluga</u>; <u>Blue Whale</u>; <u>Humpback Whale</u>; <u>Orca</u>)

If WHALE shows up, it means:

Express yourself through your voice by singing, humming, or chanting simply for the pure joy of doing so.

It's an especially creative time for you, so immerse yourself in the process, and enjoy the artistic expression of whatever emerges from the depths of your imagination.

This is a time of great spiritual expansion for you, so the more you can clear your mind (such as through regular meditation) the better.

You'll soon discover an increasing interest in esoteric information about the origins of life here on Earth.

You've been so occupied with creative and artistic projects that you're out of balance and need to step away by playing, socializing, or otherwise distracting yourself for a while.

Conserve your energy, and psychically insulate yourself by surrounding yourself with a curtain of blue or white light.

Call on WHALE when:

You have an urge to sing or play music but usually stop yourself due to self-consciousness or other conditioned inhibitions.

You've been caught up in a pool of emotions for some time and now need to come up for air.

You want to have a more consistent flow of abundance and nourishment in your life.

Your life feels so chaotic that you often feel overwhelmed, and you want to find peace and calmness in the midst of these circumstances.

If WHALE is your POWER ANIMAL:

You're self-contained, quiet, and contemplative, and you let very few people know your inner workings.

You're very psychic and highly intuitive, with a natural gift of clairaudience and telepathy.

You find yourself saying and thinking things that are quite profound and insightful without any awareness as to how or why you know these things, only later getting confirmation that these perceptions were accurate.

You're a very old soul with a connection to ancient mysteries, coupled with an intense compassion, love, and care for Mother Earth and all her inhabitants.

As you get older, you gain in your understanding and knowledge of universal truths and the origins of life on Earth, as well as our origins in the cosmos.

WILDEBEEST
(See Gnu)

WOLF

If WOLF shows up, it means:

Characteristics and behaviors that no longer serve your spiritual purpose are being culled from your consciousness.

Make cooperation a priority over competition.

Valuable insights, ideas, and new teachings are coming your way, so pay close attention.

It's important to maintain your self-esteem and integrity and deeply trust in your inner knowing, even when you feel misunderstood or misaligned.

You're being spiritually and psychically protected at all times.

Call on WOLF when:

You feel lost with regard to a relationship, project, or your career, or else you're confused about your life path and purpose.

You feel at one extreme or the other with your social ties, either feeling isolated and alone or overly enmeshed with family and friends.

You've been feeling a little too civilized lately and want to tap in to the wild and instinctual.

You're having trouble discerning the sincerity and truth of what someone is communicating to you.

You want to be more expressive in your communication, particularly by adding more body language and vocal inflection.

If WOLF is your POWER ANIMAL:

You have a strong sense of family and community, an intuitive sense of social order, and are very affectionate with your friends and family.

You would much rather avoid confrontations, but will fiercely defend yourself and your loved ones whenever necessary.

You're very expressive verbally and nonverbally and can tell a story with a great deal of passion, sincerity, and animation.

You're a natural-born teacher, imparting knowledge based on experience more than from formal education.

Although you're at ease with your closest friends and family, in most other situations you're actually quite shy.

WOLVERINE

If WOLVERINE shows up, it means:

Be assertive, stand your ground, and communicate your clear intention to do so.

This is a time to be cautious and not make any hasty or sudden moves without thinking them out.

It's important now to plan ahead by stowing away money and supplies for future availability.

Be discriminating as to whether you should fight or withdraw, knowing that your first and best choice is always to retreat.

Satisfy your hunger for education by pursuing a course of interest, whether through school or independent study.

Get yourself out in Nature, preferably the woods or forest, and spend some time there in a walking meditation.

Call on WOLVERINE when:

You find yourself in a confrontation where the other person appears to be stronger or more capable.

You feel considerable uncertainty about the times ahead and want some reassurance that your needs will be met.

You feel rather weak, like giving up, and need some additional fortification, courage, and strength.

You're seeking the truth about some situation, one that is shrouded in deception.

If WOLVERINE is your POWER ANIMAL:

You're very shy and prefer to stay in the background and out of the way, rarely putting yourself forward.

You'd prefer to avoid conflict, but if necessary you won't back down and can become quite ferocious if actually threatened.

You enjoy camping out and walks in the forest and feel like the outdoors is a second home to you.

You're rather elusive, hard to pin down, and notable for avoiding events that require you to be sociable.

WOMBAT

If WOMBAT shows up, it means:

You have all the resources you need for the dramatic changes that are going on in your life right now, but you might have to dig a bit to find them.

Strive for what you want, but stay detached about the outcome.

Speak up for yourself with confidence and self-assurance, and treat your listeners with respect and compassion no matter their reaction to what you have to say.

Practice good dental hygiene—in other words, take good care of your teeth.

Investigate herbology and herbal medicine as a course of study, starting with any condition you have that you want to treat with herbs.

Call on WOMBAT when:

You're feeling intimidated, bullied, or pushed around in some way.

You feel caught up in the rat race and want to slow down and take a break from it all, and instead put more of your energy into doing what you love.

You're ready to use the gifts that you were given, and you want to find a means of expressing these gifts.

Someone has treated you disrespectfully and you want to deal with this situation assertively and stand up for yourself without becoming overly aggressive.

Your life has been somewhat chaotic and you want to feel some steadiness and stability.

If WOMBAT is your POWER ANIMAL:

You're smart and industrious, and you have a great deal of determination and perseverance.

When you're playing, you're really playing; and when you're working, you're really working.

You're quite clear about who you are and what you want out of life, with no apologies to anyone.

You're assertive, straightforward, and clear in your communication with others.

WOODPECKER

If WOODPECKER shows up, it means:

A storm is brewing, either literally or metaphorically; but have faith, as you're protected no matter what.

It's a good time to do some drumming and/or rattling, whether on your own or with a group of friends.

You're entering into a time of abundance and plenty.

Go to a place of Nature and lie on your back on the ground, breathe slowly and steadily, and see if you can feel Mother Earth's heartbeat.

Pay particular attention to your own cycles and rhythms and do your best to honor them by aligning yourself with them, rather than being contrary to them.

Call on WOODPECKER when:

Your energy is low and you want to restore your vitality and vigor.

You're feeling prompted to get involved in drumming and rhythmic play but aren't sure how to go about pursuing this endeavor.

You're entering into a particularly busy cycle, handling a lot of different projects and demands on your time.

You're feeling trapped in some emotional turmoil and want to dig in and analyze what's going on so you can better understand these feelings.

If WOODPECKER is your POWER ANIMAL:

You're very active, hardly ever sitting still for long, hopping from one project to the next.

Your moods change rather quickly and unexpectedly, from tempestuousness one moment to quiet and contemplative the next.

You tend to cling to things and people, and can be somewhat of a nitpicker.

You follow the beat of your own drum, doing what works best for you.

ZEBRA

If ZEBRA shows up, it means:

You're looking at things with black-and-white, all-or-nothing thinking, which limits your choices and flexibility.

Regarding the conflict you're having with someone, it's better to work toward a compromise than staying stuck in a right-versus-wrong standoff.

Be willing to question what you have up to this point considered to be your reality and any illusions you may have subscribed to, and in so doing, you will expand your consciousness.

In any situation where there's disagreement, rather than being confrontational, try less direct methods such as persuasion, agreeing to disagree, or taking a time out to gain a fresh perspective.

You're about to discover some useful knowledge that has been hidden or obscured, knowledge that will come to you without seeking, so simply be open to receiving it.

Call on ZEBRA when:

You're experiencing some conflict between expressing your individuality and being a member of a family, group, or community.

You have to deal with a group process of any sort, such as a community project, and want to encourage harmonious interactions among the group's members.

You've tried various solutions, but so far nothing has worked, so you need a fresh and creative way of looking at the problem.

You're feeling uncertain that the path you're on is purposeful and want to find out if it is.

If ZEBRA is your POWER ANIMAL:

You're confident, balanced, sure-footed, and very capable of facing opposing forces and remaining stable and poised.

You have considerable compassion and would make a very effective therapist.

You enjoy a good challenge, as you clearly see it as an opportunity for growth.

You're very agile and quick, both in action and in your thinking.

You love working with groups and are able to do so and maintain your integrity and autonomy.

You love to explore the mysteries and magic of the unseen world and are willing to experiment with varying ways of accessing that world.

PART II
Whom to Call On for Specific Needs

Calling on
Animal Spirit Guides

WHEN YOU HAVE A PARTICULAR CONDITION for which you need help from an animal spirit guide, or else you want to establish or reinforce a quality or characteristic in your own makeup with the help of such a guide, this is the place to look. For most of these topics you'll have more than one choice of spirit animal, so whenever that's true, intuitively choose which animal spirit resonates with you for that particular condition or quality. Then call on that guide through prayer, meditation, shamanic journeying, or contemplation. Once you've called on the animal spirit guide of your choice, you may get immediate results, but more likely you'll get further guidance and direction as to how to alleviate the condition, or ways to bring out more of the characteristic that you want to cxhibit.

After you've determined which particular animal spirit guide you want to call on, look up that spirit animal in Part I, as you'll find additional guidance there.

Abundance and Plenty, Trusting in
Buffalo
Cow
Crane
Deer (White-tailed)
Dragon
Elk
Frog
Gnu
Jaguar
Kangaroo
    (Gray Kangaroo)
Kingfisher
Ladybug
Puffin
Python
Rat
Salmon
Seal
Swallow
Turkey
Turtle

Walrus
Whale
Woodpecker

Acceptance (Self-)
Duck (Wood Duck)
Hedgehog
Moose

Accepting New Ideas and Possibilities
Dragon
Monkey
Wasp

Accepting of Others
Dragon
Hawk

Acting, Professional or Nonprofessional
Fox

Lark
Mockingbird
Mongoose
Opossum
Toucan

Action, Taking
Antelope
Badger
Falcon (Peregrine)
Iguana
Kookaburra
Roadrunner
Squirrel

Adaptability and Flexibility
Cheetah
Chimpanzee
Dingo
Duck
Fox (Red)
Goshawk
Hare

Hawk
Hummingbird
Kite
Magpie
Polar Bear
Raccoon
Rat
Roadrunner
Seal
Starfish

Adaptability for Survival
Antelope
Camel
Coyote
Crab
Dingo
Great Horned Owl
Hyena
Llama
Polar Bear
Rat
Sparrow
Turkey

Addictions, Healing
Bear
Rattlesnake
Snake
Tarantula

Adventure and Exploration
Camel
Caribou
Deer
Dragon
Eagle
Emu
Gnu
Heron
Horse
Otter
Polar Bear
Raccoon
Skunk
Stag
Tiger
Wasp

Affection, Giving and Receiving
Baboon
Chimpanzee

Cockatoo
Mole
Moth
Quail
Sandpiper
Scorpion
Sparrow
Walrus
Wolf

Agility and Dexterity, Mental
Ferret
Ocelot
Octopus
Opossum
Rabbit
Roadrunner
Snake

Agility and Quickness
Falcon
Ferret
Gopher
Hare
Lizard
Ocelot
Osprey
Rabbit
Roadrunner
Snow Leopard
Spider
Walrus
Zebra

Altered States of Consciousness
Groundhog
Grouse
Koala
Loon
Pelican
Walrus

Amends, Making
Alligator
Cassowary
Chimpanzee
Hedgehog

Ancestors, Contacting and Honoring Your
Cat

Condor
Goose
Raccoon
Swallow

Ancient Earth, Interest in and Studies of
Blue Whale
Komodo Dragon
Lemur
Lizard
Musk Ox
Rhinoceros
Snake
Turtle
Whale

Ancient Wisdom and Mysteries, Study of
Alligator
Crocodile
Elephant
Frog
Ibis
Owl
Rhinoceros (White)
Snake
Turtle
Whale

Anger Management
Condor
Coyote
Dove
Kinkajou
Kite
Skunk
Swan
Whale
Wombat

Animals, Communication with Other
Dolphin
Raven
Snake

Anxiety and Fear, Calming
Bat
Egret
Kingfisher

Kite
Polar Bear
Snake
Spider
Squirrel

Appearances, Perceiving What's Behind
Anteater
Ferret
Gopher
Hare
Hippopotamus
Owl
Rhinoceros
Seal
Shark
Snow Leopard
Starfish
Weasel

Appreciating Nature and Environment
Chipmunk
Gibbon
Goat
Gorilla
Hummingbird
Kiwi
Roadrunner
Seagull
Unicorn
Wolverine
Woodpecker

Appreciating Your Accomplishments
Cormorant
Jaguar
Monkey
Pigeon

Appreciation, Showing and Expressing Your
Dog
Goose
Kangaroo (Gray)
Sparrow
Swan

Aromatherapy, Study or Use of
Lemur
Mole
Moths

Artistic and Creative Support
Bear
Hare
Hedgehog
Kiwi
Pheasant
Rabbit
Raccoon
Seal
Unicorn
Whale

Asking for What You Want
Armadillo
Bear
Goat
Polar Bear
Sparrow
Weasel

Assertiveness
Bear
Cougar
Great Horned Owl
Jaguar
Komodo Dragon
Otter
Parrot
Polar Bear
Raccoon
Skunk
Sparrow
Weasel
Wolverine
Wombat

Astral Travel
Jackal
Muskrat
Pelican

Attractiveness, Increasing Your
Butterfly
Meadowlark
Moth
Osprey

Authority, Establishing or Maintaining Your
Jaguar
Lion
Moose
Shark
Skunk
Wolverine

Autonomy and Independence, Support for Your
Chipmunk
Falcon
Heron
Hummingbird
Lynx
Moose
Orangutan
Owl (Screech)
Sloth
Tiger
Wasp
Zebra

Autonomy and Independence, Supporting Others in Their
Falcon
Moose

Awareness of Other Dimensions and Realities
Eagle
Grouse
Horse (White)
Moose
Ostrich
Owl
Raven
Spider
Stag

Baby Blessing or Naming Ceremony
Quail

Background, Staying in the
Black Widow Spider
Fox (Gray)
Gazelle
Octopus
Sloth

Tarantula
Weasel
Wolverine

Balance, Regaining or Maintaining
Black Widow Spider
Chinchilla
Crane
Goat
Grebe
Jaguar
Kangaroo
Magpie
Orangutan
Orca
Ram
Seal
Snow Leopard
Spider
Whale
Zebra

Balancing Intellect and Emotions
Barn Owl
Dragonfly
Flamingo
Goat
Magpie
Seagull
Spider
Wasp
Woodpecker

Balancing Intellect and Instincts
Chinchilla
Eel
Gorilla
Weasel

Balancing Masculine and Feminine Energies
Deer
Emu
Loon
Magpie
Penguin
Sandpiper
Sea Horse

Balancing Social Needs with Needs for Autonomy
Kangaroo
Lemur
Osprey
Rhinoceros
Scorpion
Sloth
Snow Leopard
Zebra

Balancing the Spiritual and Mundane
Chimpanzee
Eagle (Bald)
Giraffe
Goat
Magpie
Ostrich
Pheasant
Ram
Snake
Spider
Turkey

Beginnings, New
Antelope
Buffalo
Bull
Cuckoo
Duck
Eagle
Goat
Ram
Robin
Salamander
Salmon
Squirrel
Stork
White Cockatoo

Being Fully Present
Goshawk
Hedgehog
Hummingbird
Jaguar
Kangaroo
Komodo Dragon
Lion
Mockingbird
Parrot

Polar Bear
Raven
Rhinoceros
Whale

Blending In
Chameleon
Fox
Octopus
Sea Horse
Wolverine

Blockages, Clearing
Canary
Elephant
Robin
Squirrel
Toad
Whale (Blue Whale)

Boundaries, Setting Clear
Bear
Bull
Cassowary
Donkey
Gecko
Great Horned Owl
Groundhog
Grouse
Shark
Skunk
Sparrow
Wolf

Breaking Free of Someone
Cat (Feral)
Mongoose

Breathing, Slow and Deep
Kite
Koala

Breathwork
Dolphin
Groundhog
Koala

Calm, Remaining
Condor
Coyote
Crane

Kite
Musk Ox
Skunk
Swan
Whale

Camouflage
Chameleon
Fox
Octopus
Sea Horse
Sloth
Wolverine

Challenges and Struggles, Overcoming
Black Cockatoo
Buffalo
Condor
Eagle
Jellyfish
Musk Ox
Python
Robin
Salmon
Sandpiper
Swallow
Tiger

Challenges—Meeting Them Head On
Badger
Blue Jay
Cassowary
Eagle
Elk
Gnu
Musk Ox
Otter
Ram
Salmon
Seal
Sparrow
Squirrel
Zebra

Change of Environment
Caribou
Crab
Elk
Gnu

Grebe
Walrus

Changes, Alertness to
Crab
Egret
Hare
Raven
Roadrunner

Changes, Life
Butterfly
Chimpanzee
Cuckoo
Gnu
Heron
Impala
Kinkajou
Kite
Komodo Dragon
Polar Bear
Python
Rattlesnake
Roadrunner
Salamander
Seal
Snake
Sparrow
Spider
Swan
Tiger
Toad
Wombat

Chanting
Frog
Goose (Canadian)

Charisma and Charm
Eagle
Goshawk
Hummingbird
Jaguar
Salmon
Skunk

Cheering Up
Bluebird
Meadowlark
Parrot
Swallow

Children and Child Care
Baboon
Cheetah
Cow
Fox
Goose
Grebe
Grouse
Manatee
Musk Ox
Opossum
Orangutan
Osprey
Penguin
Python
Unicorn

Choices and Decisions, Making Clear
Chameleon
Coyote
Falcon
Hare
Lizard
Ostrich
Rhinoceros
Spider

Choosing Your Words Carefully
Bee
Hyena
Komodo Dragon
Lark
Macaw

Clairaudience, Developing or Increasing Your
Gorilla
Lynx
Owl
Whale

Clairsentience, Developing or Increasing Your
Lizard
Mole
Platypus
Rattlesnake
Snake

Clairvoyance, Developing or Increasing Your
Condor
(Turkey Vulture)
Crab
Eagle
Goshawk
Jaguar
Lemur
Lizard
Lynx
Ocelot
Owl
Rattlesnake
Sloth
Tiger

Cleansing and Detoxification, Physical
Condor
Frog
Gila Monster
Koala
Rattlesnake

Clearing and Blessing Space (such as Home or Workplace)
Barn Owl
Frog

Clearing and Releasing Spirit or Entity Attachments
Barn Owl
Raven
Wolf

Clearing Up Misunderstandings
Blue Whale
Seagull
Tasmanian Devil
Toucan

Cleverness and Ingenuity
Chimpanzee
Crow
Fox
Magpie
Monkey
Orangutan
Rabbit

Rat
Walrus

Clutter, Clearing and Cleaning Up
Beaver
Condor
Crab
Groundhog
Mongoose
Muskrat
Otter
Rat
Robin
Seagull
Squirrel
Tasmanian Devil
Toad

Color, Adding More
Butterfly
Cardinal
Macaw
Peacock
Pheasant
Toucan

Comforts of Life, Enjoying the
Echidna
Goshawk
Hedgehog
Porcupine

Commitment to a Partner
Goose
Jackal
Macaw
Manatee
Meadowlark
Ocelot
Swallow

Commitment to a Purpose
Falcon
Goose
Great Horned Owl
Jaguar
Mongoose
Osprey
Penguin
Polar Bear

Salmon
Wolf

Communication, Clarifying
Chimpanzee
Dolphin
Impala
Seagull

Communication, Clear
Blue Whale
Chimpanzee
Chinchilla
Chipmunk
Cockatoo
Dolphin
Gecko
Giraffe
Gnu
Gorilla
Humpback Whale
Kingfisher
Loon
Magpie
Monkey
Orangutan
Seagull
Squirrel
Stork
Swan (Trumpeter)
Tasmanian Devil
Wolverine
Wombat

Communication Skills, Improving
Canary
Chimpanzee
Cockatoo
Dolphin
Gorilla
Macaw
Mockingbird
Parrot
Seagull
Toucan
Wolf

Communication with Spirits
Blue Whale
Condor

Dolphin
Eagle
Echidna
Raven
Toucan
Unicorn

Community, Belonging to a
Caribou
Dog
Dingo
Elk
Gazelle
Gnu
Hyena
Prairie Dog
Turkey
Wolf

Community Leadership
Kookaburra
Moose
Wolf

Companionship or Company
Cat
Dog
Duck
Flamingo
Gibbon
Gorilla
Hyena
Kinkajou
Llama
Meerkat
Penguin
Prairie Dog
Wolf

Companionship, Seeking
Impala
Penguin

Compassion and Care
Chimpanzee
Cow
Cuckoo
Dolphin
Dove
Flamingo
Gecko

Gorilla
Grebe
Horse
Kangaroo
Kiwi
Kookaburra
Llama
Macaw
Penguin
Pigeon
Rattlesnake
Snake
Starfish
Turtle
Whale
Wombat
Zebra

Compatibility with Another, Checking
Flamingo

Complexity, Comprehending
Chimpanzee
Kinkajou

Concentration
Crane
Falcon (Kestrel)
Goshawk
Hawk
Lobster
Praying Mantis

Confidence, Boosting Your
Bull
Chipmunk
Cockatoo
Cougar
Egret
Gibbon
Kangaroo
Kingfisher
Owl
Peacock
Polar Bear
Ram
Raven
Skunk
Swan
Tiger

Toad
Zebra

Confidences and Secrets, Keeping
Alligator
Bobcat
Echidna
Lynx
Ocelot
Scorpion

Conflict Resolution
Baboon
Beaver
Dolphin
Dragon
Gecko
Jellyfish
Moose
Robin
Zebra

Confronting Another Person
Komodo Dragon
Lion
Ocelot
Otter
Skunk

Confronting Judgment or Negativity in Others
Boar
Cuckoo
Elk

Confronting Your Fears
Gibbon
Jaguar (Black Jaguar)
Kookaburra
Snake
Spider

Confusion, Clearing Up
Antelope
Black Widow Spider
Blue Whale
Moth
Swan

Conserving Your Energy
Eagle
Gila Monster
Koala
Polar Bear

Containment, Emotional
Cuckoo
Dragonfly
Grebe
Koala
Opossum
Puffin
Ram
Salamander

Containment—Keeping Ideas and Activities to Yourself
Chipmunk
Cobra
Fox
Kangaroo
Moth
Ram
Snow Leopard

Containment—Keeping Your Goals or Intentions to Yourself
Fox
Hare
Jackal
Leopard
Meerkat
Ocelot
Octopus
Ram
Snow Leopard

Contemplation and Self-Reflection
Blue Whale
Cat
Chimpanzee
Dragon
Meadowlark
Mole
Mouse
Muskrat
Praying Mantis
Toad

Turtle
Whale

Cooperation with Others
Barred Owl
Bee
Dolphin
Egret
Horse
Jackal
Orca
Pelican
Salamander
Wolf

Courage
Bear
Chipmunk
Eagle
Falcon (Peregrine)
Fox (Kit)
Jaguar (Black)
Kingfisher
Lion
Mongoose
Musk Ox
Otter
Owl (Screech)
Skunk
Sparrow
Wolverine

Courtship
Flamingo
Grebe
Ibis

Creative and Artistic Expression
Beluga Whale
Black Widow Spider
Crow
Fox
Grebe
Hare
Hedgehog
Hippopotamus
Humpback Whale
Kiwi
Ocelot
Osprey
Quail
Seal

Turtle
Unicorn
Whale

Creativity, Unleashing Your
Grebe
Hedgehog
Hippopotamus
Kinkajou
Pheasant
Rabbit
Turtle
Unicorn
Whale

Criticism and Negativity, Shielding Yourself from
Cormorant
Fox (Arctic)
Frog
Goat
Hawk
Hedgehog
Hippopotamus
Horse (White)
Hummingbird
Mongoose
Penguin
Rhinoceros (Black)
Scorpion
Shark
Tarantula

Curiosity and Exploration
Chimpanzee
Chinchilla
Chipmunk
Emu
Ferret
Gibbon
Hedgehog
Heron
Hippopotamus
Horse
Kinkajou
Monkey
Otter
Pheasant
Platypus
Porcupine
Raccoon
Ram

Dance and Movement
Grouse
Impala
Sandpiper
Stork

Death and Dying, Assisting with
Groundhog
Jackal
Octopus
Raven
Scorpion

Death and Dying—Psychopomp Work
Dove
Egret
Jackal
Kite
Scorpion

Decisiveness
Cobra
Cougar
Cow
Falcon
Gibbon
Hawk
Kiwi
Owl
Raven

Defending Yourself or Your Family
Crab
Gila Monster
Mongoose
Moth
Ostrich
Porcupine
Raccoon
Rattlesnake
Skunk
Sloth
Swan
Wolf

Defending Your Territory
Bear
Blue Jay
Cassowary
Dragon
Goose
Great Horned Owl
Grouse
Hare
Swan
Wolf

Dependencies, Breaking Away from Unhealthy
Cat (Feral)
Tiger

Depression, Lifting
Butterfly
Canary
Cardinal
Coyote
Emu
Hawk
Hummingbird
Robin

Detachment
Eagle
Egret
Gecko
Gila Monster
Heron
Koala
Lizard
Musk Ox
Ram
Salamander
Salmon
Snake
Wombat

Details, Attention to
Mouse

Determination and Perseverance
Badger
Cougar
Dingo
Dog
Elephant
Goat
Great Horned Owl
Hippopotamus

Otter
Tortoise
Wasp
Wombat

Detoxification, Physical or Emotional
Chinchilla
Cobra
Condor

Devotional Practices
Ladybug

Dexterity and Flexibility
Goshawk
Hummingbird
Octopus
Opossum
Snow Leopard

Dexterity, Manual
Baboon
Chimpanzee
Gorilla
Otter
Raccoon
Squirrel

Diet, Changes in
Cassowary
Condor
Flamingo
Goshawk
Kinkajou
Orangutan
Osprey
Panda
Platypus
Red Panda
Sandpiper
Shark

Diet, Eating a Healthy
Cardinal
Chimpanzee
Chinchilla
Falcon (Peregrine)
Kite
Manatee
Quail

Dignity and Self-Respect, Maintaining Your
Bear
Cassowary
Cobra
Cougar
Dragon
Grouse
Kookaburra
Lion
Moose
Pelican
Polar Bear
Python
Shark
Skunk
Stag

Direction with Your Life
Giraffe
Salmon
Starfish
Wolf

Discerning Another's Motives
Bobcat
Crow
Fox
Great Horned Owl
Lynx
Ocelot
Opossum
Owl
Raccoon
Roadrunner
Shark
Wolf

Discerning Meaning of Body Language and Vocal Characteristics
Chipmunk
Cuckoo
Fox
Great Horned Owl
Impala
Mockingbird
Orangutan
Orca
Puffin

Seagull
Wolf

Discerning Truth from Deception or Falsehood
Aardvark
Armadillo
Blue Jay
Bobcat
Chipmunk
Crow
Dragonfly
Fox
Great Horned Owl
Hare
Hippopotamus
Hyena
Lynx
Muskrat
Opossum
Owl
Peacock
Raccoon
Wolf
Wolverine

Discerning Whom to Trust
Echidna
Goat
Gopher
Hare
Hyena
Kookaburra
Lynx
Owl
Salmon
Skunk
Weasel
Wolf

Discretion in Communication
Bobcat
Moose
Moth
Parrot

Distractions and Interruptions, Dealing with
Mongoose
Tarantula

Tortoise
Turtle

Domesticity
Dove

Dreaming, Lucid
Beluga Whale
Grebe
Groundhog
Jackal
Loon
Penguin
Rattlesnake

Dreams, Understanding and Interpreting
Bat
Beluga Whale
Blue Whale
Coyote
Crab
Eel
Gecko
Giraffe
Grebe
Groundhog
Iguana
Lizard
Muskrat
Rattlesnake
Raven
Seal

Drumming and Dancing
Grouse (Ruffed)
Stork
Woodpecker

Education and Studying
Blue Jay
Blue Whale
Cockatoo
Echidna
Elephant
Groundhog
Hyena
Meerkat
Ostrich
Owl
Ox (Bull)

Python
Ram
Starfish
Toucan
Wolverine

Eliminating Self-Defeating Behaviors
Caribou
Opossum

Emerging into the World
Crab
Gazelle

Emotional Cleansing and Clearing
Blue Whale
Frog
Pelican
Seal
Toad

Emotional Comfort, Finding
Duck
Flamingo
Grebe
Muskrat
Osprey
Pelican
Swallow
Turtle

Emotional Strength
Lion
Musk Ox
Polar Bear
Sandpiper
Sea Horse
Seal
Wolverine

Emotional Sweetness
Cardinal
Hummingbird
Robin

Emotions, Effectively Managing
Humpback Whale
Macaw
Pelican

Shark
Stork
Whale

Emotions, Feeling and Expressing
Chameleon
Crane
Duck
Egret
Grebe
Humpback Whale
Orangutan
Polar Bear
Seal
Squirrel
Toucan
Turtle
Whale
Wolf

Emotions, Releasing Suppressed
Duck
Frog
Grebe
Polar Bear

Empathy
Cheetah
Chimpanzee
Dolphin
Gorilla
Grebe
Horse
Koala
Starfish

Empowerment
Dingo
Horse
Jaguar
Komodo Dragon
Polar Bear
Python
Raven
Stag
Swan
Tiger
Unicorn

Encouragement and Support
Butterfly

Hyena
Jackal
Lark
Meerkat
Orca
Panda
Salamander
Stag
Wasp
Whale

Encouraging and Supporting Others
Lynx
Moose
Scorpion
Starfish
Unicorn

Endurance and Stamina
Bull
Camel
Deer
Elk
Gazelle
Goat
Horse
Lizard
Llama
Moose
Musk Ox
Penguin
Pigeon

Enduring Difficult Times
Camel
Eagle
Gazelle
Lizard
Llama
Moose
Musk Ox
Penguin
Pheasant

Energy Boost
Antelope
Orca
Otter
Ram
Sandpiper

Snake
Sparrow

Energy, Replenishing
Camel
Orca
Polar Bear
Ram

Entrepreneurial Skills
Walrus
Weasel

Environmental Concerns
Gorilla
Humpback Whale
Seagull
Tasmanian Devil
Unicorn

Errors, Learning from Past
Baboon
Iguana
Penguin
Toad

Escaping from Threats or Problem Situations
Caribou
Eel
Ferret
Porcupine
Quail
Rabbit
Snake
  (Boa Constrictor)
Squirrel
Swallow
Turtle

Evolution of Humans, Study of
Chimpanzee
Gorilla
Monkey

Evolution, Study of
Komodo Dragon
Lemur
Lizard
Musk Ox

Exercise
Chinchilla
Kingfisher
Loon
Woodpecker

Expressing Yourself Clearly and Concisely
Chimpanzee
Dolphin
Gorilla
Kingfisher
Orangutan
Sparrow
Squirrel
Wolf

Faith, Increasing or Keeping Your
Camel
Dog
Giraffe
Kinkajou
Ladybug
Polar Bear
Puffin
Stag
Swan
Wolverine

Faith in Having Enough Provisions and Supplies
Barn Owl
Boar
Buffalo
Cow
Coyote
Gila Monster
Jellyfish
Kangaroo
Kingfisher
Rat
Salmon
Turkey
Wolverine

Family, Dedication to and Care of
Caribou
Gibbon

Gorilla
Hawk
Kangaroo (Red)
Ladybug
Mockingbird
Musk Ox
Muskrat
Opossum
Osprey
Otter
Pigeon
Stork
Weasel
Wolf

Family Harmony
Jellyfish
Stork

Fear, Overcoming and Releasing
Gorilla
Great Horned Owl
Jaguar (Black)
Kingfisher
Kiwi
Ladybug
Pelican
Polar Bear
Snake
Spider
Whale

Fearlessness
Black Widow Spider
Great Horned Owl
Jaguar
Orca
Owl (Screech)
Polar Bear
Skunk
Snake
Sparrow
Squirrel
Weasel

Feminine Essence
Cardinal
Lemur
Otter
Spider

Fertility
Duck
Hare
Mouse
Rabbit
Rat

Flow, Going with the
Butterfly
Cuckoo
Deer
Grebe
Hawk
Heron
Jellyfish
Kite
Octopus
Platypus
Prairie Dog
Swan

Focused, Getting or Staying
Crane
Donkey
Eagle
Falcon (Kestrel)
Ferret
Goat
Goshawk
Great Horned Owl
Hawk
Mouse
Muskrat
Octopus
Ostrich
Panda
Praying Mantis
Shark
Squirrel
Tiger
Tortoise
Wasp

Foresight or Prescience
Crane
Crow
Fox
Giraffe
Kangaroo
Kinkajou
Leopard
Mole

Owl
Peacock
Puffin
Rat
Swan

Forest or Bush, Spending Time in the
Barred Owl
Cassowary
Deer
Gibbon
Impala
Kinkajou
Kiwi
Lemur

Forewarning of Danger
Jackal
Macaw
Squirrel

Forgiveness
Coyote
Pelican
Penguin

Freedom from Burdens and Responsibilities
Albatross
Gila Monster
Horse
Mole
Praying Mantis
Tortoise
Unicorn

Freedom from Feeling Trapped
Beaver
Hawk
Horse
Python
Spider
Unicorn
Woodpecker

Friendliness
Dolphin
Giraffe

Fun, Having More
Coyote
Dolphin
Duck
Hummingbird
Otter
Puffin
Unicorn

Gardening and Planting
Dragonfly
Gopher
Hedgehog
Ladybug
Pheasant

Gentleness
Deer
Rhinoceros
Stag

Getting Unstuck
Black Widow Spider
Emu
Heron
Horse
Jellyfish
Kangaroo
Salamander
Seal
Sloth
Spider
Squirrel
Wasp
Weasel
Zebra

Giving to Others
Duck
Gnu
Kiwi
Manatee
Pelican
Quail
Sandpiper
Scorpion
Sparrow
Starfish
Turkey

423

Goals, Achieving Your
Cormorant
Cougar
Goat
Kookaburra
Llama
Osprey
Pigeon
Robin
Stag
Tiger
Weasel

Goals, Pursuing
Bear
Cougar
Donkey
Elephant
Giraffe
Goat
Gopher
Kookaburra
Mongoose
Robin
Stag
Wombat

Goddess Connection
Bee
Cat
Cobra
Cow
Deer
Elephant
Hedgehog
Horse (White)
Ibis
Ladybug
Lion
Owl
Panda
Peacock
Rabbit
Swan

Gratitude, Focus on
Crane
Quail
Swan

Grazing—Eating Small Portions Throughout Day
Anteater
Gazelle
Manatee
Red Panda
Sloth
Weasel

Grounded and Centered, Getting or Staying
Baboon
Cheetah
Dove
Emu
Gorilla
Hippopotamus
Kiwi
Meerkat
Mole
Ostrich
Pheasant
Praying Mantis
Salamander
Sandpiper
Seal
Tortoise
Wasp

Group Leadership
Impala
Jackal
Jaguar
Kookaburra
Lion
Moose
Zebra

Group Pressure, Dealing with
Cat
Heron (Great Blue)

Group Projects, Coordinating
Ant
Bee
Dolphin
Hyena
Jackal
Orca
Zebra

Group Solidarity and Camaraderie
Caribou
Dog
Elk
Emu
Flamingo
Hyena
Jackal
Jellyfish
Lion
Quail
Zebra

Happiness, Seeking
Hummingbird
Lark
Robin
Unicorn

Haven, Creating a Safe
Baboon
Osprey
Red Panda
Sea Horse

Healing, Emotional
Bear
Cow
Crow
Flamingo
Macaw
Osprey
Otter
Parrot
Platypus
Rattlesnake
Raven
Snake
Tiger

Healing, Physical
Bear
Badger
Flamingo
Macaw
Mole
Parrot
Platypus
Rattlesnake
Raven

Sea Horse
Snake
Tiger
Turtle
Walrus

Healing Relationships
Cow
Rattlesnake

Healing, Remote
Raven

Healing Skin Problems
Iguana

Healing Touch
Cat
Leopard
Mole
Tiger

Health and Well-Being, Maintaining
Canary
Chinchilla
Falcon
Hummingbird
Kinkajou
Manatee
Mole
Muskrat
Octopus
Otter
Sloth
Wombat

Herbology, Study of
Koala
Mole
Wombat

Hidden Treasures and Talents, Finding
Iguana
Ocelot
Pheasant
Walrus
Zebra

Hobbies and Recreation, Pursuing
Crane
Cuckoo

Home
Duck
Echidna
Ferret
Kookaburra
Pigeon
Red Panda
Robin
Stork
Swallow
Tarantula
Turtle

Humility
Jaguar
Sparrow
Swallow
Swan

Humor, Keeping or Regaining a Sense of
Coyote
Dingo
Duck (Wood)
Hyena
Kookaburra
Puffin

Identity, Shifting to a New
Kite
Polar Bear
Rattlesnake
Raven
Snake

Illusions and Masks, Seeing Through
Cobra
Dragonfly
Ferret
Great Horned Owl
Opossum
Zebra

Imagination and Innovation
Chimpanzee
Monkey
Owl (Screech)
Seal
Whale

Impersonations
Blue Jay
Mockingbird

Indigestion
Grebe

Information, Getting More
Aardvark
Badger
Hedgehog

Information, Processing and Assimilating
Python
Starfish

Initiations and Passages, Spiritual
Eagle
Groundhog
Horse
Polar Bear
Ram
Raven
Robin
Snake

Inner Child, Nurturing Your
Elk
Goose
Unicorn

Inner Strength, Accessing Your
Camel
Leopard
Toad
Wolverine

Inner Truth and Guidance, Following Your
Flamingo
Hippopotamus
Kite

Lion
Salmon
Snow Leopard
Stag
Starfish
Wolf
Woodpecker

Inner Wisdom, Accessing Your
Heron (Great Blue)
Ibis
Lark
Owl
Peacock
Praying Mantis
Rabbit
Rhinoceros
Salmon
Snake
Spider
Tortoise
Turtle
Wolf

Innocence and Purity
Ladybug
Unicorn

Innovation and Originality
Chimpanzee
Monkey

Insight and Understanding
Ferret
Hawk
Kinkajou
Leopard
Macaw
Platypus
Whale
Wolf
Woodpecker

Inspiration and Positive Support
Deer
Eagle (Bald)
Goose
Monkey
Orca
Parrot

Penguin
Rabbit
Salamander
Sparrow
Swallow
Walrus
Whale

Instincts, Listening to Your
Deer
Ferret
Gnu
Gazelle
Giraffe
Hyena
Impala
Moose
Praying Mantis
Rhinoceros
Shark
Toad

Instincts, Trusting Your
Black Widow Spider
Chinchilla
Cobra
Donkey
Eagle
Eel
Falcon
Hyena
Kingfisher
Kinkajou
Lynx
Opossum
Praying Mantis
Salmon
Shark
Snake
Snow Leopard

Integrity, Personal
Crow
Fox (Kit)
Horse
Wolf
Zebra

Intellectual Stimulation, Need for
Egret

Ostrich
Ram
Roadrunner

Intelligence and Ingenuity
Egret
Falcon (Kestrel)
Flamingo
Magpie
Meerkat
Ocelot
Raccoon
Swallow
Wombat

Intelligence and Wit
Hare
Fox
Jackal
Magpie
Mongoose
Monkey
Rabbit
Raccoon
Sandpiper

Intention, Clear and Purposeful
Cougar
Falcon
Great Horned Owl
Grouse (Ruffed)
Jaguar
Lynx
Magpie
Penguin
Raven
Robin
Salmon
Shark
Sparrow
Squirrel
Stag
Wombat

Introspection and Self-reflection
Bear
Chimpanzee
Heron (Great Blue)
Hippopotamus

Muskrat
Turtle

Intuition, Listening to Your
Deer
Dingo
Dolphin
Jackal
Leopard
Lizard
Mole
Moose
Panda
Puffin
Raccoon
Rhinoceros
Snow Leopard
Stag
Whale

Intuition, Trusting Your
Bobcat
Cardinal
Cobra
Crane
Ferret
Fox
Goat
Gopher
Heron
Hippopotamus
Hyena
Jackal
Leopard
Raccoon
Starfish
Tarantula

Intuitive Abilities, Developing Your
Dolphin
Moose
Owl
Pelican
Scorpion
Snow Leopard
Swan
Whale

Isolation, Breaking Out of
Elephant
Gibbon

Journaling
Gecko
Grebe
Lizard
Loon
Muskrat
Rattlesnake
Red Panda
Seal

Joy
Hummingbird
Robin
Sea Lion
Sparrow
Whale

Judgments and Assessments of Others or Situation
Antelope
Ferret
Lizard
Opossum

Karma, Law of
Eagle

Language, Learning a New
Mockingbird

Laughter
Hyena
Kookaburra
Roadrunner
Robin
Sandpiper

Leadership
Cougar
Elephant
Goshawk
Horse
Impala
Jaguar
Kookaburra
Lion
Moose

Libido, Increasing
Dove
Elephant
Goat
Grouse
Pheasant

Life Challenges, Dealing with
Albatross
Condor
Eagle
Python
Robin
Salmon
Sloth
Sparrow
Swallow

Lifestyle Changes
Kiwi
Polar Bear
Rattlesnake
Snake
Tortoise

Light and Color, Working with
Butterfly
Dragonfly
Macaw
Parrot

Lighten Up
Coyote
Dingo
Duck
Goat
Hummingbird
Meadowlark
Parrot
Pelican
Porcupine
Puffin
Roadrunner
Seagull
Skunk

Listening Skills
Dolphin
Giraffe
Gorilla
Lynx

Magpie
Seagull
Sea Lion
Tortoise
Turtle

Loss, Recovering from
Condor
Gecko
Iguana
Leopard
Lizard
Octopus
Salmon
Starfish

Love, Expressing
Butterfly
Cockatoo
Dog
Dove
Hummingbird
Kiwi
Penguin
Rabbit
Snow Leopard
Sparrow
Swallow
Wolf

Loyalty
Dog
Elephant
Horse

Magic and Mystery
Crow
Dragonfly
Frog
Goose
Goshawk
Ibis
Lark
Porcupine
Raven
Swan
Unicorn
Zebra

Manifest, Increasing Your Ability to
Beaver
Brown Bear
Crow
Duck (Mallard)
Gazelle
Goshawk
Kookaburra
Parrot
Stag
Tasmanian Devil
Wasp

Marriage
Goose
Grebe

Masculine Energy
Bull
Emu
Moose
Ram
Sandpiper
Snake
Stag

Maternal Instincts
Dolphin
Dove
Manatee
Pigeon
Sandpiper
Whale

Mechanical Items, Fixing
Raccoon

Meditation
Bear (Black)
Blue Whale
Dragon
Groundhog
Grouse
Horse
Kingfisher
Koala
Lemur
Lizard
Loon

Muskrat
Owl
Praying Mantis
Red Panda
Seagull
Starfish
Swan (Mute)
Whale

Meditation, Walking
Bluebird
Kinkajou
Kiwi
Turtle
Wolverine

Mediumship
Condor
Dove
Kite
Raccoon

Memory, Improving Your
Chinchilla
Fox (Arctic)
Gorilla

Men's Ceremonies
Bull
Cassowary
Emu
Moose
Ram
Stag

Message—Sending a Remote
Pigeon

Messages from Spirit, Receiving
Barn Owl
Blue Whale
Cockatoo
Gnu
Gorilla
Grebe
Hawk
Lemur
Toucan

Metaphysical or Occult Interests
Blackbird
Condor
Dragon
Ibis
Lemur
Magpie
Ostrich
Snake
Unicorn

Miracles, Having Faith in
Beluga Whale
Horse (White)
Rhinoceros (White)
Unicorn
White Buffalo

Money, Healing Your Relationship with
Camel
Crane
Kingfisher
Turtle
Walrus

Moon Phases, Honoring
Hare

Motivation, Increased
Ant
Badger
Donkey
Komodo Dragon
Mouse
Platypus

Movement, Leisurely
Komodo Dragon
Manatee
Platypus
Porcupine

Movement, Cautious and Deliberate
Gila Monster
Giraffe
Lion
Rat

Turtle
Wolverine

Movement, Graceful and Fluid
Deer
Falcon
Gazelle
Goshawk
Impala
Kite
Monkey
Praying Mantis
Snow Leopard
Stag
Swallow
Swan

Musical Expression
Canary
Humpback Whale
Lark
Whale

Mysticism and Mystical Arts
Dragon
Dragonfly
Groundhog
Tiger

Natural Rhythms and Cycles, Attuning to
Falcon
Gila Monster
Goat
Grouse
Jellyfish
Kinkajou
Seal
Swan
Woodpecker

Nature and the Earth, Connecting with
Blackbird
Cassowary
Gibbon
Goat
Gorilla
Hummingbird
Kiwi
Meadowlark

Praying Mantis
Seagull
Wolverine
Woodpecker

Nature Spirits, Working with
Dragonfly
Hummingbird
Kinkajou
Monkey
Orangutan
Seagull
Stag
Unicorn

Negotiation and Mediation
Crane
Gecko
Parrot
Weasel

New and Unfamiliar Situations
Chipmunk
Echidna
Peacock
Polar Bear
Robin
Snake
Turtle

Night Fears and Scary Dreams, Alleviating
Bear
Jaguar
Whale
Wolf

Nobility and Majesty
Eagle
Elk
Frog
Gorilla
Goshawk
Great Horned Owl
Hawk
Peacock

Nocturnal Activities
Fox
Gecko
Kiwi

Lobster
Moth
Ocelot
Octopus
Owl
Rattlesnake
Red Panda
Tiger

Nonconformity
Heron

Nourishment and Sustenance
Camel
Cow
Polar Bear
Wasp

Nurturing, Physical and Emotional
Cow
Deer
Manatee
Opossum
Orangutan
Sandpiper
Sea Horse
Turtle

Openness to New Ideas
Emu
Ostrich
Ram

Opportunities, Accepting Challenging
Cheetah
Jaguar
Komodo Dragon

Opportunities, Acting on
Cheetah
Cormorant
Eagle
Hare
Heron
Impala
Jaguar
Kinkajou
Loon
Magpie

Owl (Short-Eared)
Pelican
Python
Shark
Starfish

Opportunities, Making the Most of
Falcon
Ferret
Gibbon
Jackal
Kite

Opportunities, Taking Advantage of Unexpected
Cobra
Cuckoo
Rabbit
Starfish

Optimism
Giraffe
Hedgehog
Hummingbird
Pheasant
Rabbit

Organized, Getting More
Bee
Groundhog
Jellyfish
Lion
Mouse
Muskrat
Orca
Otter
Squirrel

Outdoors, Enjoying the
Cormorant
Deer
Goat
Hummingbird
Macaw
Meerkat
Otter

Out-of-Body or Near-Death Experiences
Muskrat

Octopus
Penguin

Overcoming Emotional Obstacles and Entanglements
Duck
Elephant
Goat
Hawk
Horse
Leopard
Meadowlark
Pelican
Snow Leopard

Overcoming Mental Obstacles
Kite
Lion
Meadowlark
Snow Leopard

Overcoming Physical Obstacles
Dragon
Elephant
Goat
Leopard
Snow Leopard

Pacing Yourself
Elk
Gila Monster
Leopard
Manatee
Tortoise
Turtle

Paradox, Dealing with
Coyote
Dove
Moose
Mouse
Stork

Parenting and Parenthood
Fox
Goose
Grebe
Grouse
Manatee
Penguin
Python

Stork
Unicorn

Passion and Sensuality
Jaguar (Black)
Leopard
Moth
Skunk
Tiger (Siberian)

Passion, Awakening Your
Dragon
Eagle (Golden)
Jaguar (Black)
Komodo Dragon
Ocelot
Owl (Short-Eared)
Tiger

Past-Life Connections
Cardinal
Dragon
Goshawk
Ibis
Jackal
Lemur
Pheasant
Red Panda
Robin
Snow Leopard
Tiger (Siberian)

Patience in Achieving Goals
Black Widow Spider
Egret
Gazelle
Lobster
Lynx
Pigeon
Rhinoceros
Tiger
Tortoise

Patience, Wanting More
Ant
Cougar
Donkey
Falcon
Gila Monster
Horse
Jaguar

Lobster
Owl (Snowy)
Penguin
Praying Mantis

Patience with Others
Horse
Mongoose
Penguin

Peace and Harmony
Dove
Jellyfish
Kingfisher
Puffin
Rhinoceros
Whale
White Buffalo

Performance, Giving a
Lark
Mockingbird
Mongoose
Peacock

Performing Arts
Flamingo
Fox
Gnu
Lark
Opossum

Persistence in Getting What You Want
Badger
Cougar
Elephant
Elk
Goat
Great Horned Owl
Kangaroo (Wallaby)
Leopard
Lynx
Pigeon
Salmon
Tiger
Weasel

Persistence with a Task or Project
Blue Jay

Buffalo
Dingo
Dog
Donkey
Frog
Gecko
Iguana
Kangaroo (Wallaby)
Llama
Lobster
Musk Ox
Pigeon
Roadrunner
Tortoise
Wasp

Perspective, Fresh
Gecko
Iguana
Kiwi
Monkey
Orangutan
Panda
Prairie Dog
Sloth
Snake
Stork
Swallow
Zebra

Perspective, Getting or Maintaining
Eagle
Falcon
Gnu
Hawk
Iguana
Osprey
Swallow
Zebra

Pests, Getting Rid of
Anteater
Ladybug
Mongoose
Swallow

Playful and Light-hearted, Being
Bluebird
Cat

Coyote
Dolphin
Duck
Emu
Ferret
Otter
Red Panda
Roadrunner
Sea Lion
Skunk
Squirrel
Unicorn

Playing More
Cat
Coyote
Dolphin
Ferret
Otter
Red Panda
Sea Lion
Squirrel
Unicorn
Whale

Power and Strength, Increasing Your
Bear
Horse
Komodo Dragon
Lion
Polar Bear
Python
Raven
Scorpion
Stag
Tiger
Unicorn
Wolverine

Power, Claiming and Owning Your
Cormorant
Cougar
Grouse
Horse
Jaguar
Komodo Dragon
Polar Bear
Python
Rattlesnake

Raven
Scorpion
Stag
Tiger

Power Song, Receiving Your
Lark
Raven
Robin

Prayer
Eagle
Koala
Ladybug
Praying Mantis
Puffin
Raven
Scorpion

Precision and Accuracy
Eagle
Falcon
Goshawk
Lizard
Osprey

Pregnancy and Childbirth
Hare
Manatee
Pigeon
Rabbit
Stork

Preparation
Ferret
Gila Monster
Gopher
Hippopotamus
Polar Bear
Squirrel

Presence, Strong
Eagle
Cougar
Goshawk
Hedgehog
Hummingbird
Jaguar
Komodo Dragon
Lion
Mockingbird

Parrot
Polar Bear
Raven
Wolf

Privacy, Need for
Grouse
Iguana
Koala
Komodo Dragon
Lobster
Ostrich
Panda
Wasp

Problem Solving
Aardvark
Condor
Coyote
Fox
Gopher
Monkey
Prairie Dog
Salamander
Sandpiper
Shark
Swallow
Toad
Tortoise
Walrus
Zebra

Procrastination, Overcoming
Ant
Beaver
Bee
Cougar
Manatee

Productivity
Ant
Beaver
Bee
Duck (Mallard)

Progress or Growth, Rapid
Buffalo
Gazelle
Hare
Impala
Jaguar

Kangaroo
Rabbit

Progress, Steady
Kangaroo
Rhinoceros
Robin
Salamander
Sloth
Snow Leopard
Stag
Tiger

Prophecy
Dove
Frog
Owl
Raven
Tiger

Protection, Emotional or Psychic
Armadillo
Crab
Echidna
Goose
Hawk
Horse (White)
Hummingbird
Ladybug
Lynx
Mockingbird
Penguin
Porcupine
Rhinoceros
Seal
Shark
Swallow
Turtle
Whale
Wolf

Protection from All Harm
Bear
Dog
Dragon
Gorilla
Jackal
Leopard
Polar Bear
Rhinoceros (Black)

Shark
Weasel
Wolf
Woodpecker

Protection, Physical
Blue Jay
Goose
Hawk
Ladybug
Mockingbird
Penguin
Shark
Weasel
Wolf

Protection, Spiritual
Ladybug
Ostrich
Peacock
Penguin
Shark
Swallow
Wolf

Protection While Traveling
Great Horned Owl
Jackal
Stag
Wolf

Psychic and Intuitive Development
Bobcat
Dolphin
Grebe
Jaguar
Lemur
Magpie
Mole
Puffin
Scorpion
Sloth
Whale

Psychic Skills
Dolphin
Lemur
Moose
Scorpion
Whale

Public Service
Elephant
Llama

Purification
Condor
Frog
Goshawk
Koala
Rattlesnake

Quick Thinking and Reactions
Fox
Gazelle
Lizard
Mongoose
Roadrunner
Spider

Rebirth and Renewal
Bat
Butterfly
Kite
Leopard
Python
Rattlesnake
Raven
Robin
Salmon
Snake
Stag
Stork

Reconciling Your Past
Lemur
Lizard
Penguin
Pigeon
Rattlesnake
Raven
Swallow
Toad

Recovering Lost Objects
Ladybug

Rectifying Mistakes and Errors
Dingo
Iguana

Recycling
Buffalo
Cassowary
Condor
Gorilla
Jackal
Rat
Seagull
Turkey

Reforestation, Interest in
Lemur
Panda

Reframing Your Perceptions
Condor
Snake
Tasmanian Devil

Relationship Harmony
Dove
Goose
Jackal
Meadowlark

Relaxation and Enjoyment
Jaguar
Koala
Otter
Porcupine
Prairie Dog
Rhinoceros
Seagull

Releasing and Clearing What No Longer Fits
Frog
Hummingbird
Jaguar
Kookaburra
Leopard
Lobster
Mongoose
Mouse
Ostrich
Pelican
Praying Mantis
Python
Rat
Rattlesnake
Robin
Snake
Sparrow
Squirrel
Stag
Tarantula
Toad
Wolf

Releasing Guilt and Shame
Hummingbird
Pelican
Penguin
Rattlesnake
Snake

Releasing Negativity and Judgments
Cuckoo
Deer
Emu
Frog
Hummingbird
Pelican
Rattlesnake
Snake

Releasing Toxicities
Condor
  (Turkey Vulture)
Rattlesnake
Scorpion
Snake
Spider (Brown)

Research and Investigation
Badger
Gopher
Meerkat
Wolverine

Resilience and Adaptability
Camel
Duck
Llama
Monkey
Polar Bear
Rat
Roadrunner

Resolve, Acting with
Caribou

Cougar
Dog

Resourcefulness
Barn Owl
Crow
Fox
Lobster
Magpie
Ocelot
Orangutan
Raccoon
Rat
Squirrel
Tasmanian Devil
Toad
Wombat

Respect and Care for the Earth
Jaguar
Turkey
Turtle
Whale
Woodpecker

Respect for Others
Gorilla
Great Horned Owl
Kite
Porcupine
Skunk
Starfish
Wombat

Responsibilities, Increased or Added
Badger
Bee
Bluebird
Elephant
Hyena
Woodpecker

Responsibilities, Keeping Track of
Chameleon
Seagull
Wasp
Woodpecker

Responsibility, Taking Personal
Gopher
Heron
Horse
Kangaroo
  (Red Kangaroo)
Python

Rest and Relaxation, Need for
Cheetah
Koala
Leopard
Python
Red Panda
Toucan

Retreat and Withdrawal
Armadillo
Crab
Groundhog
Hedgehog
Impala
Orangutan
Ostrich
Prairie Dog
Praying Mantis
Rhinoceros
Tarantula
Turtle
Wolverine
Wombat

Retreat into Nature
Cassowary
Dingo
Goat
Gorilla
Kinkajou
Leopard
Lynx

Retreat into Solitude
Barn Owl
Blue Whale
Bobcat
Condor
Koala
Leopard
Lynx
Rhinoceros
Tiger

Toad
Turtle

Rigid Thinking, Expanding Your
Condor
Panda
Roadrunner
Spider
Turkey

Risk-taking
Giraffe
Impala
Kangaroo
Kingfisher

Rite of Passage— Boys to Men
Stag

Rite of Passage— Girls to Women
Bluebird

Romance and Intimacy
Butterfly
Cockatoo
Dove
Elephant
Flamingo
Leopard
Meadowlark
Moth
Osprey
Pheasant
Quail
Sea Horse
Swallow
Swan

Sacred Ceremony, Creating
Eagle
Grouse
Parrot
Raven
Stag
Tasmanian Devil
Turkey
Wolf

Sacred Dance
Grouse
Stork

Sacred Geometry
Wasp

Sacred Objects, Discovering
Rhinoceros (White)

Sacred or Personal Space, Establishing
Cassowary
Grouse (Sage)
Kingfisher
Koala
Panda
Rhinoceros
Tiger

Sacredness of All Life, Remembering the
Ibis

Sacred Spiral
Grouse

Sacrifice, Purposeful
Cow
Kangaroo (Red)
Kingfisher
Kiwi
Manatee
Salmon
Sea Horse
Turkey

Safety, Discernment about
Armadillo
Rhinoceros
Wolverine

Seasonal Changes, Adapting to
Fox (Arctic)
Gila Monster
Groundhog
Humpback Whale
Wasp

Secure and Stable Foundation, Creating a
Chinchilla
Ferret
Kookaburra
Osprey
Red Panda
Sea Horse

Security, Increasing Sense of
Caribou
Deer
Dove
Rat
Red Panda

Self-care
Dove
Octopus
Roadrunner
Tarantula
Turtle

Self-confidence and Self-esteem, Increasing Your
Barred Owl
Boar
Cockatoo
Elephant
Humpback Whale
Kangaroo
Lion
Moose
Peacock
Polar Bear
Ram
Raven
Skunk
Swan
Tiger
Wolf
Wombat

Selfless Service
Dog
Donkey
Elephant
Llama
Sea Horse
Turkey

Self-sufficiency
Egret
Elk
Tortoise
Turtle
Whale

Senses, Awakening Your
Gopher
Lizard
Snake
Starfish

Senses, Sharpened
Deer
Gopher
Impala
Lizard
Snake

Sensitivity, Increasing Your
Deer
Dolphin
Ferret
Horse
Hummingbird
Hyena
Leopard
Lizard
Mockingbird
Moose
Owl
Platypus
Rabbit
Rattlesnake
Snake
Starfish
Tarantula
Turtle

Sensitivity to Environment
Crane
Deer
Hawk
Hippopotamus
Prairie Dog
Praying Mantis
Salamander
Shark
Starfish
Tarantula

Tortoise
Turtle
Walrus

Serenity and Peacefulness
Dove
Flamingo
Kinkajou
Kite
Pigeon
Rhinoceros
Sea Horse
Snow Leopard
Whale

Settling Down
Cardinal
Robin

Sexual Attraction
Eel
Elk
Flamingo
Moth
Osprey
Sandpiper
Skunk

Sexual Intimacy
Dove
Elephant
Goat
Leopard
Pheasant
Pigeon
Quail
Scorpion
Skunk
Snake

Shadows, Increasing Awareness of Your Personal
Owl
Raven

Shadows of Others, Seeing the
Great Horned Owl
Lynx
Owl
Rhinoceros

Shamanic Arts and Practices
Bat
Eagle
Groundhog
Grouse
Horse (White)
Koala
Lynx
Owl
Raven
Tasmanian Devil

Shape-shifting
Crow
Flamingo
Fox
Gnu
Octopus
Raccoon
Raven

Signs and Omens, Observing and Understanding
Chinchilla
Cockatoo
Crane
Crow
Eagle
Echidna
Falcon
Grebe
Hare
Hawk
Magpie
Owl
Raccoon
Rattlesnake
Raven
Walrus

Silence and Solitude
Ladybug
Lynx
Owl
Swan (Mute)
Turtle

Silent Retreat
Bobcat
Prairie Dog

Swan (Mute)
Weasel

Simplifying Things
Coyote
Iguana
Kinkajou

Singing or Chanting
Canary
Frog
Gecko
Gibbon
Goose (Canadian)
Humpback Whale
Lark
Macaw
Meadowlark
Mockingbird
Quail
Robin
Sparrow
Whale

Single-Parent Concerns
Emu

Slowing Down
Anteater
Chameleon
Cuckoo
Manatee
Sloth
Starfish
Tortoise
Turtle
Wombat

Sociability
Bat
Chimpanzee
Cockatoo
Egret
Gazelle
Giraffe
Gnu
Gorilla
Humpback Whale
Kangaroo
Meerkat

Monkey
Orca
Osprey
Otter
Parrot
Pelican
Pheasant
Prairie Dog
Quail
Seagull
Seal
Squirrel
Wasp
Whale
Wolf

Social Skills
Bee
Chimpanzee
Gorilla
Humpback Whale
Monkey
Seagull
Squirrel
Toucan
Wolf

Solitude, Need for
Cheetah
Cougar
Falcon
Grouse
Hare
Koala
Lemur
Leopard
Lobster
Orangutan
Panda
Raven
Rhinoceros
Scorpion
Shark
Sloth
Spider (Brown)
Tarantula
Tasmanian Devil
Tiger
Toad
Weasel
Wolverine

Soul Group, Finding Others in Your
Orca

Soul Mate, Finding Your
Swan

Soul Name, Finding Your
Quail

Soul's Path, Staying True to Your
Deer
Dolphin
Hippopotamus
Salmon
Wolf

Soul's Purpose and Mission, Clarity about Your
Cassowary
Dolphin
Gnu
Mockingbird
Quail
Salmon
Wolf
Zebra

Sound Healing
Canary
Dingo
Humpback Whale
Kinkajou
Lark
Roadrunner

Speaking or Teaching
Canary
Dingo
Macaw
Mockingbird
Seagull
Toucan
Wolf

Speaking Your Truth
Crow
Fox (Kit)
Frog
Gecko

Gila Monster
Hippopotamus
Humpback Whale
Jaguar
Kite
Macaw
Magpie
Peacock
Starfish
Toucan
Wombat

Speed and Efficiency
Cheetah
Falcon
Ostrich
Snow Leopard

Spirit Helpers, Calling Additional
Beluga Whale
Kite
Lark

Spiritual Awareness and Growth
Dolphin
Dove
Duck (Wood)
Emu
Gazelle
Giraffe
Goose
Goshawk
Hippopotamus
Horse
Macaw
Moose
Ostrich
Owl
Raven
Robin
Sandpiper
Snake
Whale
White Buffalo

Spiritual Catalyst
Eagle
Ibis
Raven
Robin

Snake
Stag

Spiritual Exploration and Adventure
Robin
Salmon
Sandpiper
Spider
Stag
Tiger (Siberian)

Spiritual Healing
Ibis
Rattlesnake
Raven
Snake

Spirituality, Study of Eastern
Cobra
Panda
Python
Red Panda
Snake
Snow Leopard

Spiritual Law
Cassowary
Crow
Goshawk

Spiritual Pilgrimage
Albatross
Eagle (Golden)
Eel
Emu
Gazelle
Gnu
Goose
Humpback Whale
Llama
Polar Bear
Robin
Sea Horse
Stag
Swallow

Spiritual Presence
Dolphin
Dove

Eagle
Goshawk
Hummingbird
Polar Bear
Raven
Robin
Snake
Whale
White Buffalo

Spiritual Revelations, Integrating
Beluga Whale
Eagle
Ibis
Robin
Snaker

Spontaneity, Increasing
Cockatoo
Dolphin
Ram

Stability and Continuity
Camel
Cardinal
Pigeon
Stag
Tortoise
Wombat
Zebra

Standing Up for Yourself
Anteater
Badger
Bear
Blue Jay
Chipmunk
Otter
Wolverine
Wombat

Starting New Projects
Antelope
Buffalo
Bull
Osprey
Ram
Roadrunner
Salamander
Sandpiper

Stork

Steadiness
Donkey
Goat

Stillness and Quiet
Cow
Ferret
Flamingo
Gopher
Kingfisher
Lizard
Lynx
Praying Mantis
Rabbit
Rhinoceros
Snow Leopard
Spider
Swan (Mute)
Weasel
Whale

Storytelling
Lark
Whale
Wolf

Strategy and Planning
Falcon (Kestrel)
Iguana
Opossum
Owl (Snowy)
Rabbit
Roadrunner
Squirrel
Wasp
Wolverine

Stress Management
Dolphin
Elk
Gila Monster
Koala
Leopard
Manatee
Opossum
Tortoise
Turtle

Stretch Beyond Your Comfort Zone

Gibbon
Giraffe
Goat
Humpback Whale
Impala
Kangaroo (Wallaby)
Lion
Opossum
Quail
Toucan

Successful Outcomes
Bee
Gila Monster
Hyena
Jaguar
Rat
Walrus
Weasel

Sunlight, Increasing Amount of
Macaw
Meerkat
Parrot

Supplies, Storing Up
Fox (Arctic)
Gopher
Mouse
Rat
Squirrel
Wolverine

Support from Family and Friends, Receiving
Jackal
Kangaroo
Meerkat
Musk Ox
Orca
Penguin
Pigeon
Whale

Support, Physical or Emotional
Bluebird
Cormorant
Cow
Crow
Dog
Falcon

Goat
Hyena
Jackal
Orca
Osprey
Penguin
Squirrel
Stag
Turtle
Wasp
Whale

Surprises, Dealing with
Coyote

Surrender and Acceptance
Condor
Jaguar (Black)
Monkey
Swan

Surviving Tough Times
Kangaroo
Gila Monster
Lizard
Polar Bear
Swallow

Suspicious Signs, Making Sense of
Antelope
Moose
Platypus

Tact and Diplomacy
Bee
Falcon
Ferret
Fox
Opossum
Parrot
Weasel

Tai Chi or Aikido, Study and Practice of
Kite
Opossum
Praying Mantis
Swan (Trumpeter)

Teachings and Lessons, Understanding

Coyote
Crab
Dingo
Platypus
Salmon
Spider
Wolf

Teamwork
Dolphin
Horse
Ox (Bull)

Telepathy, Developing Your
Whale

Threats or Intimidation, Standing Up to
Bear
Blue Jay
Porcupine

Timing, Right
Falcon
Gila Monster

Touch, Giving and Receiving
Baboon
Chimpanzee
Cockatoo
Mole
Walrus

Traditional Values
Goose
Pigeon

Transformation
Butterfly
Eel
Ibis
Lobster
Python
Rattlesnake
Salamander
Salmon
Scorpion
Snake
Toad

Transitions, Life

Alligator
Bat
Butterfly
Crocodile
Eagle
Echidna
Frog
Kinkajou
Kite
Leopard
Robin
Salamander
Salmon
Seal
Snake
Swan
Toad
Wombat

Trauma, Recovery from Physical or Emotional
Bear
Cow
Flamingo
Mole
Otter
Platypus
Raven
Swallow
Turtle

Travel, Air
Albatross
Goose (Snow)

Travel, Land
Emu
Llama
Stag

Travel, Water
Dolphin
Humpback Whale
Seal
Walrus

Trust in Divine Order and Timing
Cuckoo
Otter
Pheasant

Robin
Stag

APPENDIX

Messages from Your Animal Spirit Guide:
A Guided Meditation Journey

REVIEW THIS MEDITATION JOURNEY BEFORE TRYING IT, and do your best to follow the written guidance. You can also record it on your iPod or some other device and listen to it in your own voice, or ask someone else you know to record it. Or, get a copy of my CD of the same title, which has a version of this meditation on it.

Yet another option is to do this with a friend or even a group, where one of you reads it to the other or others, and then you can discuss what each of you came up with, using the meditation and perhaps this book, along with *Power Animals* and the *Power Animal Oracle Cards,* to make an evening of exploration and inspiration with your animal spirit guides.

Although the directions say to sit, you do have the option of lying down. If you do lie down to do this meditation, however, lift one of your forearms up to a 90-degree angle and keep it there throughout the meditation. That way if you should fall asleep, your forearm will drop and will wake you up. This is a good meditation to do first thing in the morning when you're refreshed from a good night's sleep.

Note that you'll be going to the *lower world,* which is an etheric area in the earth. It's not at all the same as what we typically think of as the underworld. It's a notion that has its origins in shamanic practices and is completely safe. In most shamanic systems, this is where the animal spirits reside.

Doing this journey, you may or may not encounter the animal spirit guide you expected. If you have a totem or power animal, you may expect it to show, but someone else might appear. The spirit animal that shows will be the one that's exactly right for your concern.

Okay, here goes:

Put on some relaxing ambient music, turn the lights down, and find a comfortable seated position. . . . Take a couple of slow deep breaths. . . . When you're ready, close your eyes. . . . Take another deep breath, and when you let it out, relax. . . . Know that you're safe at all times. . . . If you travel with a spirit animal or any other spiritual beings, call on them now to help you know you're safe . . . loved . . . protected . . . at all times. . . . Another breath. . . . Let your awareness track your breathing for the next few moments. . . . Notice how relaxed and comfortable you feel now . . . letting go of all tension . . . taking all the time in the world . . . allowing yourself to completely let go . . . breathing. . . . Now let your consciousness gently and gradually float down, into the earth, into the lower world . . . dropping comfortably down into the earth . . . knowing all the while that you're completely safe and protected at all times. . . . As you drop into the earth, notice the sensations in your body. . . . Notice your breathing. . . . Notice how relaxed you feel. . . . Now as you descend, soon you'll come to a grassy area. . . . Observe how you float down until you land gently on your feet in this meadow, feeling comfortable and safe. . . . As you arrive, look around you and see what you see . . . not too far away, a forest . . . and in the distance, the mountains. . . . On the other side of the forest is the sea. . . . Be aware of the colors. . . . Notice any sounds you hear. . . . Be aware of any smells. . . . Feel the pleasant warmth of the sun on your skin. . . . Perhaps you can feel a slight breeze. . . . Now you have a choice of staying in this beautiful meadow or wandering about. . . . Go ahead and make your choice, and if it means walking to another area, do so. . . . Take your time. . . . if you stay in the meadow, go ahead and be seated in a comfortable place. . . . If you wander to the mountains, the forest, by the river in the forest, or to the beach, once you arrive there, have a seat in a comfortable place. . . . Take a deep breath and relax into the setting you're in, using all your senses. . . . Now think of your question. . . . As you do, you soon notice an animal coming to you. . . . You realize it's an animal spirit guide, and it's exactly the right one for the question you have in mind. . . . It may or may not be your totem animal or power animal. . . . It may or may not be one that you saw in a dream or a vision. . . . But you feel confident that this is the right one for your purpose. . . . You're completely safe, protected at all times. . . . This animal spirit guide comes up to you, very friendly and willing to help you out. . . . You communicate your question telepathically to this spirit animal. . . . After you've done so, observe everything that immediately follows. . . . The information may come as a visual image, something you hear, a feeling in

*your body, or a thought in your head. . . . It may be cryptic or very
direct and clear. . . . No matter how it comes, just notice without
trying to interpret. . . . If something isn't clear, ask this spirit animal
for further clarification. . . . Take a few moments to pay attention
to what is coming to you. . . . Simply allow yourself to absorb the
information. . . .*

*Once that feels complete, turn to your animal spirit guides and
thank them in some way. . . . Notice now that this animal spirit
guide gives you a small gift. . . . It's a symbol of this journey, a
small token of this spirit guide's love and care for you. . . . When it's
offered and you receive it, first hold it to your heart. . . . Close your
eyes and take a couple of slow, easy breaths. . . . Breathe it in. . . .
Notice how it feels. . . . You're your eyes, and once again thank
this spirit animal. . . . Say your farewells to each other. . . . Your
animal spirit guide departs, and once again you close your eyes. . . .
Now you feel yourself lifting up from the lower world back into
the middle world . . . back to where you started. . . . Notice your
breathing. . . . You may want to wiggle your fingers and toes as you
bring your awareness back into your body. . . . Take your time. . . .
Let your breath be relaxed and comfortable. . . . Whenever you're
ready, open your eyes and look around to your surroundings. . . .
This helps to orient you to present time and third-dimensional
reality. . . . Once you're completely back, you may want to jot down
some notes from this journey.*

I encourage you to write down whatever happened. The message you got from your animal spirit guide may be perfectly clear
or somewhat cryptic and dreamlike. If it isn't clear, just let it work
through you during the day or evening. Often other pieces begin
to synchronistically come to you after doing this kind of journey.
You can repeat this for any type of question or concern you have,
and you'll get advice from the appropriate animal spirit guide.

Resources

Understanding Messages from Animal Spirit Guides
Books

Animal Dreaming, Scott Alexander. Project Art and Photo: Victoria, Australia, 2003.

Animal Magick: The Art of Recognizing and Working with Familiars, D.J. Conway. Llewellyn Publications: St. Paul, Minnesota, 2002.

Animal-Speak: The Spiritual and Magical Powers of Creatures Great & Small, Ted Andrews. Llewellyn Publications: St. Paul, Minnesota, 1993.

Animal Wisdom: The Definitive Guide to the Myth, Folklore and Medicine Power of Animals, Jessica Dawn Palmer. Element/HarperCollinsPublishers: London, 2001.

Animal-Wise: The Spirit Language and Signs of Nature, Ted Andrews. Dragonhawk Publishing: Jackson, Tennessee, 1999.

Celtic Totem Animals, John Matthews. Eddison Sadd Editions Ltd: London, 2002.

Druid Animal Oracle, Philip and Stephanie Carr-Gomm. Connections Book Publishing: London, 1996.

Kinship with All Life, J. Allen Boone. HarperSanFrancisco, 1954.

Magical Unicorn Oracle Cards, Doreen Virtue, Ph.D. Hay House: Carlsbad, California, 2005.

Medicine Cards, Jamie Sams and David Carson. St. Martin's Press: New York, 1988.

Power Animal Oracle Cards, Steven D. Farmer, Ph.D., Hay House: Carlsbad, California, 2006.

Power Animals, Steven D. Farmer, Ph.D. Hay House: Carlsbad, California, 2004.

Totems: The Transformative Power of Your Personal Animal Totem, Brad Steiger. HarperSanFrancisco: 1997.

The Vision, Tom Brown, Jr. The Berkley Publishing Group: New York, 1988.

The Way of the Shaman, Michael Harner. HarperSanFrancisco, 1990.

Websites

This is a list of a few select Websites. I encourage you to use a search program such as Google and type in a search word or phrase that's relevant to the topic, such as animal spirit guides, spirit animals, totem animals, or power animals, and see what you get, as new sites are popping up all the time.

Animal and Bird Totems: holistichealthtools.com/totems.html

Animal Symbolism–Animals in Art: princetonol.com/groups/iad/lessons/middle/animals.htm

Cycle of Power: Animal Totems: sayahda.com/cycle.html

Enchanted Learning: enchantedlearning.com/subjects/

How to Find Your Animal Totem: serioussilver.com/totemenergy/findtoteminfo.html

Meeting the Power Animals: rainbowcrystal.com/power/power.html

Power Animals: childrenoftheearth.org/PowerAnimals/shuffle16.html (great for older children)

The Red Road: groups.msn.com/LightWorkersandMagicalThingsCenter/americannative.msnw

Shamanism: Working with Animal Spirits, geocities.com/~animalspirits/index1.html

Totem Animals: crystalinks.com/totemanimals.html

Totems: wiccanlife.com/bos/totem.htm

Information about Animals

Books

Animal, David Burnie and Don E. Wilson, eds. DK Publishing, Inc.: New York, 2001.

Dorling Kindersley Animal Encyclopedia, Jonathan Elphick, Jen Green, Barbara Taylor, and Richard Walker. DK Publishing, Inc.: New York, 2000.

The Encyclopedia of Animals: A Complete Visual Guide, Jenni Bruce, Karen McGhee, Luba Vangelova, and Richard Vogt. University of California Press: Berkeley and Los Angeles, 2004.

The Last Big Cats: The Untamed Spirit, Erwin A. Bauer. Voyageur Press, Inc.: Stillwater, MN, 2003.

The Life of Birds, David Attenborough. Princeton University Press: Princeton, NJ, 1998.

The Life of Mammals, David Attenborough. Princeton University Press: Princeton, NJ, 2002.

National Geographic Animal Encyclopedia, Jinny Johnson, National Geographic Society: Washington, D.C., 1999 (great for children).

Scholastic Encyclopedia of Animals, Lawrence Pringle. Scholastic, Inc.: New York, 2001 (great for children).

DVDs

Africa: The Serengeti, George Casey. Slingshot Entertainment: www.slingshotent.com, 2001.

Alaska: Spirit of the Wild, George Case. Slingshot Entertainment: www.slingshotent.com, 2001.

Bears, David Lickley. Slingshot Entertainment: www.slingshotent.com, 2001.

Beavers, Stephen Low. Image Entertainment: www.image-entertainment.com, 2003.

The Blue Planet: Seas of Life, David Attenborough. BBC Video: www.bbcamerica.com, 2001.

Coral Reef Adventure, Greg MacGillivray. MacGillivray Freeman Films Educational Foundation, 2003.

Killer Instinct: Snakes, Rob Bredl, host. Starcast Productions: www.mpihomevideo.com, 2002.

The Life of Birds, David Attenborough. BBC Video: www.bbcamerica.com, 2002.

The Life of Mammals, David Attenborough. BBC Video: www.bbcamerica.com, 2003.

March of the Penguins, Luc Jacquet. Warner Independent Pictures and National Geographic Film Features: www.warnervideo.com, 2005.

Pale Male, WNET New York. PBS: www.pbs.org, 2004.

Reptiles, WNET New York. PBS: www.pbs.org, 2003.

Whales: An Unforgettable Journey, David Clark, Al Giddings, and Roger Payne. Slingshot Entertainment: www.slingshotent.com, 2001.

Winged Migration, Jacques Perrin. Sony Pictures Classics: sonyclassics.com, 2003.

Wolves, National Wildlife Federation. Slingshot Entertainment: www. slingshotent.com, 2002.

World of Raptors, Morley Nelson. Echo Film Productions, Inc: www.sts-media.com, 2003. www.image-entertainment.com, 2003.

Websites

There's an amazing amount of information on animals on the Internet. You can use a search engine to locate information about a specific animal. These are just a few that I've found useful.

All About Birds, birds.cornell.edu/programs/AllAboutBirds/BirdGuide
Animal Planet, animal.discovery.com
Animals, yahooligans.yahoo.com/content/animals (great for children)
Animals: Explore, Discover, Connect, seaworld.org/animal-info/animal-bytes/index.htm
Articles About Animals, crystalinks.com/animalarticles.html
Australian Animals, australianfauna.com
Big Cats Online, dialspace.dial.pipex.com/agarman/bco/ver4.htm
Big Cat Rescue, bigcatrescue.org
Desert Animals and Wildlife, desertusa.com/animal.html
Enchanted Learning, enchantedlearning.com/coloring (great for children)
National Geographic: Animals and Nature, nationalgeographic.com/animals
Science and Nature: Animals, bbc.co.uk/nature/animals

Organizations

The following are some organizations that directly or indirectly support the animal kingdom:

American Society for the Prevention of Cruelty to Animals, aspca.org/site/PageServer. 424 E. 92nd St, New York, NY 10128-6804. (212) 876-7700. (SPCA is international.)

Big Cat Rescue, bigcatrescue.org. 12802 Easy St., Tampa, FL 33625. (813) 920-4130.

Defenders of Wildlife, defenders.org. 1130 17th Street, NW, Washington, DC 20030. (202) 682-9400.

In Defense of Animals, idausa.org. 131 Camino Alto, Ste. E, Mill Valley, CA 94941. (415) 388-9641.

The Fund for Animals. fund.org. 200 West 57th St., New York, NY 10019. (212) 246-2096.

International Fund for Animal Welfare, ifaw.org.

National Wildlife Federation, nwf.org. 11100 Wildlife Center Dr., Reston, VA 20190-5362. (800) 822-9919.

Natural Resources Defense Council (NRDC), nrdc.org. 40 West 20th St., New York, NY 10011. (212) 727-2700.

Nature Conservancy, nature.org. 4245 North Fairfax Dr., Suite 100, Arlington, VA 22203-1606. (703) 841-5300.

Oceana, oceana.org. 2501 M Street, NW, Ste. 300, Washington, DC 20037-1311. (202) 833-3900.

People for the Ethical Treatment of Animals (PETA), peta.org. 501 Front St., Norfolk, VA 23510. (757) 622-7382.

Physicians Committee for Responsible Medicine (PCRM), PCRM.org. 5100 Wisconsin Ave., N.W., Suite 400, Washington, DC 20016.

World Wildlife Fund, wwf.org. 1250 24th St., NW, Washington, DC 20037. (800) 225-5993.

Acknowledgments

EVERY BOOK THAT'S EVER BEEN WRITTEN is a group project, and I'm extremely grateful for the contributions of all who played a part. First, a deep and humble gratitude to all the animal-spirit beings who were so helpful (sometimes to the point of being demanding), especially Hawk, Raven, Badger, Raccoon, Opossum, Owl, and Snake. As for the two-leggeds, thanks to my wife, Doreen, and her willingness to always listen to the latest piece I'd written, her tireless support for this project, and her love of the animals, including Unicorns. Thanks to Bill and Joan Hannan and our grown-up children, Chase, Nicole, Grant, and Catherine, for always asking how the book was going; and to our grandchildren, Jaden and Gena, just for their being.

My humble appreciation to indigenous peoples throughout the world, to whom these practices were second nature, and who knew in their souls our profound relationship with all of God's creatures.

Thanks to those authors and teachers who have contributed to understanding animal spirit guides and have provided such valuable inspiration, including (but not limited to) Brad Steiger, Jamie Sams, David Carson, Jessica Dawn Palmer, Ted Andrews, Philip and Stephanie Carr-Gomm, D.J. Conway, Scott King, and J. Allen Boone.

I'm grateful to the shamanic teachers and colleagues who have supported me in this work, directly and indirectly, including Michael Harner; Jade Wah'oo-Grigori; Tom Brown, Jr.; Larry Peters; Angeles Arrien; Tom Cowan; Sandra Ingerman; Hank Wesselman; Karen Palmer; Evie Kane; and Gretchyn McKay.

A special thanks to Donna Schenk for researching all the photos; Jill Kramer and Shannon Littrell for their patience and gentle editing touch; Amy Rose Grigoriou for her deft artistic touch in the design; Beverly Lu for her original artwork for the cover; Reid Tracy for believing in this project; Leon Nacson and the gang from Hay House Australia, including Heidi, Eli, Rhett, Lauren, and others; Megan, Jo, and Michelle from Hay House UK; and Louise Hay for her leadership and inspiration.

Much appreciated are the guys in my men's group who cheered me on, including Kevin, Chris, Gary M., Wayne, Paul H., Beeohbee, Gary D., Phil, and Paul C. Thanks also to other friends who loved and supported me and this project, including Rich Goodman, Jeremy Donovan, Shannon Kennedy, Edd Mabrey, Bill Lyon, Jade Wah'oo-Grigori, Lynnette Brown, Dan Clark, Debra Ann Jacobs, Liz Dawn, Ariel, Karley, and Ebony.

About the Author

STEVEN D. FARMER, PH.D., IS A SHAMANIC PRACTITIONER, ordained minister, licensed psychotherapist, and former college professor with over 30 years' experience as a professional healer and teacher. He has appeared as a guest on a number of television and radio shows and is the author of several other books and articles, including the best-selling *Sacred Ceremony, Power Animals,* and *Power Animal Oracle Cards*. He makes his home in Laguna Beach, California. For further information, please go to **www.Power Animals.com**.

We hope you enjoyed this Hay House book.
If you'd like to receive a free catalog featuring additional
Hay House books and products, or if you'd like information
about the Hay Foundation, please contact:

Hay House, Inc.
P.O. Box 5100
Carlsbad, CA 92018-5100

(760) 431-7695 or (800) 654-5126
(760) 431-6948 (fax) or (800) 650-5115 (fax)
www.hayhouse.com® • www.hayfoundation.org

Published and distributed in Australia by:
Hay House Australia Pty. Ltd., 18/36 Ralph St., Alexandria NSW 2015
Phone: 612-9669-4299 • *Fax:* 612-9669-4144 • www.hayhouse.com.au

Published and distributed in the United Kingdom by:
Hay House UK, Ltd., 292B Kensal Rd., London W10 5BE
Phone: 44-20-8962-1230 • *Fax:* 44-20-8962-1239 • www.hayhouse.co.uk

Published and distributed in the Republic of South Africa by:
Hay House SA (Pty), Ltd., P.O. Box 990, Witkoppen 2068
Phone/Fax: 27-11-467-8904 • orders@psdprom.co.za
www.hayhouse.co.za

Published in India by: Hay House Publishers India,
Muskaan Complex, Plot No. 3, B-2, Vasant Kunj, New Delhi 110 070
Phone: 91-11-4176-1620 • *Fax:* 91-11-4176-1630 • www.hayhouse.co.in

Distributed in Canada by: Raincoast,
9050 Shaughnessy St., Vancouver, B.C. V6P 6E5
Phone: (604) 323-7100 • *Fax:* (604) 323-2600 • www.raincoast.com

Tune in to **HayHouseRadio.com**® for the best in inspirational talk
radio featuring top Hay House authors! And, sign up via the Hay
House USA Website to receive the Hay House online newsletter and
stay informed about what's going on with your favorite authors. You'll
receive bimonthly announcements about: Discounts and Offers, Special
Events, Product Highlights, Free Excerpts, Giveaways, and more!
www.hayhouse.com®